THE GROANING SHELF
& other instances of book-love

THE GROANING SHELF
& other instances of book-love

Pradeep Sebastian

First published in 2010 by Hachette India
An Hachette UK company

First edition

Copyright © Pradeep Sebastian 2010

Several of these essays first appeared in *The Hindu*,
Deccan Herald, *Businessworld Online* and *The Caravan*
in a slightly different form.

Pradeep Sebastian asserts the moral right
to be identified as the author of this work.

All rights reserved. No part of the publication may be
reproduced, stored in a retrieval system, or transmitted
in any form or by any means without the prior written
permission of the publisher, nor be otherwise circulated
in any form of binding or cover other than that in which
it is published and without a similar condition
being imposed on the subsequent purchaser.

ISBN 978-93-80143-03-3

Hachette India
612/614 (6th Floor), Time Tower,
MG Road, Sector 28, Gurgaon-122001, India

Cover design by Netra Shyam

Typeset in Goudy Old Style 10.5/12.6

Printed and bound at Manipal Press Ltd.

In memory of my mother
Vatsala Sebastian

And for my father
John Sebastian

with gratitude, love and respect

Contents

Preface / x

The Pleasures of Bibliophily / 1
The Groaning Shelf / 3
Shelf Life / 9
The Magic Circle / 13

Editions / 21
The Bookman / 23
The Mystique of First Editions / 27
First Edition Fever / 33
The Tattooed Bibliophile / 36

The Browser's Ecstasy / 41
For the Cover Alone / 43
The Rock Star of Book Jacket Design / 49
The Postmodernist Always Rings Twice and Other Titles / 54
The Artists' Book / 59
ACK Title No. 11 / 68

A Gentle Madness / 73
True Tales of Bibliomania / 75
The Man Who Loved Books Too Much: Book Thief I / 80
The Tome Raider: Book Thief II / 83
Out of Circulation / 86
Marginalia (& Other Literary Curiosities) / 89
The Tireless Reader / 93
The Book Borrower / 96

The Book Eaters / 99
'The Collector of Collectors' / 101
'Our Master of Bibliophilic Revel' / 107
Bookishness / 110
A Hitchhiker's Guide to the Library / 114
Apart from the Text: Book History in India / 117

Writers / 127
Thomas Merton on a Frequent-Flier Pass: Pico Iyer / 129
Through the Looking Glass of Books: Amitava Kumar / 136
Turning the Wheel: Pankaj Mishra / 139
One Robe, One Bowl: Ryokan / 143
The Glass Family: J.D. Salinger / 146
A Genius for Suspense: Ira Levin / 150
Reverend and Mrs. Panicker's Paying Guest: Conan Doyle
(or, The Non-Canonical Sherlock Holmes) / 157
The Movie, Not the Book: Ayn Rand / 166
The Edgy Enthusiast: Ron Rosenbaum / 172
Opposites Attract Him: Craig Seligman / 177
The Second Lolita: Michael Maar / 180
The Haunted Videotape: Koji Suzuki / 184

Ruined by Reading / 191
Reading in Bed / 193
Rereading / 196
The Good Parts Version
(or 80% Austen, 20% Zombie Mayhem) / 202
Unwired, Offline, and Off-screen / 205

Loved and Lost / 211
The Unlived Life: A Literature of Failure / 213
Writers of the No / 221
Elected Silence / 224
Lost Books / 227

Bookstores / 233
The Bookwoman of Madison Avenue / 235
The Bibliophile's Dream-Bookshop / 240
At the Museum of Books / 245
Strictly Books / 248
The Ultimate Bookshop / 255
The Book in the Movie / 261
Shakespeare & Co. / 271
The Lame Duck / 274

Afterword: At the 50th New York Antiquarian Book Fair / 278
Bibliography / 291
Acknowledgments / 296

'I don't know why I believe that a book brings us the possibility of happiness, but I am truly grateful for that modest miracle.'
– Borges

Preface

I BEGAN to look at books, really *look* at them, when I stopped reading. I became a lapsed reader. (For a bibliophile who occasionally wrote a book column or two this posed a problem, but I cunningly resolved it and you will soon see how.) But buying books was such an old and compulsive habit with me that I continued to punctually stop at bookstores. At home I would pick up the book at hand, read a little, stop, and begin paying attention instead to the cover or the way the paper felt or the binding. And when I went back to reading, it was from the title page verso or the colophon.

Holding a book but not actually reading it gave me time (and put me in the mood) to reflect on the act of reading and the physicality of the book; the book as material object. (Didn't that high priest of scholar-collectors, Walter Benjamin, once make a case for the true bibliophile as the one who never reads her books?) I found myself drawn deeper and deeper into the culture and tradition of bibliophily: first and rare editions, bibliography, book history, the literature of collecting and the antiquarian book trade. When browsing in bookstores I was drawn most to books that addressed the passion for reading and book collecting.

This literary subgenre, I discovered, had a name: Books on Books, or Books about Books. The bibliophile's dream-genre. Full of bibliophilic revel and ecstatic bookishness: bibliomemoirs, bibliofiction, travels in the bookworld, true tales of bibliomania, bibliomysteries and the literature of collecting. Suddenly, I was reading again! And writing about these books. I wasn't a reader in exile anymore. A shelf-row of books about books in my book-crammed apartment soon turned into a whole shelf devoted to books on books.

I think one reason why absorption in this genre returned to me the longing to read was that it made my reading deeply personal, idiosyncratic and self-reflexive. These books described an interior world I knew intimately: the inner life of a reader. A familiar act: reading. An object I grew up with: the book. A second home: the bookstore.

The whole affair had turned bookish. And had returned to me the enchantment of reading. As Umberto Eco imagined that tireless reader Yambo in *The Mysterious Flame of Queen Loana*, this was about the reader as hero; the collector as protagonist.

In *One Way Street*, Benjamin records a strange moment: 'When a valued, cultured and elegant friend sent me his new book and I was about to open it, I caught myself in the act of straightening my tie.' Suddenly, the book had become a resonant presence.

Apart from finding antiquarian editions beautiful in their original binding, I am drawn to their intrinsic bibliographical value. The pleasures of bibliophily for me lie in fully embracing the book as material object; its bibliographical aspects – binding, edition, condition, rarity, and typography matter to me as much as their literary content.

And with so much talk around now about the printed book eventually vanishing, to pay attention to the book in this way seems to me especially important and instructive now more than ever before. For more readers to feel this way – fancy the book as object – and not just let it seem the bibliomaniacal whimsy of book collectors and bibliographers alone.

This, then, is the inner life of one reader: from re-

reader to lapsed reader to (finally when all you can read are books about books) meta-reader. Or to have it another way: from bibliophile to bibliojournalist to bibliographer. Not a scholar-bibliographer but an amateur-bibliographer of the book. And this is where I now find myself in my journey with the book. Who knows, though, what shape it will take, and where it will go, this inner life of a reader?

The Pleasures of Bibliophily

The Groaning Shelf
Shelf Life
The Magic Circle:
A Literature of Collecting

THE GROANING SHELF

A SUNDAY AFTERNOON ritual for bibliophiles is taking books off the shelves to rearrange them. I have spent the last hour getting the books down, and now they are everywhere in the apartment: on the floor, in boxes, even on the bed. What I am looking forward to is the putting back – 'you remove them in haste but you labour over the rearrangement'. That familiar moment Walter Benjamin speaks of in 'Unpacking my Library' when 'the books are not yet on the shelves, not yet touched by the mild boredom of order'.

It gives me a chance every few months to physically handle all the books, stop to look closely at the book dust jacket or re-read a passage that I remember. And then there is the anticipation of the new arrangement: how will I shelf them this time? Should I abandon the by-author arrangement and categorize them by subject instead? Why not an entire shelf of only personal favourites? Where should I put the first editions – on the open shelves or in glass-fronted bookcases?

What glass-fronted bookcases? I don't own any, and can't afford them, but it's a nice fantasy. As I begin re-shelving my books, I realize with a little amusement that there actually is a fine, ongoing and peculiar tradition of other bibliophile-writers recording this activity. The most quoted is Benjamin's essay, but others, like Geoff Dyer have picked up on this so tunefully that when speaking of unpacking *his* books, he's referencing B's essay without attribution because he knows we know who he's quoting. The title of Dyer's essay itself is a quote: 'Unpacking My Library'.

The undoubtedly fascinating author of *Jeff in Venice, Death in Varanasi* (and other equally fascinating books like *Out of Sheer Rage*) states his bibliophilic ambition: to assemble all his books in one room. He's wanted to do this his whole life. He has been relentlessly rearranging, staying up till three in the morning. 'Nothing highlights the fascination of unpacking more clearly than the difficulty of stopping this activity.' (That's the German idealist-Jewish mystic he's quoting). And this is true: lifting and carting books all day is one of the few labour-intensive activities that you don't want to see come to a halt. Because, once the books are where they should be ('coldly ranged on the shelves' as Aziz once blurted to Fielding), there is that mild twinge of disappointment that Benjamin observed.

But wait. I have just begun re-arranging, and there is at least a day's worth of nice work to be done, and at least a shelf-row full of essays about unpacking books to keep me company.

Trying to shelve authors he likes together, Dyer finds there are too many 'rogue volumes' – books of varying sizes – that spoil the arrangement. But these, and other shelving intricacies, are for this bibliomane (books are the only things he has cared to own) 'a source of unresolvable pleasure'. He looks inside the flyleaf of one book and sees he has noted where he bought it: Algiers. Then he confesses it was actually from Foyles on Charing Cross Road. It was more glamorous to put down where he had read it than where he had bought it.

The books are now finally in one room. A life's ambition is near completion, and he's content to just sit beside these books and purr. He has no desire to read the books, only touch them, perhaps smell them, because books are meant 'to be arranged and classified, shuffled around'. He feels bad, all of a sudden, for the people out there, just outside his window, who are not here in 'this lovely lamp-lit solitude, surrounded by books'.

Dyer also discovers how difficult it is to decide what books to keep and what books to chuck out. The very books he put away in a box to be sold are back on his shelf now. Part of the pleasure of shuffling books around is the illusion that you can let many of your books go – either to make more room or from an old impulse that you can do without many of these books from the past. Once, in a fit to streamline my book-cluttered apartment, I decided to cut down my library to what I hoped would be an essential collection: the kind I had when I was a student and had just begun to collect the work of writers I admired. A deeply personal collection that identified me not as a bibliomane, but simply as a bibliophile: a being that belonged to those pre-collector times. Then, there were only a handful of books but I knew every one of them intimately – I had read and re-read them all. I couldn't bear the idea of unread books on a shelf.

Books, I realized, can clutter your bookshelf and your mind. I wanted to simplify, resist complication, and did not want to be encumbered by obsession. So I began the trimming process with books and writers that I once felt a deep connection to, but who now seemed to fall away when I revisited them. It isn't the book but me that had changed – I was not the same reader I once was. Not surprisingly, I didn't find it easy to let go of them.

Ah, the joys and snares of reading – who can predict them? Now I feel the need to have books that I am yet to read, yet to open. Like friends I can call on unexpectedly. I don't like the idea of an essential collection anymore.

It seems to define me too much; as if I couldn't conceive of other friendships, enter other worlds. Luckily, we don't outgrow all the authors of our youth; some just get better. For me two writers I discovered in college continue to have my full attention now: Malamud and Salinger. I try to keep some extra copies of Salinger's Glass novels and Malamud's *A New Life* and *Dubin's Lives* (the books I admire most by both) at hand, to be able to press on readers that I feel will embrace them the way I have.

As with all previous attempts at radically trimming my book collection, this one too mysteriously failed: the more books I managed to let go of, the more books I acquired. To make up for this, I'm tossing out a lot of overrated, overwritten contemporary fiction that seems to have insidiously crept into my bookshelves. Banishing the philosophers (except the existentialists) was easy, especially since the trade-off was keeping all the mystics. (I think I heard my bookshelves actually thank me for chucking out all the encyclopaedias and autobiographies.)

The books (I should really say *editions*) that have given me the most pleasure to collect and house in my shelves are first editions, while the most sacred are the ones that have been signed and inscribed to me. The editions shelved in this part of the bookcase I take out only to gaze on them a while and carefully put back. An indulgence over the years has been keeping (harbouring?) multiple copies of rare and out-of-print books. When I see them on sale, I can't bear to leave them neglected and languishing in some dusty corner of a second-hand bookshop. I, of course, see this more as a rescue operation than hoarding.

I never seem to be able to get rid of any poetry. These slim volumes take up little shelf space and grow dearer every day. I keep all of Chekhov, Proust and Kafka: the Chekhovs because they have become part of my autobiography, the Kafkas because they make more sense by the day, and the Prousts for late in life, when all is read, and you still want to hear a companionable voice.

It isn't really a cliché that the moment you let go of a book, you miss it immediately. Isn't it always a sadness to see books that have made a home with you leave your shelf? But no such sentimental bookishness kept Joseph Epstein, ex-bibliophile, from *dismantling*, (not unpacking) his library. One day it dawned on him that books were threatening to take over his apartment, making him wonder that while books do furnish a room, 'where is it written that they have to furnish *every* room?'

He then proceeded coolly to banish his library, leaving himself 400 books out of 2,000. In his witty, delightful personal essay 'Books Won't Furnish a Room', Epstein is pleased to report the results: '…like Henry James when he shaved off his beard at fifty-seven, "I feel forty, and clean, and light."' His apartment immediately felt light and airy and spacious. Less book-bound. He made a rule and kept it: for every new book he bought, one old book went out. He stopped going to second-hand bookshops, 'those pool halls for the bibliomane'.

He kisses poor Franz Kafka goodbye, bids good day to most of Thomas Mann, and watches Walter Benjamin leave 'without registering the least fibrillation'. Except for Nabokov (but not *Lolita!*) the Russians do 'not do well in this purge'. Some of the most deadly remarks on reading are here: that reading and thinking are not always the same thing, that 'sometimes reading supplies the most cunning of all means of avoiding thought', and that it is just possible that if you are always reading, you may never discover anything. For Joseph Epstein, retired bibliomane, it was time to move beyond books to finding what else could suitably furnish a mind.

Nicholson Baker, for whom books *are* a kind of furniture for the mind, speaks of a 'best bookcase moment' in his essay from *The Size of Thoughts*. For him it is the reaching out for a book that is on the topmost shelf; the one that you have to stand on tip-toe to push out, and catch it as it falls. I don't think I have a best bookcase moment, unless you count the number of times I move my bookcases around the room. And to do this, of course, I have to first remove all the books from the shelf, and once I've found a new place for my bookcases, put them all back again.

This pleasurable, absorbing ritual of rearranging books, even trying to downsize one's library, now seems to me really about getting to know these books all over again. To pick one from the shelves, remember where and when you bought it, and recall the pleasure that finding the book gave you – this is why a book collector gets all her books off and on the shelves every year. Before you put them back, you are curious to flip the pages and see if you've stuck something in there – a note, a favourite bookmark, a photograph.

At last I have finished sorting and shelving, and discover (like Geoff Dyer), that I have put away more books *back* on the shelf than into those packing boxes. Who is to say when a book or a writer you had been indifferent to or ignorant of, can suddenly turn around and offer that thrill of mysterious connection we all seek as readers? And so, unlike in the case of Mr Epstein, it will not be the end of my days as a bibliomane, after all. Books *will* furnish my apartment and my life.

Shelf Life

I AM NOT happy with the way my new bookshelves look. Not the books on each bookshelf, but the shelf itself: it is too deep. Besides, instead of running in straight rows, the shelves have three partitions, making them look like those pockets that you see in glass showcases. Or pigeonholes. I would have liked the depth of the shelf to be exactly the width and height of a book, no more, no less. I let myself be talked into the design the carpenter had in mind. Now I wish I had been more fastidious.

In many Indian homes and offices, showcases often double as bookcases. And our educational institutions and libraries think nothing of using those slotted angle metal shelves (I am not reconciled to the slotted angle – they should be allowed to house only management and computer books. And perhaps all those writers we feel are overrated.), while most furniture showrooms display ornate bookshelves that are more tacky and overwrought than elegant.

I was surprised, then, when a friend confessed to me recently that she liked bookshelves with deep pockets. Her own, she said, were remarkably deep. Nevertheless, I said, I preferred bookshelves to be slim and running in straight rows. (A terrible temptation with deep shelves is to have a second row of books. Once books get behind other books, you can never find them when you most need them. They simply disappear. They are the Bermuda Triangle of books.) It was only when I finally saw her bookshelves that I understood why she liked depth: the books were all pushed right in. Mine – and most others I know – were all on the front edge of the shelf. When I pointed this out, she was surprised that books should be stacked that way.

'But,' she exclaimed, 'the shelf will look too two-dimensional. When they are in the back, you get a more three-dimensional impression. I reserve the space in front for keeping pencils, bookmarks, my reading glasses, even books that I'm in the middle of reading. Also, the books are easier to pull out.'

Curious, I tried doing the same, pushed them all back, and then stood a little away to appraise the effect. The shelves did indeed take on a three-dimensional depth I never knew they possessed. The books themselves looked more protected somehow. And she was right: it was easier to retrieve them. This has always proved a problem, whether it is the bookcase at home or the ones in the library: removing a book when the shelf is packed tightly. You mustn't damage the book jacket or the spine – and yet browsers always pull out books by gripping the spine and pulling hard. Or they will hook their finger on the headband of the book and drag it out. When a shelf has depth, all you need to do is push the books in either corner inside, and then any book on the shelf becomes easy to handle. I don't think I am entirely convinced that books should be in the inner recesses of the shelf but I do like the effect.

It was at the house of my former boss, Siddhartha, that I had my first glimpse of pleasing bookcases. When he has a new bookshelf made, the carpenter is briefed thoroughly before he begins work on it, and every aspect of the workmanship is carefully inspected. If the carpenter cannot meet his specifications, then he will not hesitate to dismantle the whole thing, and begin all over again by hunting for a better craftsman. Terry Belanger, founder of the Rare Book School, once wrote an amusing, erudite little pamphlet called *Lunacy and the Arrangement of Books* on the various strange to foolish ways book collectors over the centuries have categorized and shelved books. Until the 18th century, spines of books were not labelled, and the owners identified books on their shelves by colour and size. Bindings in morocco came in bright colours and the books were of all shapes and sizes.

Samuel Pepys was obsessed with trying to get books of various sizes – folio, quarto, octavo, duodecimo – looking even on the shelf *without* having to use shelves of different sizes. To accomplish this, Belanger informs us, Pepys built into his bookcases (what we could only describe as) high heels for the smaller books so every book would sit evenly. His wainscot bookcases can still be seen at Magdalene College, Cambridge, where they have been since 1724.

Belanger cites an absurd Victorian book of etiquette that suggests 'the perfect hostess will see to it that the works of male and female authors be properly segregated on her book shelves. Their proximity, unless they happen to be married, should not be tolerated.'

Alberto Manguel in *The Library at Night* speaks of a certain boredom that seizes you when arranging books in geometrical progression (alphabetical, subject, genre, series, etc.) and wonders what would happens if he became really whimsical with the bookshelves. He has always wanted, he says, a personal library full of just his most thumbed copies. Or books on a bookshelf arranged in the degree of his fondness for them. He would imagine all sorts of fantastical bookshelf arrangements in the night, and later, in the light of day, sadly dismiss them as impractical.

He quotes Maurus, the forgotten medieval essayist: 'Books have their own fates.' Some nights he has even dreamt of bookshelves that are entirely anonymous where the books are without author or title or genre converging into one dazzling narrative. In this stream, Manguel goes on to say, keeping the river metaphor afloat, the hero of *The Castle* finds passage aboard the *Pequod* in his search for the Holy Grail only to find himself deserted on an island. And it is in this way that we experience our books, our personal libraries: as One Book. No wonder Borges imagined paradise to be a kind of library.

In *The Book on the Bookshelf*, Henry Petroski tells us that in medieval times books were chained to desks in monasteries, and when it became possible a little later to privately own books, they were mostly placed horizontally on desks, windowsills, beds, chairs and all over the floor.

It was only with the proliferation of bibliophiles who often had to step over books to reach their beds, and who were at a loss to contain their books, did bookshelves become a necessity. I was astonished to learn that for at least a century books were not placed vertically on shelves, and that the spines faced inward! Since the spine didn't contain the title or the author, it didn't matter if you shelved it spine in and fore-edge out.

No bibliophile will disagree with Petroski when he concludes that from the most simply designed bookshelf to contemporary bookcases in bookstores (where the shelves are slanted and the bottom shelves flare out so that a browser can look at the titles standing up) bookshelves are a marvel of structure and engineering. When I look at a book now, I also see a bookshelf.

THE MAGIC CIRCLE:
A LITERATURE OF COLLECTING

As I NEGOTIATE my way between books in the bedroom, the passageway and the staircase landing, I stop to ask myself, not for the first time, why I collect. Why does anyone collect? Even if the objects are books, isn't collecting them another form of being acquisitive? Why should it be naturally superior to hoarding anything else? The answer is complex, and though there are poetic and erudite accounts about book collectors and what they collect, there is very little critical discussion on *why* they collect.

The ur-text of collecting is Jean Baudrillard's essay 'The System of Collecting'. Walter Benjamin's 'Unpacking My Library' too has near cult status among bibliophiles. Other more modern founding documents in the literature of collecting are Susan Stewart's *On Longing*, Susan Pearce's *Interpreting Objects and Collections*, Werner Muenstenberger's *Collecting: An Unruly Passion* and John Elsner and Roger Cardinal's *The Cultures of Collecting*.

Richard Wendorf's *The Literature of Collecting*, however, is my pick for the most illuminating and absorbing scholarly book on collecting, drawing on literary theory, psychoanalysis and fiction to dig deep into why we collect, and its veiled subtexts. Wendorf masterfully criss-crosses between theoretical texts devoted to collecting and the focus on collecting in prose fiction (John Fowles's *The Collector*, Susan Sontag's *The Volcano Lover*, Bruce Chatwin's *Utz*, Tibor Fischer's *The Collector Collector*, Henry James's *The Aspern Papers*).

He begins with an exploration of Jean Baudrillard's famous work on the subject where the writer comes to the conclusion that the objects we collect mirror us, are material representations of the self, and thus in the multiplicity of collecting, the self is extended 'to the very limits of the collection. Here lies the whole miracle of collecting. For it is invariably *oneself* that one collects.' And a collection, B is quick to remind us, is never initiated to be completed! Intriguing? There's more: he warns us that the collecting impulse is regressive, the passion, escapist and the gratification, illusory.

Why regressive? You invest in objects because investing in human relationships is hard and tricky. Also, when you are down and need to recover, you seek the company of objects. The book as the perfect pet. The elusive or missing book becomes valuable by its absence. 'The collector's passion is predicated on pursuit, not completion,' notes Wendorf.

Baudrillard balances this dramatic reading of the need to collect with how objects offer consolation in a world characterized by faltering religious and ideological authorities; objects absorb our anxieties about time and death. Wendorf explicates and glosses each of B's intriguing, melodramatic hypotheses (collecting as a jealousy system – other people can't have it; 'confining beauty in order to savour it in isolation'; how the pursuit of collecting displaces and even abolishes real time, and so on) and pushes further to look at other scholarly literature devoted to collecting, such as Werner Muensterberger's psychoanalytic study of this 'unruly passion'. For M collectibles are toys that grown-ups take seriously.

It is left to three women – three Susans to be exact, Susan Sontag, Susan Stewart and Susan Pearce – to say more pleasant things about collecting. The hero of

Sontag's novel *The Volcano Lover* trusts things because they don't change their nature. Wendorf quotes from her: 'Rare things have intrinsic value, people the value your own need obliges you to assign to them.' Pearce urges us to understand the things we collect because they bring us closer to self-knowledge; they are our other selves. (And I should like to add, with some beautiful books, our better selves.)

Stewart says collecting offers the fantasy – through the ritualized, bibliophilic activity of arranging and rearranging a shelf display, pursuing absent books, trying to complete a collection – that you are a producer more than a consumer of objects. Related to this is the feeling of being able to fashion and control your environment. Walter Benjamin famously said that a collector's passion rests on 'the chaos of memory', and this dictum could be extended to seeing collecting as a desire to control this chaos.

For Thomas Tanselle, for instance, a collection is a magic circle, and a quest for order and 'a feeling for mastery' are at the heart of collecting. The most transcendent explanation that Wendorf takes us to is the one offered by Philip Blom (author of *To Have and to Hold: An Intimate History of Collectors and Collecting*): the collector's devotion infuses life into these dead objects, forming a bridge 'between our limited world and an infinitely richer one, that of history or art, of charisma or of holiness,' a world, he concludes, 'of ultimate authenticity and thus a profoundly romantic utopia.'

While granting the views of Baudrillard and other theorists who see collecting as a 'glorious, if illusory, gratification', Wendorf counters their arguments with his own – and it is his reading that I lean most closely towards.

He notes that there is a richer, many-sided texture to book collecting than that allowed by the theorists who don't fully explore the complex relationship between things and owners. Collecting is based on 'desire, curiosity, knowledge, observation, patience and pursuit'. It is a way of finding oneself. Wendorf writes: 'I see personal collecting in particular as part of the complicated project of self-projection, self-fashioning, and self-fulfilment.'

Another elegant, beautifully written and idiosyncratic scholarly work on collecting is Judith Pascoe's *The Hummingbird Cabinet: A Rare and Curious History of Romantic Collectors*. It's not a book that surfaces easily when exploring books on collecting because it isn't academic or populist but a rare, pretty thing that won't be caged like the hummingbird on its cover. I wasn't surprised then when at some point in the book she says, 'Academic writing often does a poor job of capturing the sensuous appeal of collecting.'

Pascoe's lyrical introduction begins with an account of a self-styled, self-made Percy Bysshe Shelley collector who buys, in 1898, a beautifully crafted Italian guitar that the Romantic poet once owned. (He eventually gives it away to the Bodleian library.) Edward Silsbee became the basis for Henry James's protagonist in *The Aspern Papers*.

Collecting things once touched by the Romantic poets had just become an obsession; people went after Shelley watch fobs, Shelley snuffboxes, and Shelley hair. 'There may also be extant,' Pascoe records, 'or so it is hoped, a volume of Keats's *Poems* found in the drowned Shelley's pocket. This sodden volume was seen in Shelley's jacket when his body washed up on shore.'

Another collector, Fred Holland Day, a Keats enthusiast, owned a framed portrait of Keats with a lock of his hair under the glass, and a series of letters the poet wrote to his beloved Fanny Brawne. But his golden treasure, the high point of his collection, was a copy of Keats's 1817 *Poems* inscribed to Wordsworth. Judith Pascoe's interest in all this is 'to reveal the entanglement of literary and collecting aesthetics'. It wasn't until the late 18th century that collecting was democratized and individuals began private collections of their own. Until then collecting was a sport for the rich and the aristocratic. (This led eventually to the Victorian institutional practice of opening public museums.)

Pascoe shows us how the philosophical and literary movement of Romanticism spurred the idea of collecting with its strong aesthetic notions of devotion, beauty, and the fetishizing of objects. She explores the grip that 'objects have over their owners and the ways in which romantic structures of feeling – a longing for permanence, a fascination with perfect beauty, a preoccupation with authenticity, a propensity for grandiose endeavours – contribute to this hold.'

The literature of collecting is a tiny but intriguing sub-genre of Books About Books. More recently, however, academics have begun to show more interest in making critical inquiries into the subject of collecting.

There are now a handful of scholarly and theoretical books on the discourse of collecting. Interestingly, their primary focus has been not books but museum collections: the burgeoning field of museum anthropology or museum studies that looks at questions of connoisseurship and display.

Leah Dilworth, editor of the anthology *Acts of Possession*, notes that this has resulted in meta-museum studies – museums studying their own collecting practices. 'The appeal of collecting,' notes Dilworth, 'is that completeness and closure are impossible… it is a process of continual inquiry and endless desire.'

The Cultures of Collecting, edited by John Elsner and Roger Cardinal, are essays on the psychology, history and theory of the compulsion to collect. I've already mentioned how, in the psychoanalytic writings of Baudrillard and others, collecting is viewed as a pathology, linked to obsession and fetishism. There's an interesting essay in this anthology that reveals what an obsessive-compulsive collector Sigmund Freud was. He collected antiquities of which, by the time he died in September 1939, he had 3000 pieces. Apparently he kept them in the two rooms where he worked (and he always had a Vishnu figurine on his desk).

Susan Stewart examines the work of the painter Charles Wilson Peale who is a key figure in understanding the evolution of museum collecting: the museum he founded in 1786 is considered the first museum to be ever set up in the West. Peale made a sort of self-portrait that is today an iconic image for collecting and collectors, and which you find reproduced in most literature of collecting: *The Artist in His Museum*, 1822. You see him raising a curtain to reveal his collection. In the foreground, the giant jaw and tibia of a mastodon can be seen. Further inside, a woman is holding up her hands in astonishment at the mounted giant mastodon. Peale developed his museum, says Stewart, 'as an antidote to war's losses, and as a gesture against disorder and the extinction of knowledge'.

In their introduction, the editors come back to this idea of collecting as a stay against time using a most unusual and thrilling example: 'Noah was the first collector. Adam had given names to the animals, but it fell to Noah to collect them… In the myth of Noah as ur-collector resonate all the themes of collecting itself: desire and nostalgia, saving and loss, the urge to erect a permanent and complete system against the destructiveness of time.'

The line is thin between bibliomania and bibliophilia (because 'the act of acquisition is not an end but a beginning') but there *is* a line. And in returning to my earlier question – whether book collecting is not another form of hoarding and acquisitiveness – the distinction becomes important. The just published *Oxford Companion to the Book* (edited by Michael Suarez, H.R. Woudhuysen, 2010, the first ever reference books about books published) urges us to distinguish between the two.

While the bibliomaniac has 'a rage for collecting and possessing books', the bibliophile is 'a book collector of refined judgment, the quality of whose library reflects his or her exacting bibliographical standards in respect to such criteria as rarity and condition with their chosen fields'. A bibliophile is also distinguished from a bibliomane 'by the degree of discrimination used that is exercised in acquiring books'.

The great bibliophile-collectors are also the most passionate bibliographers, chasing after the actual object to learn from it. The life and practices of such collectors and the politics of collecting seduce me, instruct me, reveal to me my own relationship to a lifetime of reading, pursuing and possessing books. And as a modest collector, even if I'm not fully conscious of it, even if this is not what is on the minds of book collectors when they acquire rare books, I – we – collect because they are some of the most valuable and venerated objects in a culture.

EDITIONS

THE BOOKMAN
THE MYSTIQUE OF FIRST EDITIONS
FIRST EDITION FEVER
THE TATTOOED BIBLIOPHILE

THE BOOKMAN

In 1988, RARE book dealer Rick Gekoski offered the first English edition of *Lolita* in his catalogue for £3,250. A few weeks later, Graham Greene wrote to him, saying, 'Dear Mr Gekoski, If your copy of *Lolita*, which isn't even the true first edition, is worth £3,250, how much is the original Paris edition inscribed to me worth?' The Olympia Press *Lolita* is a finer edition and a copy inscribed by Nabokov to Greene would have to be special for many reasons. 'Dear Mr Greene,' wrote back Gekoski, 'More. Would you care to sell it?' Greene already owned another first edition, also inscribed by Nabokov, and felt he could sell the Olympia edition. Gekoski bought it for £4,000.

He opened the book and read the inscription, 'For Graham Greene from Vladimir Nabokov, November 8, 1959'. It was followed by a drawing of a large green butterfly.

By the next morning, Gekoski had sold it to a rich book collector (Bernie Taupin, Elton John's long-time lyricist) for £9,000. The moment it had gone out of his hands he regretted selling it. He had wanted to keep it with him. In 1992, Gekoski traced the book and bought it back for £13,000. After owning it for a short while, he couldn't resist selling it for a much higher sum to a book collector. In 2002, the book appeared at a Christie's sale and sold for an astounding $264,000.

Greene's involvement in *Swami and Friends* is a familiar literary legend; from Gekoski's *Nabokov's Butterfly and Other Stories of Great Authors and Rare Books*, we learn it was Greene who also brought *Lolita* to the notice of a reading public when he chose it as his best book of the year in 1955. *Lolita* had been fairly obscure till then since it had been published by Maurice Girodias in Paris. His Obelisk Press usually published classy pornography. In *Nabokov's Butterfly* (in some editions titled as *Tolkien's Gown*) Gekoski tells the stories of twenty rare books that passed through his hands, and includes a short publishing history of each book.

There are many books about book collectors, but only a handful on rare book dealers. David Meyer's *Memoirs of a Book Snake*, Larry McMurty's *Books; A Memoir*, John Baxter's *A Pound of Paper: Confessions of a Book Addict*, and *Book Row: An Anecdotal and Pictorial History of the Antiquarian Book Trade*, are also absorbing accounts of book scouts and dealers. Gekoski's specialization is rare 20th-century books. (Recognized for his distinction in the field, he was made a judge for the 2007 Man Booker prize: the first book dealer to be on the panel.)

In the 1960s, as a post-graduate at Merton College, Oxford, Gekoski found himself living in the same college house as Tolkien. He now kicks himself every day for not getting Tolkien to sign first editions of *The Hobbit* or *The Lord of the Rings*, which would now fetch $135,000 and $90,000 respectively. Tolkien was nearly reclusive but would gladly inscribe a book for a Fellow from the same college.

One day, Gekoski found out from the college porter that Tolkien was getting rid of things from his room. Hopeful of making a discovery, Gekoski was disappointed when no first editions or signed copies turned up.

What he did find was Tolkien's old college gown. It even had a name tag sewn on it. Being a Tolkien fan he felt compelled to keep it. Decades later, when he was putting out his book catalogue, he thought it a good idea to list the gown as well. Shortly after the catalogue went out, Julian Barnes, then a young novelist, phoned to ask if Gekoski was interested in Joyce's smoking jacket or perhaps Lawrence's underpants and Gertrude Stein's bra? Gekoski got the point and took the gown off the catalogue.

While working on William Golding's bibliography, he toyed with the idea of buying the manuscript of the *Lord of the Flies*. Evaluating, buying and selling a first edition, he notes, is easier than estimating the price of a manuscript of a modern classic. A nice crisp first edition of *Lord of the Flies* with a fine dust-wrapper, for instance, is sold usually at $9,000 – the manuscript for anything between $90,000 and 430,000. But Golding, he tells us, thought even this too cheap.

One of the highest sums ever paid for a manuscript was two million dollars for *On the Road*. It makes you wonder what the manuscript of *Catch 22* or *The Catcher in the Rye* might be worth. There are perhaps only a hundred signed copies of *Ulysses*, and at a 2002 Christie's sale one of them sold for $460,000: a considerable price for a 20th-century book. Gekoski owns a first edition that he treasures so much, he's never felt the temptation to sell it. First editions of *The Great Gatsby* and *The Sun Also Rises* with dust-wrappers have even broken the 90,000-dollar barrier. What is crucial to these editions is that they also possess fine or near-fine dust jackets.

Is there in the book somewhere a story about *The Catcher in the Rye*? There certainly is, and it has to do with more than just a first edition: Salinger wanted to sue Gekoski for possessing archival material (correspondence, notes, transcripts of interviews) relating to Ian Hamilton's unauthorized biography of the writer. Salinger pleaded with Hamilton not to write a biography but when Hamilton went ahead, the author took him to court. Salinger won and, years later, Hamilton decided to sell some of his research material (and the correspondence that followed) to Gekoski.

Eventually, the book dealer had to return most of the material to Salinger. (In exchange, Gekoski wanted Salinger to inscribe his first edition of *The Catcher in the Rye*. Salinger refused, of course.) But there were a few letters he sold to private collectors and libraries for a small profit.

Rick Gekoski was also one of the publishers included in the fatwa against Rushdie. Much before the controversy broke out, Gekoski and Rushdie had worked out an arrangement to print signed, numbered and specially designed limited editions (50 in all) of *The Satanic Verses*. Rushdie was closely involved with the book's production (a Bhupen Khakar illustration was the cover) and took pleasure in choosing the typeface himself. Each copy was sold for a fabulous sum, and when the fatwa was declared, they became even more valuable.

These limited signed editions are usually worth more than most first editions because they are numbered (there can be only 50 of them in the world, with number 1 being most valuable and 50 the least). Interestingly, notes Gekoski, the first editions themselves in this case were worth even less than the Penguin paperbacks which became scarcer because they were quickly pulled out of the market.

There are more stories of rare books in *Nabokov's Butterfly*. There is one even about the Harry Potter books in which the book dealer refuses to deal in Potter mania, believing more in the literary power of Philip Pullman. He doesn't mind, as he says somewhere, a reader preferring Enid Blyton to Tolkien but if you say Blyton is a better writer than JRR you are either 'a very unsophisticated child, or an idiot'. Apparently the bookshop Gekoski owns in London stocks only 50 books. But each is worth a fortune.

The Mystique of First Editions

For me, it began with Donna Tartt's *The Secret History*. One day, quite by chance, I happened to look at the imprint of my copy and noticed it was a first edition. I pulled down all the hardbacks off my shelf to see if I owned other first editions, and found out I had at least fourteen in my possession – and I hadn't even known. Since then, whenever I come across a hardcover book, I am quick to check the title page verso. What, though, is the mystique of a First Edition?

The lure of a First Edition is perhaps best known to someone who loves a particular book so intensely that she has to have the book when it was *born*, so to speak. A rather weak parallel I can think of to explain the value of a first edition is that it is like owning an original painting. Later editions – however new, however beautiful – can only be copies.

To be exact: what a book collector collects is the first printing of the first edition – the first print run, that is, or the first issue. But why is a first printing coveted when it looks exactly like the later printings? Take a book like *The Catcher in the Rye*, worshipped by its readers with a cultic devotion: it is not enough to own a paperback or even a hardback of the book but a copy that rolled off the printing press in 1951.

The first printing is also the edition closest to the author – the first print run that the author was directly involved with. I haven't gone as far as some collectors have – buying an expensive book only because it is a first printing, and not because they want it or care for it. For me (as for most bibliomanes) the importance of a first edition is in the value the book holds for me personally – not its market value. Which is why, for instance, I would gladly trade the more expensive and scarcer *The Catcher in the Rye* for *Franny and Zooey*: I happen to love the latter more. Or why a Maugham fan or a Wodehouse fan wouldn't think twice about trading her priceless Hemingway first edition for the vastly cheaper Maugham or Wodehouse first editions.

First editions, says Jeanette Winterson in her essay 'The Pyschometry of Books', have a presence not found in other editions, not even in old books. They have 'isotopic qualities, and the excitement a collector feels is not simply bibliographical – it is emotional… The text will transcend its time, the wrapper and the binding and the paper and the ink and the signature and the dedication can't. All that is caught (or lost) at a single moment.'

Has anyone explained the special lure of first editions better?

What is all this fuss, I often hear people ask me, about condition and value? Dust jackets protected in Mylar, fine editions in locked bookcases, exorbitant prices simply because a book is a first printing, and a vibrant, worldwide antiquarian book trade that deals (and thrives) in buying and selling rare and fine books. The fuss is about cataloguing, preserving and pursuing what is valuable in (and to) a culture. India becomes a classic instance where few understand that collecting first editions and fine bindings has more than monetary or personal value – that its value is cultural.

Three hundred years of a culture of bibliophily around the world, and we seem to have completely missed out on it. Where and when was the last time you came across, in an Indian bookstore or in a reader's personal library, a hardcover *first printing* of *The Guide* or *The God* of *Small Things*, or *Midnight's Children*? Seldom probably, or perhaps never. And if at all you got lucky and did chance on even one of these, what was the condition you found it in? Soiled, very surely, with the dust jacket torn or entirely missing. Which makes the value of the copy exactly zero.

The last time I found not one but six first editions of Narayan was in a used and rare bookstore in a small town near Boston. Three UK first editions (from Hamilton, Nelson, Heinemann) in a near fine condition, dust jackets nicely sheathed in Mylar, and three Indian paperback first printings from Indian Thought publishers, Mysore, in near mint condition. Elsewhere, in a London bookstore, I found a first printing of Roy's book, its dust jacket cozily wrapped in Brodart. Ditto for that winner of the Booker of Bookers – stashed away in a quaint, crumbling Hay-on-Wye bookshop.

So, to find some fine, desirable copies of an Indian author you have to comb bookstores across oceans. Thanks to these foreign booksellers who instinctively recognized they had something valuable in those first printings, we now have at least a few existing copies of first editions of our writers in decent to fine condition. And I don't have to tell you that the value of preserving the works of our best writers in their original editions is a cultural enterprise, not acts of bibliomania or cold-blooded commercialism.

Walk into any Indian bookshop – first or second – and you would be hard-pressed to find a shelf (let alone a section), devoted to first editions from anywhere. (Also missing from the trade are book scouts – book hunters – who track down rare books for a fee.) What you can find, scattered with the rest of the books, are some hypermoderns: contemporary first editions. A first edition of a Sue Grafton or a John le Carré. If you get lucky, you might find something more interesting – as I have from time to time: first editions of *The Silence of the Lambs*, and Arturo Pérez-Reverte's *The Club Dumas*.

A Modern First, of course, would be a modern classic – something by Kafka, Joyce, Faulkner, Greene, Chandler, Fitzgerald, Márquez, Tagore and so on. It is fairly easy to identify hypermodern first editions. The publisher clearly states it in the copyright page; or indicates it is a first edition with a number sequence running from 10 to 1. I bought a copy of Thomas Harris's *Hannibal* when it was just out, in the hope that the first imprint would have to be a first edition. It was a first, all right – a first Trade edition. Which probably means that x number of signed copies were printed first and sold privately as a limited edition to collectors.

Sometimes the imprint will read 1st UK or 1st US In this case, you have to 'follow the flag' – is the author American or British? – to find out which is the more desired true first. Identifying antiquarian and modern first editions is trickier. Because here a book may have two or even three first editions. How does this happen and how do you make out which was absolutely the first? To identify a true first edition, for example, you'll have to know how to differentiate between a 'first state' and a 'second state'.

The first state is the part of the first printing before they found the mistakes. Sometimes during the first print run, the publisher notices that there is a mistake. They stop, correct it and continue printing. But by now they've already printed several copies. Thus by default these x number of copies become the first *first* edition. More typos, and it becomes the second state. To differentiate between states, you have to become familiar with the various 'Points of Issue' in a book – that's bibliospeak for the errors that separate one state or issue from another.

For instance the first state of Steinbeck's *The Moon Is Down* will have this typo on page 112: 'talk.this'. The period in the middle of the sentence (talk.this) is one Point of Issue. Each printing or state could have several Points or mistakes. You can also turn to books about book collecting such as *Book Collecting: A Comprehensive Guide* by Allen and Patricia Ahearn, the *Pocket Guide to the Identification of First Editions* by Bill McBride, Edward N. Zempel and Linda A. Verkler's *First Editions: A Guide to Identification*, and rare book catalogues that describe existing editions of rare first editions.

The market value of a first edition depends on its condition. (And condition, as they say, isn't all, it's *everything*.) The more pristine it is the better, particularly the book jacket. The book minus its dust jacket is worth (in all but a few cases) nothing. Or if it is 'foxed' (stained with brownish, yellow spots) and 'rubbed' (if the spine is chafed or weak). The first thing a rare or antiquarian book dealer will tell you is not to use the word 'rare' casually. Many books that we think of as rare are to the dealer only 'out of print'. Antiquarian dealers frequently come across out-of-print books and editions in their daily workday.

It is only the retail bookstore and its patrons, namely us, who find it hard to come by a book that is no longer in print. A large portion of a book dealer's stock consists of out-of-print or limited editions. A book that even a dealer sees only seldom is termed 'scarce'. A scarce copy. It's only the book(s) that the dealer sees once in a decade – and sometimes a lifetime – that will be bestowed with the term, 'rare'.

One such legendary 'high spot' (book trade term for a rare item) is, of course, the *true* first edition of Scott F. Fitzgerald's *The Great Gatsby*. Why *true* first edition?

Because this is one book that has at least three or four states of printing! There are perhaps a handful of copies of the first true edition (first edition, first issue) of this book circulating in the market: that is, a good book jacket (if not a bright one) with all the points intact. It is notoriously hard to come by one which has both: if the points are intact – that is all the errors and typos from the very first print run are duly present – the jacket will have a tear or would be faded or entirely missing.

But what would be considered a rare Indian book? I'm curious about the antiquarian book trade here. Does one exist at all? Little or nothing is known about the Indian rare book market. What, for instance, are the existing rare or antiquarian Indian books? Who sells them and who buys them? (Possibly the only place or time I've had a glimpse of the antiquarian trade here is at the Osian's ABC series auctions.) Do we have rare book collectors here? If so, who are they and what kind of fabled prices do they pay for these antiquarian books?

What would we regard as a modern first or a hypermodern here? Books by R.K. Narayan could be modern firsts, while my bets are on *English, August* for a hypermodern. And just how rare would a first edition of Narayan's *Swami and Friends* be, anyway? Or a signed first edition of Upamanyu Chatterjee's *English, August*? Would Gandhi's *My Experiments With Truth* qualify as antiquarian? And if I happen to accidentally stumble on a rare manuscript, where would I get it evaluated and how much could I get for it?

First Edition Fever

'First Edition Fever' is how Lawrence and Nancy Goldstone describe the hunt for first editions. And they should know: the Goldstones went from first balking at paying $60 for a first edition of *Goodbye Mr. Chips* to wantonly paying $700 for a first edition of *Bleak House*. *Used and Rare: Travels in the Book World* was the Goldstone's first book about book hunting in second-hand bookshops. *Slightly Chipped: Footnotes in Booklore* was the sequel. The couple's third, *Warmly Inscribed: The New England Forger and Other Book Tales*, is perhaps the weakest in the trilogy but none the less indispensable to bibliophiles.

What sets this trilogy apart from other books about books is that they are not academic essays but a lively and knowledgeable narrative of their visits to several remarkable used, rare and antiquarian bookstores. The Goldstones discovered that they were primarily interested in modern firsts. While they would go happily without hypermoderns, the couple would have dearly loved to possess rare editions if only they could have afforded it: a first edition of *Gulliver's Travels*, they discover, is $40,000. In their first ever visit to a used bookstore they discover that the more beautiful the edition, the more suspect it is. They stare longingly at a row of classics bound in leather.

The owner of the shop comes over to them and dismisses the leather bounds. And the Goldstones wince because 'he said "leather bounds" the way Harold Bloom might say Judith Krantz.' But what was wrong with them? – they were finely bound, had gilt edging and there were even ribbons to keep your place with. They are worthless, insists the bookseller. The only edition that really matters, they learn, is the First Edition. And it is not long before the First Edition fever grips them. 'We didn't want condition,' they write, 'we wanted character.' My favourite part in their books is the lore on rare books, and what classic modern firsts are priced at. The Goldstones illustrate what a typical description of a scarce first edition in a book catalogue would look like:

> STOKER, BRAM. DRACULA. London: Archibald Constable, 1897. First Edition, First printing, first issue. Front hinge cracking, back hinge just barely started, small cloth tears at the top and the bottom of the spine, light foxing and minor soiling. $9,500.

To their utter astonishment, the Goldstones discover that the most expensive first edition is not something by, say, Dickens or Austen but *Tarzan of the Apes* by Edgar Rice Burroughs, priced at $50,000.

Ayn Rand's own copy of *The Fountainhead* is $15,000. *Catch 22* is $500. Raymond Chandler's *The Big Sleep* is $8,500. The very rare *Call for the Dead*, John le Carré's very first novel is $20,000. A Wodehouse ranges from $150 to 250. *Dracula* is $ 9,500. H.P. Lovecraft first editions are so rare that even a reprint will go for as much as $10,000. *The Prime of Miss Jean Brodie* is $50.

Tom Wolfe's *The Right Stuff* and Norman Mailer's *Armies of the Night* are for as little as $15. *Psycho* is $2,600 and is collected more for its vintage cover art. And Michael Ondaatje's 1974 Wall Calendar, which is 'extensively annotated by him in his hand as to his family activities on an often daily basis' is also for sale at $250! By a delicious coincidence, my own copy of *Warmly Inscribed* turns out to be a first edition. A first edition about first editions! Unlike *Used and Rare* and *Slightly Chipped*, *Warmly Inscribed* moves away from bookshops to the history behind unique copies, writers and libraries.

It's a bit disappointing not to have the Goldstones foraging in bookshops in their third instalment. The most interesting chapter from *Warmly Inscribed* is on rare book selling on the Internet. While the Goldstones are only too aware of the benefits of buying and selling on the Net, they lament it. What, after all, can take the place of browsing in a bookshop, meeting knowledgeable booksellers and actually seeing and holding a book?

The Tattooed Bibliophile

After first editions, what next? wonders the book collector. This isn't greed but a natural extension of the collector's longing to connect with everything associated with the book as object. Collecting broadsides and letters of a cherished author for instance, and by extension, special/limited/signed editions, galley/advance proofs, book jackets, vintage paperbacks, literary bookmarks, printed book catalogues, and even notebooks and bags with literary motifs (quotes/sketches of famous authors).

A Nabokov devotee I know asked his friends going abroad to search for Ticonderoga No. 2 pencils, because that's what the author used when sketching or writing. Paul Theroux once profiled an Anthony Burgess collector (probably fictional but no less interesting for it) in the *New Yorker*, who, in addition to owning everything Burgess had ever written, also possessed two old passports of Burgess, some concert tickets he had once used and an umbrella he had left behind at a bookshop.

I like to think of these as literary accessories, or to use a term from the rare book trade, literary ephemera. And to such literary accessories I've just added t-shirts.

It began as one of those souvenir larks – to make certain when visiting a bookstore abroad that you grab a t-shirt from there before exiting. But now I see them for what they are: highly desirable collectibles to go with my books. I've even gone and ordered one from the Internet. I saw it advertised when I was intently browsing through a high-end online bookstore called Between The Covers. I couldn't help noticing a weirdly wonderful sketch on the site: a fat, bald, fearsome looking man being tattooed with the names of famous authors. It was called 'The Tattooed Bibliophile'. A closer look revealed that it was the bookstore's way of advertising their wares. On top of the sketch was the bookstore's name, and below it, the legend: 'Not Just Another Bunch of Book Geeks'. It spoke for all of us book geeks who didn't want to be messed with. The sketch was by none other than their renowned resident artist, Tom Bloom.

While conducting a virtual inspection of the t-shirt, my eyes wandered to something that looked even more intriguing: a set of fifty trading cards, each card holding the picture of the original book jacket of a first edition high spot (a very rare and expensive first edition) and a description of condition, points and price. In other words, a stack of cards with photos of famous book jackets. I could see how reasonable and thoughtful these bookstore people were: first a kind of WWF book geek t-shirt and now sports cards converted to literary trading cards. (Why should only philistines and jocks have all the fun?) I sent for the Between The Covers t-shirt and the trading cards.

One of the more interesting ephemera I've spotted on eBay (I'm not an eBay groupie, but this one was too special to resist) is a seller who specializes in custom-made literary bookmarks. Is there a favourite author that you want to turn into a nice bookmark? You can have one that comes laminated and with pretty tassels. The bookmark will contain several book jacket images of the author's work, three of the author's best photos, and a small passage from her best-known book. I bid for Fitzgerald and Nabokov, and won. Later, I added a guilty pleasure: J.D. Salinger. Strictly verboten, actually, but I couldn't resist. That's a collectible bookmark if I ever saw one.

A further transgression in ephemera-collecting was

when I ordered, online, a facsimile book jacket of a first edition *Catcher in the Rye* from 'The Phantom Bookshop'. An artist named John Anthony Miller keeps countless book lovers across the globe happy (and well fed) by making high quality facsimile book jackets of famous books. From Stoker's *Dracula* to Burroughs' *Tarzan the Terrible* to that holy grail of jackets, Fitzgerald's *The Great Gatsby*. Made from the original source, the material is digitally scanned 'and meticulously restored on a pixel level many times more'. Miller sees it as an art form. And indeed when I received that facsimile *Catcher* (and it very clearly states *facsimile*) wrapped in a Mylar-protected cover, it was breathtaking. It looked bright and sharp, like it was printed yesterday (which it was).

I had with me a jacketless first edition of *Catcher* and I – as they say in the antiquarian trade – married jacket to book. Salinger won't approve, of course, but that jacket in the true original is scarce and expensive.

My newest literary accessory is the book catalogue. Our booksellers have never had a tradition of putting out catalogues (those booklets in black and white don't count), so I've taken to asking bookstores abroad to post it to me, which they are glad to do. Until now, the experience of browsing for books through a catalogue was an unfamiliar one for me. I recommend it – it's a new bibliophile high. Book catalogues today are, however, not as common as they once were. The contemporary trend to browse for books on the Net has altered book-buying practices everywhere.

Once booksellers (and not just antiquarian dealers) regularly printed catalogues and sent them out on request. Today, they mostly post a pdf version online. It still does the job, but in so many ways is a lesser and diminished experience than (as they used to say) perusing a sumptuously done book catalogue.

An exemplary book catalogue is the Bruce Kahn Collection, offered jointly by Between The Covers Rare Books and Ken Lopez Bookseller, another highly sought after and respected book dealer in high-end modern editions. Catalogues are traditionally focused on antiquarian items, and so it is a particular delight to encounter an entire catalogue devoted to just modern first editions. And what editions! What condition! How often can you find near-mint copies of first edition high spots? And, fantastic as this sounds, it is all the collection of just one man: Bruce Kahn, a successful lawyer turned book collector.

Among numerous treasures in the catalogue is a limited signed edition of Paul Auster's *New York Trilogy* ($7500), a near flawless copy of Cain's *The Postman Always Rings Twice* ($27,500), a signed copy of Raymond Carver's scarce first book of poems, *Near Klamath* ($12,500), the nicest possible signed copy of *Catch 22* ($12,500), *On the Road* in a perfect dust jacket ($25,000), a beautiful copy of *The Catcher in the Rye* in an un-restored dust jacket, and that exceptionally scarce first issue of *Raise High the Roofbeam Carpenters* lacking a dedication page.

In his catalogue introduction, BTC's owner, Tom Congalton, who has been book-dealing with Kahn for two decades, clues us in on how the lawyer put together such a stunning collection. 'He always wanted his books to be in perfect condition,' notes Tom, 'and even the slightest flaw would be either unacceptable, or if he finally decided he could overlook some nearly microscopic flaw, it had damn well better be mitigated by being a unique copy or an exceptionally rare book, or an important association copy, or preferably both. What's a bookseller to do? This set a pretty high standard for selling him books, and to some degree it is amazing that he has managed to assemble a collection of about 15,000 books in beautiful condition…'

Ken Lopez in his introduction notes that Kahn 'collected in the style of the old-time book collectors – that is, he collected authors in depth, pursuing all their published titles, variant editions such as proofs, advance copies, and broadsides… As a result, the author collections themselves end up being bibliographically significant, especially for those authors for whom there is not yet an "official" or definitive bibliography. Bruce has had a particular interest in the writings of Jim Harrison, and his collection contributed significantly to the forthcoming Harrison bibliography.'

Making a print-worthy catalogue – writing, illustrating and designing it – is an art. I am grateful to all these booksellers who still take an interest in writing and printing catalogues. The production costs for fine catalogues are obviously high, and they can easily just stay with an electronic version – and yet these booksellers print them because both the aesthetics of such a thing and its place in antiquarian bookselling feel important to them.

And perhaps even more vitally for the reasons Howard Prouty (who runs ReadInk, an online rare bookstore that also issues catalogues) pointed out to me: 'There's a little anxiety about the future of the printed book, especially given the increasing availability of digitized text. Printed catalogues are expressions of faith in a future world in which books will continue to be objects of interest to many people, and demonstrations of confidence in the continuing viability of the book trade itself.'

The Browser's Ecstasy

For the Cover Alone
The Rock Star of Book Jacket Design
The Postmodernist Always Rings Twice
& Other Titles
The Artists' Book

For the Cover Alone

I WOULD OFTEN hear T.G. Vaidyanathan, teacher, culture critic, and ardent bibliophile, tell me that he had bought a particular book for its physical beauty. He had no intention of reading it, he would tell me, as he caressed the book and put it back on the shelf. Once he had even cello-taped (with the thin, transparent kind) the edges of a book whose cover he was smitten by, so that it would stay unopened. I didn't understand this fetish then, but now I find myself buying books just for their covers or because the edition is beautiful.

Browsing in bookshops has become a veritable feast for the eyes. Book jackets are an art form. In some cases, the book jacket *is* the best thing about a book. Sooner or later it happens to all book lovers: coveting books in a physical sense. For the way they look and feel. And smell. Is it possible then to think of some books as objects (bright, beautiful, shining – not shiny) and not feel guilty that you aren't reading them because they were bought not to be read but to be looked at and lusted after?

I have been meeting more and more bibliophiles who seem to be doing likewise – and I must rush to add that this kind of books-adorning-our-bookshelves is not the same as that philistine practice common in so many of our homes where twenty-five books or so are displayed in the showcase (the top row is usually five or ten volumes of an encyclopaedia followed by religious, self-help and health books, popular paperbacks, and Readers' Digest Condensed Books) along with other trophies.

For the longest time I actually preferred second-hand books – mostly paperbacks – to new books. I could afford them and I loved the way they smelled. Well into the early '90s I remember our sidewalks being full of hawkers selling old paperbacks. Occasionally I'd stop, bargain and buy one or two at five or ten rupees each. Today there are fewer pavement booksellers and they now mostly flog new paperbacks, either pirated bestsellers or contemporary thrillers. The paperbacks I found once upon a time here are what are called in the book trade 'vintage'. And vintage paperbacks are collectibles.

Vintage paperbacks are collected for their cover art. Not to be read – although the collector is welcome to read them – but it's the cover art that one is really after here. The work of the graphic artists on these vintage covers was often superior to the writing inside. The paperback would be trashy or mediocre but its cover art redeemed it and made it special. Vintage paperback covers were done by artists trained classically as painters. (Compare this to the poor cover art of our paperbacks of that time.)

The genius of vintage paperbacks is that the cover artist created these small masterpieces without trying for it – much the same way some of the best pulp writers wrote without any self-conscious design of making art. Many of these cover artists went on to become giants in the art of illustration, and often paired off with a writer to do a whole series. Some of the best known were Robert McGuiness and his deadly femme fatales in the Carter Brown mysteries, Frank Frazetta and his bizarre covers for the *Conan the Barbarian* series by Robert E. Howard, the busty women of Bill Ward and James Avati's steamy paintings.

Avati is also famous for his cover art for the paperback of *The Catcher in the Rye* showing a young boy with a suitcase, red cap worn back and a scarlet scarf around his neck. Holden Caulfield, if you remember, 'horses around' by wearing the cap backwards. Avati, unlike many paperback illustrators, actually read the books before he designed the cover.

The first book to use the term 'science fiction' in the title was also a vintage paperback, an anthology called *The Pocket Book of Science Fiction* edited by Donald A. Wollheim (Pocket Book no. 214) from 1943. Needless to say, this is a huge collectible and anyone finding a copy of this edition will have struck collector's gold.

In the past, we've never had a culture of collecting foreign hardbacks in India. Our bookstores stocked so few of them and they were – and still are – expensive. Paperbacks – new and old – are what we saw in abundance and that's what we bought and kept (quite proudly and contentedly) on our shelves. The habit of collecting hardbacks is perhaps finally here with several Indian publishers bringing out reasonably priced, nice to stunning looking hard-covers.

Paperbacks were functional – to use and discard. Not anymore. They look so collectible these days: especially those Vintage paperbacks (the work of Sonny Mehta of Alfred Knopf) which are more exquisite than even some hardbacks. I delight in those bright, bold, irresistible colours used on the covers, and the artful and pleasing way the cover design combines a photograph with an illustration. It took me years to be weaned away from paperbacks (I missed the blurbs, for one thing) to hardbacks. But it is with the hardbacks that you really first encounter the physicality of books. It begins with their size and weight, their heft, and the way it feels in your hands. Then you become aware of the dust jacket (there's a way of reading a book with the dust jacket on which I'm yet to learn, so I take it off when reading on account of how it keeps slipping).

It's a little strange for us to think of a time when books had few or no dust jackets, but pre-1910, dust jackets were scarce, making them invaluable today to collectors and bibliographers. Books were issued in plain wrappers or had a hole cut into the jacket to reveal the title and author. It was only post 1910, with increasing competition in the book trade, that publishers began using dust jackets as a way to market a book. In April 2009, Michael Turner, head conservationist at Oxford's Bodleian Library uncovered a dust jacket dated 1829, making it the oldest known book dust jacket. It had been separated from its book, and Turner found it while sorting through an archive of book trade ephemera. The book itself was hardly notable, some sort of British annual, a gift book. The oldest dust jackets in literature on record are probably for Lewis Carroll's *The Hunting of the Snark* (1876), Conan Doyle's *The Adventures of Sherlock Holmes* (1892) and Kipling's *The Second Jungle Book* (1895). Two of them were issued in blue pictorial jackets. The first *Jungle Book* probably had no wrapper at all. There are only two or three known copies in their dust jackets of *The Wind in the Willows* (1908) and *The Hound of the Baskervilles* (1902), making them not only the scarcest jackets in the world, but the most sought after by collectors. A copy, if found, of any one of these books in their dust jackets would usually fetch a price of £80,000 and upwards at an auction. An increasingly rare modern wrapper is the dust jacket from the uncommon first state edition of *The Great Gatsby*.

The fascination with books as beautiful objects doesn't stop with dust jackets – it begins there. It's when you strip the book off its jacket that you see how elegantly crafted it is – paper, ink, cardboard, glue, thread and binding. For instance, for some time now I've been delighting in hardback books with untrimmed fore-edges – making the book look and feel old; wonderful and priceless to the touch.

I've also begun paying particular attention to a book's colophon, the page at the back of the book where the publisher credits the printer and her choice of typeface for the book: 'A Note on the Type' says the page's text, followed by something along the lines of: 'This book was set in Monotype Dante, a typeface designed by Giovanni Mardesteig (1872-1977). Dante is a thoroughly modern interpretation of the venerable face'. This has led me to a new appreciation of bibliopoesy, the making of books, and bibliopegy, bookbinding as a fine art.

When it comes to handling books I confess that I am what Anne Fadiman in *Ex Libris* called a courtly lover as opposed to a carnal lover. The courtly lover is obsessed with keeping, maintaining and preserving a book in good condition. For the carnal lover a book's words are holy – not the paper, cloth, ink and binding. And so the carnal lover wantonly writes in margins and fly leafs, underlines passages, dog-ears pages and keeps books face down, straining the spine.

T.G. Vaidyanathan was another courtly lover. The subject of his first English Lit lecture in my M.A. class was on handling books. 'First wash your hands, then dry them well. Now lightly apply some talcum powder to your palms, then pick up the book – that's how you keep from dirtying the covers of books. When you open a paperback, read it keeping the other side of the page upright or at a slight angle, never completely open – it creases the spine.' He demonstrated with two paperbacks he had brought with him.

I didn't always use to be a courtly lover. Reading in school and college, I would often dog-ear pages and keep the book spread-eagled on the bed. The book as an object was invisible to me. Only the writing inside mattered. Now that I read less, and I'm not the bibliophagist that I once was, I'm looking more at the book! Now I know that books are more than beautiful objects on the bookshelf – they offer presence.

The Rock Star of Book Jacket Design

The Tyrannosaurus silhouette on Crichton's *Jurassic Park*, the titles flying off the page from James Gleick's *Faster*, the spoon and fork sleeping beside each other from Vikram Seth's *All You Who Sleep Tonight*, the clear acetate jacket and the enlarged doll's head in Donna Tartt's *The Secret History* and *The Little Friend*, the simple but arresting typography on Katherine Dunn's *Geek Love*, the bloody close-up of a dead man's eye in Richard Lattimore's translation of *The New Testament* and the panels of red and blue in Orhan Pamuk's *My Name is Red* are all images on book jackets that have become iconic.

And they are all the work of Chip Kidd, the rock star of book jacket design.

Kidd – associate art director at Alfred Knopf who has designed more than 1,500 covers – is so sought after that authors stipulate in their contracts that he design their book jackets.

At a time when most graphic designers experimented with typography and illustrations, he used a collage of photographs, illustrations and typography. The design for *Chip Kidd: Book One*, a monograph of his work, is itself tantalizing. Kidd picks more than 800 of his best book covers and lavishly and playfully showcases them here, along with commentary by the authors he designed these jackets for. His signature style is not to have an obvious cover image but something oblique – even wild – that would still evoke the book. He often blurs and crops photographs, and is fond of using pop culture images to suggest wit, irreverence and zip.

Kidd readily admits that it was his boss at Knopf, Carol

Devine Carson (who pioneered conceptual photography on covers) who inspired him. Knopf's legendary editor, Sonny Mehta, is his other mentor. Kidd's work is not just slick. It has edge and depth. Updike notes in the book's introduction, 'Kidd reads the book he designs for and locates a disquieting image close to the narrative's dark, beating heart.' In another evocative, slim and finely produced monograph on Kidd's work (titled *Chip Kidd*) by Veronique Vienne, the author notes that Kidd 'uses every surface of a hardcover jacket – the spine, the back, the flaps – to escape the two-dimensional world of graphic design.'

In *By Its Cover*, an intelligent, analytical and richly produced book that looks at the history of book jacket design, the authors, Ned Drew and Paul Sternberger, tell us that it was the cover of Joyce's *Ulysses* that signalled the arrival of modern book jacket design. Ernest Reichl's now-famous cover used 'elongated typography that seemed as modern as Joyce's book'. Until the 1970s, modern book design seems to have largely experimented with typeface and illustrations – designers such as Paul Bacon who used a combination of typography and illustration for *Catch 22* and *One Flew Over the Cuckoo's Nest*. 'With the 80s,' notes *By Its Cover*, 'book design moved to post-modern collage... constructing post-modern jumbles that challenged modernist notions of continuity and creative individuality.' And it was the design team at Alfred Knopf that first met the challenge of postmodern book jacket design by using collaged imagery. The gifted Knopf team – Archie Ferguson, Barbara deWilde, Abby Weintraub, Gabriele Wilson, Peter Mendelsund and John Gall – are by no means the only high-profile book designers. Equally noteworthy are Michael Ian Kaye, (Farrar, Straus and Giroux; Little, Brown), Rodrigo Coral, Paul Sahre,

Angela Skouras, Jonathan Gray, Christine Kettner and Susan Mitchell to name only a few. (Book design has been so central to publishing for more than a century, it makes you wonder, doesn't it, what role it will play in the e-book?)

While many Indian publishing houses use freelancers, some of them have begun to build their own in-house design teams.

Bena Sareen, art director at Penguin India who has designed many of their best covers (she met Chip Kidd once, and he told her that he was surprised people knew his work in India) told me, 'As a book cover designer you only have so much space to convey many hundred pages of thoughts. And only a fleeting moment to catch the reader's eye amid the many titles screaming for attention in bookstores. Mine is a two-pronged strategy – either a cover should be arresting or have layers of meaning to trigger curiosity. I tend to judge a cover (and a designer) by its typeface usage. Some of the timeless cover designs display a sense of minimalism with simple stark typography. It is important to strike a balance between the aesthetic and the commercial. For instance, we rejacketed the Vikram Seth poetry backlist in an attractive, small hardback format, gave a series look and were delighted to see sales figures shoot up. A truly satisfying experience when the author and the sales team are pleased!'

For Shruti Debi, Picador India's chief editor, the main thing about cover design 'is to have the jacket capture some of the mood of the book. Our covers are all by freelance designers, the majority by artists of the pen, paper and paintbrush variety (quite the opposite of Chip Kidd, as it were), who have been absolutely superb at translating and distilling a book's tone and content into a singular image.' In 2009 Faber&Faber, one of the last of the great independent publishing houses left in the world, turned 80. Faber celebrated it with a lavishly illustrated book of their best book covers. In *80 Years of Book Cover Design*, Joseph Connolly, an ardent collector of Faber first editions, demonstrates the art and beauty of these magnificent covers. Faber's familiar typography, brush lettering and hand painted covers were largely the work of its great art director, Berthold Wolpe.

He designed two new typefaces – Hyperion and Albertus. When in 1941 he became the resident jacket designer for Faber, he began using these over-scaled typefaces to create his book covers. Apparently, he would hand-paint some of these covers in just an hour, after a last-minute change had been called for. He designed more than 1,500 jackets for Faber. The Faber covers that I know well are the jackets for those Lawrence Durrell books (*Justine, Balthazar*), Eliot's *Four Quartets, Old Possum's Book of Practical Cats* (1939), Becket's *Waiting for Godot*, Golding's *Lord of the Flies*, Sylvia Plath's *Ariel, The Faber Book of Children's Verse*, and Larkin's *Girl in Winter*.

When Wolpe retired in 1975, and Pentagram, an independent design company began to do the covers, Faber books weren't instantly recognizable anymore. Pentagram experimented a good bit with geometric design and black and white photography. And before Faber put together its own in-house design team, Pentagram had come up with that unmistakable Faber colophon: **ff**.

The more recent Faber covers have broken away from their signature lettering. Rohinton Mistry's *A Fine Balance*, Vikram Chandra's *Love and Longing in Bombay*, Vikram Seth's *Three Chinese Poets, More Kinky Friedman* (this one is far-out), Ted Hughes' *Birthday Letters*,

Jonathan Lethem's *The Disappointment Artist*, P.D James' *The Murder Room*, Manju Kapur's *Home* and the strikingly unFaber-like Aniruddha Bahal's *Bunker 13*.

What Orhan Pamuk once noted about book covers and faces seems a fitting tribute to the work of Kidd, Wolpe and other gifted book jacket designers: 'Book covers are like people's faces: either they remind us of a lost happiness or they promise blissful worlds we have yet to explore. That is why we gaze at book covers as passionately as we do faces.'

The Postmodernist Always Rings Twice
& Other Titles

THERE'S SOMETHING THRILLING about a good title. The best titles are small literary constructs in themselves, almost poem-like. And amazing for the way they can reverberate with meaning. I collect titles. Consider these: *First Love and Other Sorrows*, *More Die of Heartbreak*, *A Sentimental Education*, *The Long Goodbye*, *The Object of My Affection*, *The Size of Thoughts*, *Totally, Tenderly, Tragically*, *In Praise of Shadows*, *The Importance of Elsewhere* and *Jeff in Venice, Death in Varanasi*.

The above titles are for me some of the most beautiful in the language. *The Interpreter of Maladies* and *The God of Small Things* are so good, I can actually picture their authors smacking their lips in satisfaction. Amit Chaudhuri seems to invent the loveliest titles. What could be more beautiful than *A Strange and Sublime Address*? Amitav Ghosh's *The Shadow Lines* is imaginative and haunting; *In An Antique Land* is evocative for its formal, classical beauty. *English, August* feels quaint, and doesn't mean anything until you begin reading the book. And then the title lights up with rich comic possibilities. Well chosen, Mr Chatterjee.

Titles can fool you: I've so often been the victim of fantastically titled books that turn out to be duds. A lot of contemporary fiction – particularly Indian fiction in English – falls into this category: often the title is the only remarkable thing about the book. And so they end up feeling pretentious – the books never live up to their titles. The more gimmicky the title, the less interesting the book! And I have to wonder: the simpler the title, the better the book?

What is a good title? Not only one that is fitting, but also evocative and stylish. *The Gutenberg Elegies* is about the fate of reading in an electronic age. *The Bachelor of Arts* is simple, pleasing, fitting. *Hours in the Dark* is such an evocative and stylish title for a book of film reviews and essays on cinema. *A Year in the Dark* is a year spent reviewing movies in the dark of a theatre. Joe Queenan's irreverent book on Hollywood is titled *Confessions of a Cineplex Heckler*. *Love and Hisses* is a collection of 'for and against' film reviews on the same movie! Nicholson Baker's *U&I* is a meditation on his non-existent friendship with John Updike.

It's delightful when titles are borrowed and played around with. A great example of such title-skewering is when culture critic Gilbert Adair called his book on literary theory bashing *The Postmodernist Always Rings Twice*. A spin-off, of course, of James M. Cain's *The Postman Always Rings Twice*.

Sometimes the same book will have two titles. In Britain, Salinger's collection of short stories was called *For Esme, With Love and Squalor*. But Salinger was insistent that he wanted the American edition to be called, simply, *Nine Stories*. As lovely as the *Esme* title is, I think he was right about *Nine Stories* – there's a quiet, unpretentious (Zen-like, I'm tempted to add) quality to it. (*Franny and Zooey*, *Raise High the Roofbeam Carpenters* and *Seymour, An Introduction* are special because they are about the Glass Family and carry a private meaning for those who know Salinger's literary family).

The title that Umberto Eco most wanted for *The Name of the Rose* was 'Adso of Melk'. His publishers would not let him, and a working title for the book was 'The Abbey of the Crime'. In his postscript to the book, Eco tells us that the final title came purely by chance and he was happy with it because the rose was so rich in meaning as a symbol that it had lost all meaning or any one meaning. 'A title must muddle the reader's ideas,' Eco notes, 'not regiment them.'

Authors have used titles to speak of their subject in rich metaphor: Andrew Solomon's book on depression is titled *The Noonday Demon*, Jeffrey Masson's book on the emotional life of animals is *When Elephants Weep*, Robert Thurman's classic introduction to Tibetan Buddhism is titled *The Jewel Tree of Tibet: The Enlightenment Machine of Tibetan Buddhism* (the unusual, scientific-sounding conjunction of 'enlightenment-machine' does the trick), Richard Preston's book on the small-pox virus is *Demon in the Freezer*, and Pico Iyer, writing about lonely places in the world, titled his book *Falling off the Map*.

Some book titles are so quirky and arresting that even non-readers know them by heart: *The Man Who Mistook His Wife for a Hat*, *The Unbearable Lightness of Being*, *Zen and the Art of Motorcycle Maintenance*, *One Hundred Years of Solitude*, *Six Characters in Search of an Author*, *A Confederacy of Dunces*, and *Publish and Perish: Three Tales of Tenure and Terror*. Perhaps the most oddly ravishing title I came across recently is the eccentric fantasy-adventure novel by G.W. Dalquist, *The Glass Books of the Dream Eaters*. An unforgettable title, and an unforgettable jacket design that pokes your eyes out from where the book sits on the shelf.

All those beloved classics with proper and personal names – *Jane Eyre*, *Hamlet* (!), *Wuthering Heights*, *David Copperfield*, *Madame Bovary*, *Anna Karenina*, *Shakuntala*, *Kanthapura* – are now established titles. But how very easily they could have all been known by other names... even for the sake of it I don't want to speculate what else

Hamlet or *Anna Karenina* or *Shakuntala* might have been called by their creators.

There are titles that acquire a mystique because of what the book has come to mean, such as Isak Dinesen's *Out of Africa*. Turn that into 'Out of America' or 'Out of England' and the title evaporates. (Her *Anecdotes of Destiny* is really more like it).

The title of Peter Hoeg's remarkable Danish thriller was translated as *Smilla's Sense of Snow* (the one that stuck) but I prefer the other translation – *Smilla's Feeling for Snow*. Simon Winchester's book about the making of the Oxford English Dictionary was called *The Surgeon of Crowthorne* in Britain and in America, *The Professor and the Madman*.

The mystery genre has its own set of rules when it comes to titles. The titles usually belong to a series that is coded: John. D. McDonald's Travis McGee series, for instance have a colour coding: *The Deep Blue Goodbye*, *The Dreadful Lemon Sky*, etc. And then there's Sue Grafton's alphabetical series: *A is for Alibi*, *Q is for Quarry*, *L is for Lawless* and so on. Do mystery writers resort to this because it solves the problem of coming up with a decent title? What will Grafton do when she runs out of alphabets?

Raymond Chandler never took the easy way out: his books are some of the best-titled mysteries: *The Big Sleep*, *The Long Goodbye* and then there's his classic essay: 'The Simple Art of Murder'.

However, not everyone feels the same way as I do about titles: a poet friend of mine refuses to title her poems. (And that's long before she came across e.e. cummings.) When she comes across a poem in an anthology, she avoids looking at the title if she can help it. The title, she feels, defines the poem too much. I suspect many artists would like to leave their work untitled if they had a choice. e.e. cummings published a book without a title. Apparently, to this day, copyright clerks and librarians continue to be haunted by the problem of recording and categorizing it.

Whether the best titles are pure inspiration and spring out of nowhere, or they need working at before they're found, one thing is for sure: coming up with a good title is itself half the achievement.

The Artists' Book

Put simply, an artists' book is a book made by an artist. A book designed and produced by an artist. The artist executes each step of a book's production, and has control over every aspect of the book. It could be handmade or from a hand press. A modern example: Claire Van Vliet's *The Tower of Babel* (1974), a set of unbound folios of haunting lithographs accompanied by letter press printed texts by Franz Kafka about the imagery and myths of Babel. The artists' book is part of a larger discipline – Book Arts, which encompasses all aspects of the physical book: bookbinding, typography, papermaking, letterpress and offset printing, illustration, book design, paper decoration, calligraphy, the sculptural and the altered book.

My familiarity with collecting beautiful books has been limited to special editions brought out by 'fine presses'. But this is *not* the artists' book. The artists' book takes this expression further: the entire book as crafted by an artist. Early instances of book arts is William Blake illustrating and binding his own poems, and perhaps most famously William Morris and the books from his Kelmscott Press (1860s), especially the renowned Kelmscott Chaucer with its fine illustrations of vines twisting and spilling around the text.

When someone remarked that Morris' Kelmscott was overdressed, he said: 'If the modern book that gives you words and pictures is enough I say that your interest in books in that case is literary only, not artistic, and that implies I think a partial crippling of the faculties; a misfortune which no one should be proud of.' I was struck by this: that one's interest in a book can or should be beyond merely literary! But of course if you care for the book as an object of art, the artists' book is the ultimate in the poetics of books, no?

Take the book form that preceded the artists' book: the deluxe edition. The 1935 deluxe edition of Joyce's *Ulysses*, illustrated by Henri Matisse in a craft binding by James Brockman. Only 250 copies printed, with each book signed by Joyce and Matisse. Even if you couldn't afford to own it, you'd want to see it and touch it, wouldn't you?

In *No Longer Innocent: Book Art 1960-1980*, (the first comprehensive history of the book art movement) Betty Bright, a long-time participant in the books arts environment, notes that the book artist makes the entire book her material. It goes beyond illustrating a writer's work – the traditional book itself is reconfigured, altered. Bright, an independent scholar and historian and book art curator, writes on her website that 'Artists' books transform the reading experience into a participatory interaction involving intellect and emotion, the body and the senses.'

An offshoot of book art is the altered book: old books recycled by rebinding, cutting or folding them into shapes. One that stunned me was *Lolita* altered to the shape of a pistol. What the artist is doing here is taking soiled or discarded copies of *Lolita*, and sculpting it in the shape of a gun. The sculpted book is avant garde, used as an installation or a performance piece. Great contemporary artists like Brian Dettmer and Ed Ruscha have been passionately involved in the book arts environment.

The artists' book can also be political, points out Bright, as in Richard Minsky's *The Crisis of Democracy*, where Minsky bound the book in leather and wrapped it in barbed wire.

Minsky is the founder of the Centre for Book Arts in New York. Book Arts is practised largely within a community of non-profit arts organizations. Many contemporary book artists have also begun making use of technology to make their work available to a larger public – offset printing, photocopy machines, computer-assisted images, and flatbed lithography. One book artist noted that what they are doing '…is not dependent on approval by a publisher. It doesn't require a lot of capital. The scale is human. Our medium doesn't need batteries. It produces no radiation and is portable.'

There are fine presses devoted to just bookwork; some of the best known are Janus Press, Granary Books, Brighton Press, Lapis Press, Arion Press and Crooked Letter Press.

Tara Books in Chennai is a marvellous example of a fine press for handmade books. Not just finely drawn, handcrafted and designed but interesting for their emotional, intellectual and political content as well. *The Night Life of Trees*, silk screened and hand bound, is filled with 'luminous, intricately drawn visions of trees', featuring the art work of three fine artists from the Gond tribe: Bhajju Shyam, Ram Singh Urveti and Durga Bai. At the 2008 Bologna Children's Book Fair, *Trees* won the 'Ragazzi New Horizons' award, making it the first Indian book to do so. No less an art critic than John Berger described it as 'A book where the nightingale sings until morning.' Shyam also illustrated another hand-bound book, *The Mermaid's Story*, which re-visualizes the Andersen fairly tale in a tribal cosmos.

One of their first books, *The Very Hungry Lion*, featured illustrations in the Warli style of painting, setting the tone and style for the rest of the books that would follow, featuring traditional visual art. Tara made another publishing decision, audacious for an independent publisher but ultimately inspiring for the way it succeeded: to use quality paper and printing. Tara is probably the only fine press to have published more than 160,000 handmade books, all of them from workshops run on fair trade practices.

The books from Tara that I am fondest of, and connect with deeply, are the ones on popular culture. *Baby!* is a book that takes you straight back to your childhood and those calendars you saw everywhere (offices, schools, barber shops) of the Agricultural baby, the Military baby, the Nehru baby, and all those crazy, impossible, bureaucratic-government-imagined babies in caps and uniforms and on tractors.

We dismissed it as kitsch art, and in time, came to be embarrassed by such calendar and picture postcard art. Tara's genius was to recognize that these pictures and images had actually become our emotional past, making us instinctively long for more such picture books. The *Match Book* is my personal favourite. Pictures of Indian matchbox labels: Cheetah Fight, Judo Deluxe, Tip Top, and Chaavi, to name only a few brands from nearly a thousand colourful labels; the collection of just one man, Shahid Datawala. The book is even designed like a matchbox, and comes in a slipcase.

The 9 Emotions of Indian Cinema is another exciting creation: an homage to those wild, giant-sized, exploding-with-colour cinema hoardings that once festooned our main thoroughfares. The paintings by the Chennai hoarding artists featured here (who were behind all those huge, vibrant Tamil movie cut-outs on Mount Road) were commissioned for the book, each illustrating an emotional trope from our cinema. The book is illustrated by M.P. Dakshna.

Tara is now collectively owned by those who run it. It works as a collective of writers, artists and designers, and this seems to be in keeping with the spirit and tradition of book arts environments everywhere.

The more children's picture books I see, and the more familiar I become with their illustrators, the more I'm convinced the best of them can be looked upon as, if not the Artists' Book, the work of true artists. For the last couple of years the section I head straight to on entering a bookstore is the children's picture books. It's always a small section in most Indian bookshops, almost negligible, but this is where I make my most ecstatic discoveries. No kidding.

When I head off for the picture book section, I get amused looks from friends rushing off to browse through the latest *Granta* or the new Booker winner. And when I invite them to join me to flip through these picture books, I get a you-can't-be-serious look. Later, examining our loot over chaat and coffee, I'll pass these books around to show them what they missed. After flipping a few pages hastily, they always pause and flip back the pages to look more closely at the illustrations, and nine times out of ten I'll see a new respect in their eyes. I'll see hands caressing the pages from a need to get close to the drawings.

Some of the most beautiful and artistic books I've had the pleasure of encountering lie amidst piles of mediocre children's literature. (And they are invariably deeply discounted or dumped in bargain bins). I've found at least four *hardcover* Maurice Sendak books, and I've had the joy of feasting eyes on the work of dozens of other brilliant illustrators, only not as famous.

Sendak is 81 now. He wrote and illustrated *Where The Wild Things Are* in 1963. I first heard of this author and his legendary book from a friend while in college. By that time, it was already a children's classic in the West and Sendak was regarded as the picture book artist who had forever changed how picture books would look and feel in the future. But few readers – children and adults – seemed to know the book or its author in India, and it wasn't until many years later that I finally saw the little book myself.

For the first few encounters with the book, I found myself, unexpectedly, not very impressed with the illustrations or the story. The wild things the boy meets – what admirers and detractors of the book had found either remarkable or troublesome – didn't do much for me. Since then, however, I've kept running into the book here and there and found that with each new browsing of *Where the Wild Things Are*, I began entering Max's adventure with more empathy and enjoyment, until I became the little boy.

The deep power of Sendak's drawings and words don't spring at you, but enter your imagination subtly. His secret, by his own admission, is that he recalls the mind and emotions of a child with a vividness, clarity and affection few adult artists remember or know how to. I think his drawings of children and animals are enchanting for their detail and beauty. No picture book artist I know can describe a child's emotions and subconscious dream world in the truthful, unfinished way Sendak's books have.

The stories really have no sense of completeness or wholesomeness – the characters tumble from one fanciful, silly, transcendent situation to another and when you reach the end, the fantasy has no meaning. No lessons are learnt (at least nothing typical) and no morals are drawn. Sendak has illustrated more than 100 books over nearly seven decades. And each book, small or big in scope, is unfailingly and uncommonly good. They have continually challenged the conventions of children's literature and spoken powerfully and indelibly to adults as well.

Many contemporary artists working in the picture book genre are sophisticated graphic novelists who leave behind all the dark stuff they do for adults and imagine something gentle and funny and happy. For instance, the work of Maira Kalman (among all the famous *New Yorker* magazine covers, her 'Dog Reads Book' cover is my great favourite).

She has a series with a dog named Max Stravinsky who is a dreamer and a poet. And in *Swami on Rye*, Max the poet-dog takes off to India. There he meets a garrulous guru, a suave swami who introduces himself as: 'Vivek Shabaza-zaza-za, that's za-zaaa-za, not za-za-za-za or za-za za za za, please.'

Shabaza-zaza-za then declares that Max is 'an old soul and that life is a wheel.' Max thinks: 'What, I'm wearing old shoes and life is a banana peel?' Everywhere Max goes he sees huge movie poster hoardings. One is for a major motion picture titled 'Guru To Go', with hand illustrated faces of Sri Devi and Rekha. And Max says, 'You have to be a real falooda not to love a movie.' He also goes around exclaiming: 'Holy Madras!'

The enchanting *Library Lion* is a book I'm tempted to thrust on *everyone*.

'One day, a lion came to the library,' is how it begins. Written by Michelle Knudsen and illustrated by Kevin Hawkes, *Library Lion* is a children's picture book that can beguile the most jaded adult. At storytelling time, the lion raptly listens with the children. Soon, he's doing errands around the library, licking envelopes, dusting shelves with a switch of his tail, and letting the children ride on his back.

I break into a broad grin each time I see Hawkes' magisterial, lovable lion, which must now be counted as one of literature's unforgettable characters. Knudsen's text is witty, moving, and bookishly imaginative. A perfect tribute to books, libraries and reading.

Perhaps the most staggering picture book I have ever seen, a masterpiece unlike anything else in the genre, is Shaun Tan's *The Arrival* (2007). I'm unable to believe anyone could imagine up and draw the things Tan has. The book is wordless. Tan uses a mix of hyper-real and surreal illustrations to introduce us to a world that is old and new. Familiar things lie side by side with strange things. *The Arrival* is a story of the immigrant disguised as science fiction. We see a man leave his family and enter a world he has never seen before.

In the apartment he takes residence in, he discovers a flatmate who looks like a cross between a fish and a cat. Though they cannot speak each other's language, the fish-cat is friendly and makes the man feel more comfortable in this new city where he hopes to find work. The colour throughout is sepia and indeed the images resemble old family photos. The challenge is to draw a city that is both old and new to every reader on the planet, and Tan's imagination and artistic skills astonish us page after page. His last, *Tales of Outer Suburbia*, figured in nearly every critic's top ten list of notable 2009 picture books.

Robert Sabuda is the prince of pop-up artists. The pop-up book is the one kind of picture book that is seldom seen in our bookstores. (If you see a few, they are invariably second hand and damaged enough for the pop-ups not to work). A pop-up book is basically the work of a paper engineer. The garden variety has illustrations that open out in a three-dimensional way (they pop up when the page is opened), and of course most adults dismiss it as kid's stuff.

Ah, but there are pop-up books and then there are pop-up books. The work of the genius paper engineer Sabuda simply astonishes and pushes the boundaries of the pop-up book beyond what any paper engineer has dared or imagined. He's done mind-blowing pop-up versions of classics like *Alice in Wonderland*, *Wizard of Oz*, a science series on prehistoric animals, and several different Christmas fables and fairy tales. His greatest achievement is his last, *The Chronicles of Narnia*. Each pop-up here illustrates a key image or scene from each chronicle. They are sheer magic, an unsurpassed feat of paper engineering.

And, of course, like almost everyone around the world, I love the drawings of E.H. Shepard (*Winnie the Pooh*), Ludwig Bemelmans (*Madeline*) Beatrix Potter (*Peter Rabbit*), Arthur Rackham (*Brothers Grimm; The Wind in the Willows*), John Tenniel (*Alice in Wonderland*), Quentin Blake ((Roald Dahl), and Edward Gorey. I also delight in the work of Peter Sis, Sara Fanelli, Elena Odriozola, Raymond Briggs, Øyvind Torseter and Maurizio Quarello, to name only a few among the hundred or so brilliant illustrators at work today.

There is much stylistic variety and vibrancy among picture book artists, with each illustrator bringing his own graphic language to the book, her own visual eloquence. Which is why Sendak said that the stars of picture books are illustrators.

ACK Title No. 11

IN A BAZAAR in Mumbai's Santa Cruz, a rather attractive American professor of religion is combing the wares of those familiar footpath book sellers for old issues of *Amar Chitra Katha*. As strange and curious as this may seem, it is why she is here in India: to study these comics.

On a September afternoon in 2001, Karline McLain makes a little discovery that first puzzles, and then excites her: she finds, amidst the raddi, a tattered copy of the *Krishna* comic book.

Karline notices that this version differs from the one in circulation. Here, the miracles are absent: Krishna is not holding aloft that mountain. She wonders if, even before the first print run of this famous title no. 11 from the ACK stable in 1969, there had been another smaller print run that had completely disappeared. But why? Had she stumbled on the true first edition of the *Krishna* comic book?

Teaching at Bucknell University, McLain was already deeply engaged in exploring visual culture in modern India, with an emphasis on representations of popular devotional art in the region. Bazaar art: calendars and posters of gods and goddesses that often, to our peril, we dismiss as kitsch. Fascinated by ACK, she packed her bags for Mumbai in 2001, feeling driven to take her research deeper. She began at the Amar Chitra Katha studio where she was given a desk and access to the staff, the readers of the comic book and its founding editor, Anant Pai. Earlier, she had corresponded with Pai, and he had welcomed the project.

Out of this emerged *India's Immortal Comic Books:*

Gods, Kings, and Other Heroes, her engaging book on the ACK comics. Though the origins of *ACK* are well known, Karline provides many sparkling insider details on the working of the studio. This, and the reprints of the original cover art of *ACK*'s classic titles (*Rama, Jataka Tales, Birbal, The Gita, Shakuntala, Pandava Princess, Savitri, Mirabai, Akbar, Tulsidas, Tansen*) in the book, makes *India's Immortal Comic Books* a genuine find. It's both scholarly and accessible, narrating the history of the comic, the way its readers have apprehended it, and its present-day incarnation.

For her study of *ACK*, Karline began with its readers, flung far and wide. And, then again, right there in Mumbai where she spoke with college students. What she heard over and over again, from old and young readers, was the ubiquitous presence of the comics in not just their growing up, but in shaping an Indian sensibility. One of her scholarly objectives here is to show how these comics construct a middle-class Hindu identity.

For many of its middle-class Brahmin readers it was clearly a nationalist or Hindu sensibility. But even its non-Hindu readers gushed that the comics had inspired in them an emotional sense of feeling Indian. Like the many readers represented in McLain's book, I too came fresh from a reading diet of *Phantom, Mandrake* and *Tarzan* to ACK. I remember it was a little infra-dig to be seen with a *Krishna* or a *Tansen* or *Shakuntala* comic when you could be looking hipper with Marvel or Tintin. But coming from a slightly evangelical Christian home, I couldn't get enough of these comics, and it was a back entry to Hindu mythology which I had begun to grow fascinated with.

Karline McLain also spoke to grandparents, and families in diasporic Indian communities, and what the scholar repeatedly heard from them was that the comic books seemed to almost radiate a spiritual force. In many households, other comics were seen as a waste of time and discarded, but ACK was preserved carefully. She notes that the panels featuring gods and goddesses were drawn looking slightly left so as not to induce darshan or gaze. Uncles willed *Amar Chitra Kathas* to their nieces and nephews; fathers handed whole bound sets to sons as legacies, and grandmothers carefully preserved the comics with brown paper as if they were school books or religious icons.

When she asked younger readers if they thought the comics were also political, she discovered a range of responses with one group saying it was 'insane to think it as being part of a political agenda' and the other declaring it as 'damn Hindutva propaganda to brainwash children'. One reader wrote this: '*Amar Chitra Katha* embraces globalization without giving in to homogenization: India is a country with an equally great past as any European country. While it is important to embrace modernity, it is important to do so on one's own terms.'

I asked Karline what first drew her to these comics: 'The moment that stands out to me is this: I had already studied a number of the ACK issues. But then I was spending some time in Udaipur, Rajasthan studying Hindi literature, this would have been in 1999, and I kept running across the comics in English and in Hindi everywhere I went, and was able to see firsthand how kids responded to them. One day I was buying a stack of the comics in Hindi (for more language practice), and there was a boy standing with his mouth open in awe that I was buying so many at once. So I gave him a couple of issues, and he was thrilled – he just sat right down in the dusty lane to read them on the spot.'

After a few months at the *ACK* studio she had become more than familiar with all the *ACK* comics. And when she found the miracle-less *Krishna* copy she took it to Anant Pai and asked him to explain the mystery of this unorthodox edition. His background as a chemical engineer, he told her, had made it uncomfortable for him to keep the miracles as part of the mythology. So they did a first print run of the Krishna story without too many spectacular miracles. But he soon changed his mind when he realized it was exactly that aspect of *ACK* that readers were so charged by, and reprinted the comic with the miracles intact. *Krishna* has been reprinted more than 60 times, selling more than a million copies.

Once Pai had convinced H.G. Mirchandani of IBH to publish comics with stories from Indian mythology, he set about looking for illustrators. He found them in Bombay's advertising companies: Yusuf Bangalorewala, Pratap Mullick and Ram Waeerkar. At first the ACK comics sold slowly, and then began outselling Indrajal comics. They had to be careful not to imitate the style of those comics, and evolved their own style of panel drawing. The comics focused on writing, inking and drawing stories about Hindu gods, saints, Muslim kings, British villains, musicians, and modern patriots.

McLain's interest in the project is to look at these comics as 'a unique opportunity for the study of the definition and negotiation of a modern middle class Indian identity… They also draw upon Indian visual and literary culture. In mixing mythology and history they create a national canon of heroes – where Bose and Rama are side by side.' She observes that they even go some way in defining an Indian in post-colonial times, and so have a power and significance that other comic books from other cultures seldom possess.

Karline's new research interest is the *Vivalok Comics*, founded by Rukmini Sekhar in New Delhi in 2001. 'Sekhar acknowledges her indebtedness to *ACK*,' McLaine told me, 'which she fondly recalled reading as a child, but stated that in her comics she tries to "draw out the undercurrents and subtleties of mythology, to use comic books for rigorous inquiry".'

Thus in her *Godavari Tales* comic book, she presents a local version of the *Ramayana* epic as it is retold among village women in the Godavari River valley today. 'In this version there is no happily-ever-after ending as in the *ACK Valmiki's Ramayana* comic; instead, the women focus on Sita's banishment and question why Rama might do such a thing, thereby drawing out the moral ambiguities of the epic.'

She continues to pursue further research on the devotional usage of posters and calendars, which she first became interested in when tracing the relationship between the *ACK* comics and earlier images (including those of the Ravi Varma press). Several art historians in India and abroad have done very good work with the history of such images, but little attention has been paid to their devotional side, and this is what the young American professor hopes to focus on next.

A Gentle Madness

True Tales of Bibliomania
The Man Who Loved Books Too Much:
Book Thief I
The Tome Raider: Book Thief II
Out of Circulation
Marginalia (& Other Literary Curiosities)
The Tireless Reader
The Book Borrower

True Tales of Bibliomania

Some bibliophiles confess to having nicked a book or two in the past. Others speak of having wanted to but not daring it. 'God, I wanted to lay my hands on it so badly,' they will say of a particular book. Some will just grin brightly and you must understand that the notion has crossed their mind. There's something about bibliokleptomania that makes people want to excuse it.

The reasons for stealing books and the methods seem to vary. Much of it happens when you are a student and can't afford to buy a new book. In college, there were a few students who didn't always return books to the public library. They saw this largely as a rescue operation. Their rationale was that no one else would care for these books as much as they did. Also, Indian public libraries being what they are, they felt the books would soon fall apart from neglect.

Years later when I met other bibliophiles, I heard the same thing. 'We couldn't believe they actually had a copy of *A Sentimental Education* sitting there!' Or, 'Imagine, Kenneth Rexroth's translation of Greek and Chinese poetry collecting dust on the stacks. The borrower's slip showed that no one had taken it out in ten years! It was as if the book was waiting for me to come possess it.'

When a friend heard I was talking to people about stolen books, she told me of once borrowing a book from the British Library, falling in love with it and deciding not to return it. She ignored the notices sent to her. Some five years later she felt compelled to tell them she had 'stolen' it. She walked into the library one morning and did just that.

A well known biographer and historian I know is convinced that borrowing books from friends and acquaintances and forgetting to return them is a subtle, decent, grown-up form of pinching being practised today. He gave me the example of another well known writer and book lover who would never return his books.

'Did you try asking for them back?' I asked. 'Of course!' he shot back. 'Of course I tried asking him – several times. And do you know what he'd say? "My need of it is greater than yours."' The underlying reason for stealing books – whether from a bookstore, library or a person's house – is always the same: no one else deserved the book as much as they did. And it was not about possessing just any old book; it was about possessing *that* book.

Why, there was even a time when I had to steal my own books! This is how it happened: a 'friend' couldn't remember having borrowed books from me. One day when he had left his room for a bit, I quickly ransacked his shelf and found them tucked away in the second row. I helped myself to the two books I wanted back rather badly and left the rest.

We're talking here of fairly harmless biblioklepts; books nicked because someone was too poor to buy a book they needed or felt it had to be rescued and brought to light from some library or bookstore that didn't care for it. But there are other kinds of biblioklepts in the book world, those for whom it is more than a passion: it is an obsession, a madness. And then there are professional book thieves who commit major book crimes for profit.

'Bibliomania', Flaubert's first published story (he was 15) is about a Spanish monk who was 'literally willing to kill to possess a book he wanted for his collection.' He based it on a true case of bibliomania. In 1830, a Spanish monk named Don Vincente looted his own monastery's library of rare books, left the order and a few months later surfaced as an antiquarian bookseller in Barcelona! People grew suspicious, but those were the early days of bibliomania and few knew how exactly the mania manifested.

Soon, the former monk turned book dealer was showing more interest in buying books than selling them. 'For own use only', he would say when someone asked to buy a book from his bookshop. In 1836 a rival bookseller won the bid at a book auction for a coveted rare volume, the only surviving copy of *Edicts for Valencia*, printed in 1482 by Spain's first printer, Lamberto Palmart. Don Vincente bid everything he owned for the book in the auction but was outbid by a syndicate of rival booksellers led by Augustino Paxtot.

Three days later Paxtot was found dead in his bookshop. The clues pointed to Don Vincente, and the authorities found all the books that had gone missing or had been stolen in Barcelona. The former monk had not sold a single item, although he could have become rich by putting them on the market. 'I am not a thief,' he declared at his trial. And added that sooner or later people had to die, but books needed to be preserved, looked after. But the true nature of Don Vincente's bibliomania would only surface at the end of the trial.

Trying to establish his innocence, his lawyer unearthed another existing copy of the *Edicts* in Paris and used it as evidence to show that Vincente's book was not necessarily Paxtot's. The monk went into shock. From that day until the day of his death, he was heard to mumble constantly, 'My copy is not unique, my copy is not unique, my copy is not unique.' A year later, word of this monk's deeds reached the ears of young Gustave. Flaubert shaped this into a twisty little tale about a bookseller's homicidal quest to own the only known copy of a book to exist in the world.

In May 2002, a naval officer named Stanislas Gosse was caught with three suitcases containing 300 ancient religious manuscripts and precious illuminated books that he had plundered over the years from various monasteries. He would sneak the volumes out at night, and his getaway vehicle was a bicycle. In 2005, a book thief who was also a master of disguise – William Jacques alias David Fletcher – was arrested for stealing books worth more than a million pounds from the London library.

And in January 2009, a sixty-year-old Iranian businessman and book collector called Farhad Hakimzadeh was found stealing pages from rare books in the Bodleian library. He had been doing this for seven years and had gone undetected. He was snipping out pages, he later said, to augment his own fine collection of antiquarian books. One of the pages he had cut out was a 500-year-old map worth 32,000 pounds. Before passing sentence on Hakimzadeh, the judge paused to say, 'You have a deep love of books, perhaps so deep that it goes to excess.' And the British press noted that Hakimzadeh, 'slowly nodded his head'. These men liked to call themselves 'gentlemen thieves'; obsessed academics who offered their bibliomania as defence: that they were rescuing these books from being abandoned in libraries.

The most infamous book thief in history is probably Stephen Blumberg who stole 23,600 rare books from 268 libraries, estimated at 20 million dollars. Though he had only passed high school, he would masquerade as a professor in university libraries. His modus operandi ranged from wearing long coats with specially sewn long pockets inside to hiding in the library after it closed.

He didn't see it as stealing – he saw it as building a

unique collection of books. At his trial he said he always meant to return them. He had preserved them carefully in an old house, storing the books in 180 bookcases that went from floor to ceiling. To get the glue off the library cards he would lick them. He licked the glue off a hundred books a day and would stop only when he got sick.

His lawyers pleaded insanity as defence but the judges wouldn't buy it. Librarians were outraged and felt Blumberg had given bibliomania a bad name. Some book collectors saw his passion for books as something noble, even romantic. The problem with both arguments is that they are too cut-and-dried.

Perhaps part of the reason why we find ourselves drawn to such bibliomania is that they seem to say something about the nature of our relationship to books? That it is more intimate and more complex than we imagined?

THE MAN WHO LOVED BOOKS TOO MUCH:
BOOK THIEF I

ON MARCH 14, 2001, a man named John Gilkey called the Brick Row Book Shop, a well known antiquarian bookstore in San Francisco and said, 'I'm looking for a gift. Something in the two thousand- to three thousand-dollar range.' The bookstore suggested a special two-volume set of *The Mayor of Casterbridge*, a first edition priced at twenty-five hundred. Gilkey then read his credit card number to the bookstore clerk and said he would pick up the book in the afternoon. The bookstore had it wrapped and kept ready for the book to be picked up. Later in the day a man rushed in, said he was in a hurry, and left with the book.

For several years between 2001 and 2003, this was typically how the rare book thief Gilkey operated: using stolen credit card numbers he would place the order over telephone and tell the bookstore that he was too busy to come himself and would be sending someone to pick up the book on his behalf. He would stroll into the bookshop a few hours later and ask for the book. Only weeks later would the bookseller realize the charge was fraudulent. Among the many first or rare editions he stole were *Catch 22* ($3,500), *Lord Jim* ($3,000) Samuel Becket's *No's Knife* ($850), Kerouac's *On the Road* ($4,500) and first editions of *Winnie-the-Pooh*. In all, perhaps books worth $200,000.

In her absorbing book, *The Man Who Loved Books Too Much*, Allison Hoover Bartlett tells the story of not just Gilkey and his rare book theft escapades, but of his nemesis, the rare book dealer turned 'bibliodick' Ken

Sanders, and how he stalked and captured this century's most relentless and successful book thief. Her book is also a seductive look at the obsessive world of rare books, collectors and dealers. What set John Gilkey apart from most book thieves is that he did not steal for profit but to collect. He had come under the spell of first editions and fine books, and wanted to own them.

He didn't have the means to buy them, so he helped himself to these books because he felt entitled to them. He didn't think of it as stealing – he is quoted as saying that taking a book from a library would be stealing. Like that other notorious biblioklept, Stephen Blumberg, Gilkey stole for the love of books. Another stunning instance of bibliomania gone wrong. Bartlett, who interviewed Gilkey several times, recounts that he visualized himself as a Sherlock Holmes 'with a smoking jacket and an old library. I'd have a big antique globe and read next to it.'

How did he get access to stolen credit card numbers? From receipts left by customers at the famous Saks department store he worked in on and off for several years. Once he had collected several credit card numbers, he would begin his round of telephone calls. Ken Sanders who owns a fine rare book store in Salt Lake City had been appointed as head of security for the ABAA (Antiquarian Bookseller's Association of America), and it was while serving his term here that he began investigating a series of book thefts by fraudulent credit card numbers.

He had requested all ABAA affiliated bookstores in the country to report book thefts, and kept them updated with everything he could gather about this book thief. On a Tuesday in January 2003 John Gilkey, armed with a new set of card numbers, dialled the number of Ken Lopez Bookseller, one of the most high-end dealers in modern first editions, and asked for a book in the range of $5,000 to $7,000. Lopez suggested *The Grapes of Wrath*. The caller wondered if he should also purchase a clamshell box to keep the book in. Immediately, Lopez was reminded of another man who had called six months earlier asking if he should get a clamshell for a first edition of Ken Kesey's *One Flew Over the Cuckoo's Nest*.

Lopez asked Gilkey to call back, and then alerted Ken Sanders. When the thief called back next, the trap had been set. Ken Lopez accepted the card number and the sale went through. However, Gilkey said he would like the book delivered to his hotel, and wouldn't be picking it up himself. Lopez now played a joke – one that would fool the man who had been fooling all of them: he sent a worthless facsimile edition of the book. Gilkey was nabbed trying to pick up the book.

Allison Bartlett notes that for many collectors the goal is 'to stumble upon a book whose scarcity or beauty or history or provenance is even more seductive than the story printed between its covers'. While researching and writing about this world of literary obsession, the author wondered what her own position was as a bibliophile: was she a bibliomaniac? And if she was, how far would she go to own a book she coveted? Bartlett's honest self-scrutiny all through the book bonds her with the reader, who will have to ask similar questions: what kind of bibliophile am I?

Even rare book dealers confess to moments of temptation when they ache to hold a book that they don't possess. But they fight the impulse and the moment passes. 'We were all tenacious hunters,' Bartlett concludes. 'Gilkey for books, Sanders for thieves, and me for both their stories.' In the end, what her book is really about she notes is 'people's intimate and complex and sometimes dangerous relationship to books.'

The Tome Raider: Book Thief II

In the late evenings of the spring of 1994, Daniel Spiegelman, a small man in his late thirties, stole several rare manuscripts and maps from Columbia University's Butler Library. By the time the thefts were discovered, Spiegelman was already in Europe, trying to sell them on the open rare book market. Spiegelman's crime, his eventual capture and trial is the subject of Travis McDade's fascinating book, *The Book Thief: The True Crimes of Daniel Spiegelman*. McDade's book is the first book-length account of a book thief.

Columbia's Butler library is equipped with high-tech security systems, and yet Spiegelman broke in. Like all old libraries, McDade tells us, Columbia's Butler also had one small security flaw. And one flaw was enough. Butler had still not sealed off its dumbwaiter shafts, which were basically mini-elevators that were used to send books up from one floor to the other. Only a child could squeeze into one of those and hop out when it reached a floor, but Spiegelman had practice: he had been in a Soviet prison as a child and had crawled out from there. The book thief found one of those shafts on stack 11, which could take him up to stack 13.

It was Consuelo Dutschke, the curator of the medieval and Renaissance collection, who first discovered the missing manuscripts. Jean Ashton, the director of Columbia's Rare Book and Manuscript Library, was notified. As in most cases of library rare book thefts, McDade informs us that suspicion first fell on the staff. It took months for their names to be cleared, and for the true thief to be identified.

Among the many rare items that Spiegelman stole were 17 medieval and Renaissance manuscripts, including Euclid's *Elementa*, three *Books of Hours*, two papal bulls, eight Arabic and Persian manuscripts dating from the 10th century to 1887, and 237 individual maps razored out of a 17th-century version of Blaeu's *Atlas Major*. In all, he stole rare books, letters, manuscripts and maps worth several million dollars. (On an aside, a rich excursion into the arcane world of map collectors and map thieves is Miles Harvey's *The Island of Lost Maps: A True Story of Cartographic Crime*.)

McDade points out that there are two kinds of book thieves – those that steal to make a profit, and those who steal to collect. It is the second who is the most dangerous to libraries because the material, once taken, vanishes. Luckily, Spiegelman was stealing to sell and it was only a matter of time before these manuscripts and maps turned up on the open market.

In the second chapter, 'Smart Thief, Bad Crook', he describes the capers of at least a dozen book thieves who have been stealing from rare book repositories. Some worked as a couple, some were professors and graduate students with access to rare book rooms and a few were even librarians. Stephen Blumberg, the author reminds us, ended up serving only a five-year sentence. However, in what was one of the most extraordinary sentences in recent criminal history, Judge Kaplan declared that 'rare books and manuscripts are vital to understanding the world and often are irreplaceable objects of study for scholars who add to our knowledge of ourselves and our environment.'

Kaplan then sentenced the book thief to '60 months in prison, three years of supervised release and 300 hours of community service towards increasing adult literacy and pay restitution to Columbia.' McDade's intention in *The*

Book Thief is to show us that Spiegelman's punishment is important to deter other book thieves. And that Kaplan's verdict has now set a court precedent for the prosecution of other book thieves. Another heroic figure from the trial is rare manuscript librarian Jean Ashton who spent many days in court, persuading people about the importance of these rare manuscripts and maps.

McDade told me that he was drawn particularly to the legal aspects of the story: 'I had thousands of pages of documents and court transcripts to sift through, but I didn't mind doing it; it was like hunting for clues to solve a mystery, trying to uncover neat little bits of information from the smallest scrap.

'For example: There was a photocopy of a receipt that didn't mean anything at all to me at first. I put it in the "useless" pile and forgot about it. Then, when I'd run out of good material to use, I went back to the "useless" pile to see if anything in there made any sense. That receipt turned out to be for one of the safe deposit boxes Spiegelman used to store some of the stolen items; it had a box number, the address of the bank, the alias he used, when he rented the thing and how much he paid.'

What is interesting to note about the book crimes of Spiegelman is that it is a story of destruction and greed, and not, as in Gilkey's case, a dark tale of bibliomania gone wrong. Gilkey and Spiegelman were professional book thieves with very different aims. One loved books and stole them to take possession; the other didn't care for them and did it for the money. As we have seen, among professional book thieves the most dangerous is the one who steals not to possess but to profit from it. Once Gilkey was caught, the bookstores could at least recover some of the stolen material, but with a thief like Spiegelman, they vanished on the open rare book market.

Out of Circulation

While raising our book-haunted voices to toast bookshops, let's not forget to pay homage to that humble, hole-in-the-wall affair we have come to call the private circulating library. To me they seem a singularly Indian phenomenon. The local lending library is unique to us – the rest of the world has public libraries. Every Indian city has – or has had – at least one legendary private circulating library. These libraries are usually treasure houses of out-of-print paperbacks and comics. For many of us, our first real contact with books happened here, at these local libraries. And if anyone was responsible for transforming us into inveterate readers, they were. We owe them that.

My earliest memory of imaginative and intellectual pleasure (though I didn't know that then) as a child was the ritual walk I took every day to my local library to exchange my comics. All day I looked forward to coming back from school, kicking off my shoes, chucking the uniform for something comfortable, slipping into chappals, snacking on something hurriedly, and then waiting impatiently for the library doors to open. And then would come the best part: returning the previous day's comic (which by now I would have read several times) and browsing for a new one. On my small deposit, I could borrow only one.

But what would it be? *Korak* if I had finished all the *Tarzans* or an old *Phantom* or *Mandrake* for the seventh time if the issue featured the Cobra. I would move to the Marvel pile only if I couldn't find an Indrajal or Gold Key comic I wanted to re-read. And if Marvel let me down, then it would be the Junior Illustrated Classics. Later, I delighted in *Chandamama* and *Amar Chitra Katha*. In Chennai one of those legendary, old libraries was Easwari. Here you could once find books and comics that were hard to come by in bookshops. Books and comics you can't even buy for the love of money because they aren't in print anymore.

At a treasure house like Easwari, you never know what you'll turn up: anything from *Billy Bunter* to *The Saint* to Victorian soft porn. Those familiar with Easwari know what a labyrinth of pleasures it was: dark, tiny partitions that lead off from the front room, filled with secret nooks and crannies stashed with the rarest and quaintest of books. Most of it pulp, of course, but the kind that they don't print anymore. I've spent many hours burrowing in those musty shelves in the early '90s. Unfortunately, the owner Mr Palani, had taken to subjecting all the books to library binding, reducing the value of these collectible vintage paperbacks.

My favourite ritual at Easwari after browsing was paying for the books. You had to first get them entered in those thick, old ledgers and then you plonked your armload of books on the owner's desk at the entrance. Palani would give the pile a swift, sharp glance, pick the lot up, bang them lightly on the table to shake the dust off, weigh them in his hands, and then shoot off the reading charge: 'Fifty rupees.' Fifty rupees for a large pile of books! Women – mostly Triplicane mamis (Chennai's affectionate nickname for middle-class, middle-aged Brahmin women) – would come here with large shopping bags to carry away a basketful of books (mostly racy, sexy bestsellers) to last them for the entire month.

Stepping into these old libraries, you could get high just on the smell of old books and comics. New libraries with their shiny books and comics that smell of fresh ink never seem to turn you on the same way. But things changed in the late '90s. Circulating libraries – pardon the pun – went out of circulation. Libraries closed down or were run down from neglect. Some of them were vandalised – readers stole books or lost them or just forgot to return them. People blamed it on cable television, the price of books shooting up and the sudden, steep increase in reading charges – 10 per cent of the book's cost. But in truth, it wasn't that: people just stopped reading. They found other distractions. In the end, the faithful were the children who still preferred comics to Cartoon Network and the women who needed their fix of Silhouette romances.

There's a corner I turned from child to adolescent that I associate with these circulating libraries: moving from Enid Blyton to Alfred Hitchcock and The Three Investigators to adult pulp fiction to accidentally stumbling on 'literature' – *Of Human Bondage*, *The Outsider* – you can fill in the names of all those modern classics you first found at your library that shook up your life. Chances are you discovered your first Georgette Heyer and P.G. Wodehouse here too. These libraries were an addiction. They got me through countless hours of boredom (especially those torpid Sunday afternoons), not to forget the many hours of pleasure I got from curling up with a library book. They gave me my longest standing identity – that of a reader.

Marginalia (& Other Literary Curiosities)

I MYSELF HAVE never been able to scribble in the margins of a book, but several of my friends never begin a book without a soft pencil in hand. When she is not making graceful, nearly invisible soft pencil jottings, an illustrator friend uses minuscule post-it notes along the margins, to keep or remove at will.

Are there really only two kinds of readers then? Those who write in books, and those who don't? In *Marginalia: Readers Writing in Books*, H.J. Jackson notes that the reader-annotated book feels like 'a scruffy thing' to some readers who can't stand the sight of yellow highlighters in books. But for the 'marginalist' or 'marginalian', making these margin-jottings is a form of conversation, turning monologue into dialogue. Many marginalists use non-verbal codes, notes the author. Private signs and symbols recognized only by them, while other jottings vary from casual scribbles such as 'how true!' to lengthy arguments and discursive notes.

Jackson offers a marvellous fictional example of marginalia that turns up in Brontë's *Wuthering Heights*, when Lockwood, unable to sleep, examines a few of Catherine's musty, old books and discovers: '...scarcely one chapter had escaped a pen-and-ink commentary... covering every morsel of blank the printer had left'. In a real life instance, Maurice Sendak was asked by an anxious child at a book signing not to spoil her book by autographing it – and Sendak agreed wholeheartedly, returning the book back unsigned.

It was Coleridge, a compulsive book scribbler, who first called it marginalia. Lamb would lend books to Coleridge, and they would come back annotated. Rather than being upset with his friend, Lamb valued such personal jottings. Other well documented marginalists include William Blake, Conan Doyle, Virginia Woolf, Gertrude Stein, Northrop Frye and Vladimir Nabokov.

Readers writing in books usually take the form of notes in the side margins of a book, though there are those who will scribble on the flyleaf or fill up the endpapers. (It occurs to very few readers that they can use the endpaper to make notes in.) Most browsers in used bookstores like the idea of finding a book filled with marginalia: it increases the value of the book for them. In *84 Charing Cross Road*, Helene Hanff writes, 'I love inscriptions on flyleaves and notes in margins, I like the comradely sense of turning pages someone else turned, and reading passages some one long gone has called my attention to'.

Jackson is one among several scholars who have recently turned their attention to what another Jackson – Kevin Jackson – referred to as literary curiosities in *Invisible Forms*, a lively, witty study of dedications, titles, epigraphs, footnotes, prefaces, afterwords, indexes, stage directions, first lines and last lines. He refers to these as invisible paratexts in a book: we constantly see them or come across them but (unless you are an obsessive bibliophile) seldom view them as serious text.

If I were to tell you that 'He Do The Policeman in Different Voices' is a landmark in modern poetry would you believe me? Or that 'Tom All-Alone's Factory That Got Into Chancery and Never Got Out' is a great Victorian novel, while 'The High Bouncing Lover' (or 'Trimalchio in West Egg', take your pick) is considered the greatest American novel ever written? With well earned glee, *Invisible Forms* informs us that these were the original titles of Eliot's *The Waste Land*, Dickens' *Bleak*

House and Fitzgerald's *The Great Gatsby*, respectively. (Long after the book had become beloved, the author still lamented losing 'The High-Bouncing Lover' as the title for *The Great Gatsby*!)

We learn that the lowly footnote is not really a lowly paratext in Anthony Grafton's *The Footnote; A Curious History* and Chuck Zerby's *The Devil's Details: A History of Footnotes*. A study of footnotes is revealing and rewarding, conclude both scholars. For it is the footnote that tells the reader the Byzantine paths taken by a scholar in her research. The fascinating details are there, below the actual text. These books trace the history of the footnote, provide examples of the earliest documented footnotes to what footnoting has become today: endnotes relegated to the back of a book.

The reader-annotated book is also the focus of *Used Books* (by William H. Sherman), a lively and learned study on how librarians, literary bibliographers and historians of reading have begun to uncover and document marginalia to view how readers personalize a text.

'When I revisit a book,' says my friend Cheriyan, 'which I have previously marked, perhaps a decade or more ago, it always reminds me of Ariadne's thread. Ariadne is this character in Greek myth who accompanies Theseus on his dangerous expedition to the heart of the labyrinth to kill the dreaded Minotaur. In order to make it easy for them to find their way out through the maze, Ariadne unrolls a ball of yarn all the way from the entrance. After Theseus kills the monster, it is Ariadne's thread that makes it possible for them to navigate the maze. The markings in a book, the remarks scribbled in the margin, all help one traverse the labyrinthine recesses of a richly textured, highly nuanced tome.'

On the other hand, when I asked Rosamma, a book

editor for whom reading has meant a kind of sweet solitude, she responded with: 'A printed page with text neatly laid out and smart margins – how does one bring oneself to mark the sides, to mar such perfection? Especially if the book isn't your own, but borrowed from a library?' One good old friend stoutly disagrees, and merrily marks up pages: generations of people may read after us, and we are doing them all a good turn when we mark things intelligently, underlining and commenting on the sides. The good parts of the book just spring out at you. Her advice: 'Feel no qualms about ruining books – they perish like all things else; while they last, keep the conversations, the asides, going.'

Though not a marginalist myself, I'm buoyed enough by that to have a pencil or two lying close to me the next time I reach for a book.

The Tireless Reader

YAMBO THE ANTIQUARIAN book dealer wakes up from a coma and remembers only the books he has read. Not his name, not his job, not his wife. Just whole chunks from books. This is the mischievous premise of Umberto Eco's *The Mysterious Flame of Queen Loana*. Though Eco isn't giving us the one thing we so badly want from him – a sequel to *The Name of the Rose* (since *Foucault's Pendulum*, he hasn't given us anything as exciting as those erudite medieval mysteries that mixed low and highbrow with such jolly and startling scholarship), he comes closest in this book to such Borgesian mischief. From page one, Eco delights us with planting pop culture references without telling us from which book or movie or comic book they come from, so that we can have fun spotting them for ourselves.

When the book begins, Yambo answers the questions posed by the hospital doctor from an encyclopaedic fog. His responses, spoken and thought, are lines and titles from books he has read such as 'Call me Ishmael', 'April is the cruellest month' and 'The Man Who Mistook His Wife for a Hat'.

And then, like the pages of an encyclopaedia floating in his head, the book dealer summons literary references from his otherwise amnesiac head: 'Where fog hovers between the towers like incense dreaming? Elementary, my dear Watson, there are ten little Indians... Finally I came into a vast chasm and could see a colossal figure, wrapped in a shroud, its face the immaculate whiteness of snow. My name is Arthur Gordon Pym.'

By now, anyone reading this with some knowledge

of literature and pop culture would have caught most of the references. But as the book progresses the references, in typical Eco fashion, get more obscure and strange and wondrous. 'Often have I encountered the evil of living. Nothing can shake my belief that this world is the fruit of a dark god whose shadow I extend.' With sneaking suspicion the reader suddenly realizes that some of these quotes could be Yambo's own version – a conflation of what he has read and his own riffs on them!

For, after all, that is the kind of delightful inter-textual mischief Eco has been up to all along – juxtaposing theology and detective fiction, the ancient and the contemporary (Yambo's Ph.D. thesis we learn was on the 'Hypnerotomachia Poliphili' – a pop reference and in-joke on *The Rule of Four*) text and image. 'Quotations,' confesses Yambo, 'are my only fog lights.' *The Mysterious Flame of Queen Loana* is illustrated: black and white and colour pictures from highbrow and popular culture – Flash Gordon, Phantom, Mandrake, Fantomas, Verne, Wells, Dumas, lovely volumes with an ancient air, cigarette boxes with exotic foreign sounding names (including Gold Flake!), postage stamps and the original drawings that accompanied the Sherlock Holmes stories in *The Strand*.

The illustrations and plates, so rich and magical and nostalgic, alone are worth the price of the book, but, happily, even the text is a joy. This is the book Eco has been reaching to write all along: a story with words and pictures. Yambo, the Milanese rare-book-dealer hero of the book (a fictitious version of Eco himself?) can only recall words, not images! Each antiquarian book in Yambo's collection (numbering more than 5,000) is 500 hundred years old and more expensive than a Porsche. His wife calls him a 'tireless reader' with an 'iron memory'.

The Mysterious Flame of Queen Loana goes on a bit too long, and the brisk pacing, the buoyant comic tone and the pop culture loaded first part of the book gives way to (meandering, and slowly paced) history, romance and a detailed description of Eco's childhood reading. Is Eco, sly entertainer, hinting that readers invent the books they read and even their own characters? Reading this odd and beguiling ode to childhood reading, all book lovers will recognize some part of themselves in Yambo, the tireless reader who loves even the sound and feel of the thumb flipping the pages of a book in reverse. This is the reader as hero, the reader as character, the reader who becomes the book.

(I was lucky enough to find a signed U.S. first edition – it was not as expensive as it could have been, the true first being the Italian edition – of the book in the rare books floor at the Strand, New York, in May 2007. Now, admittedly, the truly great find would have been a signed edition of *The Name of the Rose*. But considering any signed copy of an Eco book is scarce, it was a nice little thing to run into. And its provenance? Eco had visited Strand and they had got him to sign as many copies as they could.)

The Book Borrower

LIKE MOST lovers, book lovers are possessive, too. I have to confess that anyone flirting with my bookshelf makes me nervous. The scene I dread is a classic one that repeats itself – most book collectors will know this moment well:

A visitor wanders over to your bookshelf and begins browsing. You're hoping he'll become bored and return to his chair. But no – he has begun pulling out books and is now examining them closely, fondling them. He has lost all interest in you. When he finally does return to his chair, a small pile of books from your shelf accompanies him. You know what's coming but you are prepared. He'll ask and you'll say – not a chance!

After all, this is not the first time that this has happened. The moment finally comes. The poor chap is just as nervous as you are, as he works up the courage to ask the question.

'Oh', he says almost absentmindedly, as he gets up to leave, 'can I borrow these books?'

'Of course, no problem.'

'I'll return them in a week.'

'Take your time.'

'You don't mind, do you?'

'Mind? Why should I mind?'

'In theory I like lending,' says my friend Usha, 'but in actuality, I'm very careful nowadays about whom I loan books to. I first test them out by loaning them paperbacks, and if those are returned on time and in undamaged condition, then I might think about lending my favourite books. Otherwise, I'll conveniently keep putting off finding the book to lend! Oh, but borrowing, I love and do borrow, but that's because I know I'll be good to the books and I'm particular about returning them too.'

I asked a few book collectors what made lending a book so traumatic. The three most common answers were:

'Few borrowers return the book when they say they will. I mean, how could they forget? I haven't been able to think of anything else since I lent it.'

'It isn't even about returning it late – they can take their time – it's that they mishandle the book. It'll come back dog-eared or soiled or with a creased spine.'

'I don't mind when it comes back or what state it comes back in. What disappoints me, what crushes me, is that – after all those months – they haven't read the book.'

But we weren't always possessive, were we? One of the (uncontemplated) pleasures of childhood and adolescence was how rigorously we exchanged comics and books with our buddies. As adults we seem to have lost that joy. As children we were eager to swap comics with schoolmates; in college we freely lent books to each other. There was always a favourite writer or book we were urging our classmates to read.

'You mean you actually haven't read any Wodehouse? I'll get you a whole bunch of them tomorrow.'

'I'm reading this really amazing book – *Zen And The Art of Motorcycle Maintenance* – you can take my copy the moment I'm through.'

I remember this classmate passing on his copy of *Catch 22* to the entire class – he felt no one could afford to not know something that funny. I myself buttonholed strangers with copies of *The Chosen* and *My Name Is Asher Lev*. And all this free lending was at a time when none of us could afford to buy new copies of our favourite books in case they were mishandled or lost. But we lent (and borrowed) unstintingly. The main thing was to get someone else to read a book that mattered to us. It filled you with evangelical purpose, and it made friendship possible. Reading the other's favourite writer was – is – such an intimate thing to do. Between readers nothing seals a friendship or deepens a relationship the way book transactions can.

One of the more endearing and generous gestures I've seen a book lover perform – time and time again – is my friend Prasanna inviting her friends to her bookshelf to borrow a book of their choice. 'I'm a compulsive lender,' she confessed. 'However impractical this may seem, in the end it is a deeply fulfilling gesture. I like the idea of a book I care for in the hands of a friend.'

The Book Eaters

'The Collector of Collectors'
'Our Master of Bibliophilic Revel'
Bookishness
A Hitchhiker's Guide to the Library
Apart from the Text: Book History in India

'THE COLLECTOR OF COLLECTORS'

IN THE EARLY '90s, Nicholas A. Basbanes, a journalist covering 'the book beat' (reporting on rare book auctions and exhibitions, profiling people in the book trade, etc.) for his newspaper signed a deal with Random House to expand his pieces into something more book length. It was to be about 90,000 words and completed in eighteen months. As Basbanes began researching the subject, his journalist's nose for a deeper story kicked in, and he began following a very different book premise.

His trail led him all over Europe and he completed the book seven years later at twice the projected length for Henry Holt, not Random House. What Basbanes had envisioned as a tidy little book on the antiquarian book trade turned into an obsessive adventure that produced the first comprehensive popular history on bibliomania. Titled *A Gentle Madness*, it was also the book that revived the non-fiction genre of books on books or books about books. Or, defined more expansively: books that speak of other books, bibliophiles, reading, book collecting, book history, book arts and book culture.

A Gentle Madness, now in its twentieth printing, has sold more than 120,000 copies. (One of the most prized possessions in my library is a signed, inscribed – alas, though, not to me – first edition of this book). Today, with five more books on the history of the book, Basbanes has become a highly respected bookman. A book series that is, in the author's own words, 'a comprehensive guide to the literature, history, romance, apocrypha, folklore, and the mechanics of book collecting'.

Basbanes is often introduced as a 'collector of collectors', and he confesses that he feels a sense of possession towards all these bibliomanes he has so accurately and lovingly profiled. It is from this 'roving chronicler of book people' that we learn there were equally great women book collectors from antiquity, mighty women book hunters.

The Grolier Club, the world's premier bibliophile club, devoted an entire exhibition once to honour women collectors over five centuries, from Diane de Poitiers to Amy Lowell to Frances Hooper. A modern legend in bookselling is Priscilla Juvelis, who specializes in rare and fine books in the areas of contemporary book arts and women authors.

In exploring the origins of the word bibliomania, he notes several early instances of its first recorded use that made the word popular: 1750, when Philip Stanhope, fourth Earl of Chesterfield, 'sent a haughty letter to his illegitimate son warning him of book buying as a consuming plague'; Dr John Ferriar, who published a satirical poem with the same title in 1809; and perhaps, most famously, Reverend Thomas Frognall Dibdin, who popularized the word in his book, *Bibliomania or Book Madness* (also 1809). (The first time the word crops up in fiction, interestingly, is in the first story Flaubert wrote, when he was fifteen.)

I wrote to Basbanes asking if he could throw some light on who first coined the word, and he replied that he didn't think anyone knew for certain. He told me, however, that he has now noted an even earlier use of the word that he found cited in both, the *OED* and the recently published *The Oxford Companion to the Book*. Thomas Hearne, librarian and book collector, who seems to have used it in his diary in 1734: 'I should have been tempted to have laid out a pretty deal of money without thinking my self at all touched with Bibliomania.'

'When that diary may have been made public, I have no earthly idea,' added Basbanes. 'Regardless of who used it first, we credit Dibdin with giving it the life it enjoys today. I'm hoping at some point in the next year or so to bring out an updated version of *Gentle Madness*, in which case I'll revisit the matter. But that'll have to wait until I conclude the book at hand.'

Basbanes' *Patience and Fortitude*, is the definitive account of contemporary collectors, booksellers and rare book institutions. My favourite chapter here is his fascinating portrait of Umberto Eco and his library of 30,000 volumes. He offers us ample instances of driven but sane bibliophiles, from antiquity to the present. In *Among the Gently Mad*, the last in the book collecting trilogy, he offers perspectives and strategies for the 21st-century book hunter.

The newest manifestation of his 'gentle madness' is *Editions and Impressions* (brought out in a limited edition *and* a deluxe edition by Fine Books Press; both editions are signed), short, entertaining journalistic pieces gathered from twenty years on the book beat as a reporter. Nicholas Basbanes' profile of Eric Waschke, a bookseller obsessed with far-flung bookshops – he's visited three thousand bookstores across 53 countries, an odyssey to explore 'the known book world' through bookstore visits at every stop – is one among several other remarkable book people and places that turn up here.

On one December morning in 1990 Basbanes set off to the famed auction house of Sotheby's with great excitement and some nervousness. He would be bidding, that day, for a book dealer acquaintance who couldn't attend the auction herself (in a postscript he reveals it was none other than the legendary bookwoman, Priscilla Juvelis), and had permission to play around with – if it came to that – half a million dollars. He would be locking horns that morning with 'such stalwarts as Quaritch of London, Pierre Beres of Paris, Heritage Book Shop of Los Angeles, and H.P. Kraus of New York'.

With a prominent paddle ready, Basbanes, on most lots, shrewdly enters the contest only when it has reached a higher bid of $25,000. And is surprised, each time, to find himself folding very early because the closing bids on most lots were as unimaginably high as $100,000 to $125, 000. What books would command such prices? Not really books, as it turns out, but illuminated manuscripts, aquatints and woodcuts.

An item that Basbanes captures (for $28,000) is an illuminated Book of Hours in really fine vellum. His total expenditure for the day comes to $59,625. 'This wasn't my money,' the author observes wryly, 'but I have to admit, it was a kick.' The Schiff Library – from where these lots came – was thought to bring in 1.4 million, notes Basbanes. But it finally went for a total of $2 million – 'evidence that while prices in the paintings market have gone into a tailspin, rare books have held their own'.

A few days later into the week, he attends a small, local auction, bidding with his own money. And gets very lucky. One item being auctioned here was something titled *The Sketch Book of Geoffrey Crayon, Gent*. A quick look earlier had told our bookman this was something very scarce and a genuine find. It was, though no one else except Basbanes at the auction realized it, a collection of stories by Washington Irving, the father of American literature. Crayon had been one of Irving's pseudonyms. *The Sketch Book* actually contained the first ever hardback appearance of *The Legend of Sleepy Hollow*. An item worth thousands – our bookman snaps it up for a cool $20.

Basbanes other books include *A Splendour of Letters:*

The Permanence of Books in an Impermanent World, Every Book Its Reader and *A World of Letters*. He is working on a yet to be titled book for Alfred Knopf on paper and papermaking.

At the end of a sensational book auction he's asked on a television show why he thinks someone would pay six and half million dollars for a Shakespeare folio or $941,000 for an original of Blake's *Songs of Innocence and Experience*, and he offers one of the best answers I've heard for why certain first editions are precious: Blake, as you know, points out Basbanes to the audience, not only wrote the poems but printed them, engraved them and bound them himself: the collector who just bought *Songs* is handling a copy that the poet once held. Imagine, says Basbanes, the interaction between the owner and such a book on a daily basis – the privilege and pleasure of communing with such a copy every day.

Basbanes' own joy in being a bookman is contagious, tempting even the common reader to become a serious book collector. I asked him what it felt like to have spent a lifetime passionately and meticulously researching and writing about bibliophiles and their relationship to books, and he wrote back saying: 'As a professional writer who has devoted so much of his adult life to writing about books and book culture, it is a measure of great satisfaction for me to know that I not only have readers for what I write – since nobody likes writing into a vacuum – but even more rewarding, to have the reassurance of knowing that what I write resonates with so many kindred spirits out there. And because books still matter, regardless of where the technology is taking us, it is worthwhile, I think, to have as many champions for them as we can muster.

'I am by no means a Luddite, but I also believe in productive coexistence. And if I can be a voice for that,

I have my epitaph. (Although I must say I much prefer for my tombstone the description of me printed in a newspaper in Honolulu when I arrived in 2005 with my wife to give a lecture at the University of Hawaii. The headline – tongue, to be sure, very much in cheek – read: "Bibliomaniac in Paradise".)'

'OUR MASTER OF BIBLIOPHILIC REVEL'

ONE AFTERNOON IN 1964 in a Buenos Aires bookstore, a blind man walked up to a sixteen-year-old who worked there and asked if the lad would be interested in a part-time job reading to him in the evenings.

This is how Alberto Manguel met Jorge Luis Borges, and from this chance encounter emerged this century's most intelligent, eloquent and witty bookman. Manguel's celebrated *A History of Reading* (1996) is a classic in the genre of books on books.

Manguel is a magnificent, impassioned reader among bibliophiles. His erudition and scholarship are unorthodox, eccentric and capacious. There's poetry and wit to his writing – unusual in bookmen who mostly chronicle or report. His books are steeped in breathtaking anecdotes and strike-you-dead aphorisms, like this one by Beckett: 'To restore silence is the role of objects.'

In 2006 Alberto Manguel published a slim memoir called *With Borges* that lovingly recounts that brief time he spent reading to the enigmatic Argentinean literary genius. For several years the bookstore clerk would turn up promptly at Borges' apartment at Maipu 994 and read the book the blind writer had chosen for that evening. Manguel would also take dictation, mostly Borges' poetry, which he would call out with punctuation in place.

In *The Library at Night*, Manguel notes that 'libraries have always seemed to me pleasantly mad places, and for as long as I can remember I've been seduced by their labyrinthine logic.' The idea for this book came when he was creating a vast library for himself in a 15th-century home he had bought recently in France.

Imagine now that the library is closing, the doors have been locked, and the lights go out. Somewhere else, in a house (in many houses) someone puts a book that she was reading back on to her bookshelf, and turns out the light, leaving the room. Now, what do you think the books do once they are alone? In *The Library at Night*, Manguel imagines them slowly settling down for the night – to converse, make love, breed more books, even do battle with each other. 'During the day, the library is a realm of order,' he observes. 'The library at night seems to rejoice in the world's essential, joyful muddle.'

His starting point for the book became his childhood library. Beginning his tour there, he takes us deep into book-lined labyrinths (with striking images and photographs) old and new: from the vanished Alexandrian library to Google. In between we learn of the personal libraries of Borges and Dickens, of an Afghani bookseller who kept his store open even during the war, and the imaginary library of Count Dracula. Most nights Manguel sits in this newly constructed library which he calls a 'shapeless universe', warmed by all the lamp lights spilling on his books and around him, breathing in the smell of the 'musky perfume of the leather bindings'.

Before he built this library, his apartment in Toronto had virtually become a gigantic warehouse with books crammed in bedrooms, bathrooms and even the staircases, leaving his children amused and exasperated that 'they required a library card to enter their own home.' Talking about the world wide library, Manguel perceptively observes that the Internet has changed the library that contained everything to the library that contains anything. He values the sense of a library or collection with a defined space, a personal focus. What you exclude from a library is just as important as what you include!

Manguel was born in Buenos Aires in 1948, and went to school there. Disillusioned very early by academic life, he never went to university, preferring to teach himself by reading prodigiously. His father was the ambassador to Israel when Manguel was growing up, and he was partly raised there. In 1984 he adopted Canada as his country, and for the first time could see himself as a writer there. He is a gifted essayist, anthologist, translator and novelist. His little-known *Stevenson Under the Palm Trees* is a delectable little murder mystery featuring Robert Louis Stevenson – one of his all-time favourite writers. The book is accompanied by Stevenson's own woodcuts.

Bride of Frankenstein is an engaging piece of film criticism, *Into the Looking Glass Wood* is a fine collection of essays, *A Reading Diary* – which is exactly that – a diary. *God's Spies: Stories in Defiance of Oppression* is an unusual anthology and *Reading Pictures: A History of Love and Hate* is art criticism at its most unconventional and invigorating. This list hardly exhausts his work – there are several more that I haven't mentioned. His newest book *A Reader on Reading* (2010) collects 39 of his best essays in one volume. (In one of these pieces he notes that on his bookshelves 'shiny young Penguins sit happily side by side with severe-looking leather-bound patriarchs'.)

'For the cosmopolitan reader,' noted Manguel once, 'a homeland is not in space, fractured by political frontiers, but in time, which has no borders... I wouldn't define myself as a writer. I would define myself as a reader.'

It is because he sees himself this way that he is, as one critic put it, 'our master of bibliophilic revel'.

Bookishness

I seem to have become somewhat of a lapsed reader, becoming nostalgic for the kind of serious reader I once was. Michael Dirda to the rescue: he makes you feel the pleasure books give him, makes you covet bookishness. He got me thinking about what bookishness once meant, and what it means now. It was something you didn't want to admit to; being bookish meant you weren't tough and practical and worldly. Now, suddenly, it's a new virtue, even a goal, because reading is seen as hard work. I don't want to offer that cliché about a generation lost to video games, the Internet and TV, but they seem to have ambushed us; we don't anymore embrace a book and lose ourselves in it with the abandon and excitement we reserve for watching a movie or surfing the Net.

Are books simply too serious for us? asks Dirda, and calls for a return to bookishness – to pick up a real book, even a difficult book and to 'hunger for seriousness'. This engaging literary critic renews your passion for serious reading. *Bound to Please: An Extraordinary One-Volume Literary Education*, a collection of his book reviews and essays, skips contemporary writers in favour of classical and modernist masters. Just what I needed – seduced by genre fiction and waylaid by historical thrillers, I've been guilty of neglecting serious literature. Dirda offers Herodotus, Emerson, the Bible, Proust, the *Arabian Nights* and Pepys as though they were the latest literary sensations you can't afford to pass by.

But these are only six out of more than a hundred reviews that include what he calls serious entertainers – Wodehouse, Terry Pratchett, Philip Pullman, Avram

Davidson, K.C. Constantine, Vernon Lee – and neglected or little known literary masters such as Fernando Pessoa, Djuna Barnes, Ronald Firbank, Italo Svevo, Flann O'Brien and Machado de Assis. His method is a close reading of their work. 'Think of these articles as old fashioned appreciations,' he writes, 'a fan's notes, good talk. My primary goal is to… convey something of each book's particular magic, strength, or excitement.'

Bound to Please is not only a textbook in the craft of book reviewing, it is a primer on how to write a good review on a tight deadline: Dirda is usually given five days to review a book and write a 1,800-word piece, and in the space of a month, he writes five such pieces!

Dirda's secret (which he eagerly shares with us) is that you have to be a certain kind of reader – a deliberate reader – to write a decent review. In his introduction, he talks a little about the way he goes about writing a book review. While reading and browsing, he accumulates notes, and anecdotes and facts and even 'thoughts', all of which are set down in a bound composition notebook with black and white speckled covers. To mark key passages he 'pencils vertical lines in the margins of that week's uncorrected page proofs… sometimes I'll scribble an idea on the endpapers, or make a list of pages to refer back to.'

Dirda dispels the myth of the writer for whom words simply flow onto the pages. 'I work hard at word choice, balance, rhythm… I write slowly, by methodical, almost geological accretion, setting down one sentence at a time, saying it over to myself, then adding another… always listening to the sound of the words.'

My favourite Dirda anthology, however, is *Readings*, a collection of personal, wryly humorous essays on the bookish life that he terms 'literary entertainments'. (I can't think of a better way to describe what he does with books).

Here in a witty, affectionate piece titled 'Bookish Fantasies', Dirda asks us to indulge him in the pulpy fantasies of the ordinary reader and writer, which might even include a note from Salinger that says 'you alone understand me'. I was so tickled by this piece that it got me wondering what the dream life of a bibliophile would be. Curious, I asked a handful of readers about their favourite literary fantasies.

'I get a letter out of the blue saying: "Among all my fans you alone understand why Seymour killed himself. Sincerely, J.D. Salinger."'

'What you need is rest. I'm recommending to the principal that you be excused from teaching for three months. You are not to read anything heavy or syllabus-oriented but only detective fiction and graphic novels.'

'E-mail: "I loved your book and wish I had written it. Signed, Vikram Seth. P.S.: I ran into Salman the other day and he told how much he envied your style."'

There's another fantasy that readers are a little bashful to discuss: the one about being able to enter a book and meet your favourite hero or heroine. When Woody Allen wrote those two masterful parodies of the literary life, *The Kugelmas Episode* and *The Whore of Mensa* (which you can find in *The Complete Prose of Woody Allen*) he was fantasizing for all of us. In *The Kugelmas Episode*, a bookish Jewish professor of literature finds a magician who can actually send him, body and soul, into any fictional work of his choice.

The academic ends up sleeping with Emma Bovary. Noticing this, students studying the book at that very moment in various classrooms ask 'Who is this character on page 100? A bald Jew is kissing Madame Bovary.' A professor declares that this is a mark of a classic: that you can reread it and always find something new.

The Whore of Mensa, which I think is Allen's masterpiece, is about a high-class brothel that has women cater to your intellectual needs. For a price, Allen tells us, they'll come over to your apartment and discuss Proust, Yeats, anthropology. Or you could go over to the joint where 'girls with black-rimmed glasses lolling around the sofas, riffling Penguin classics provocatively… for two hundred bucks you could get a blonde and a brunette to explain Noam Chomsky to you.' Or a 'Jewish girl will let you read her Master's thesis and fake a suicide of your choosing.'

I often envy non-readers for all the wonderful books out there that they have never read. Imagine the number of books that await them and the joy of encountering these great works for the first time. Thus, another favourite literary fantasy of mine has been to turn amnesiac (like Eco's amnesiac bibliophile, Yambo) for a year and read all my favourite books as though for the very first time.

A Hitchhiker's Guide to the Library

A VILLAIN NAMED Acheron Hades has entered *Jane Eyre* and kidnapped its protagonist. Using a Prose Portal, a detective named Thursday Next jumps into the book, giving chase. Meanwhile, characters from *Jane Eyre* escape from the book into the real world. If you're not already a fan of the Thursday Next series, welcome to the parallel literary universe of author Jasper Fforde where that seminal dream of every bibliophile – the desire to step into the universe of a favourite book – comes true.

To this literary fantasy, Fforde adds a new dimension: fictional creations are able to escape into the real world. In the bookish universe created by him (*The Eyre Affair, Lost In a Good Book, The Well of Lost Plots, Something Rotten, First Among Sequels*), literature has become central to everyone's life. Like the alternative universes in his books, his work crosses many genres: mystery, fantasy, science fiction, meta-fiction. Thursday is a woman in her mid-thirties who lives with her pet dodo, Pickwick, and is a literary detective in the real world who finds herself immersed in this bizarre 'BookWorld'.

In Fforde's Britain, books are more fun than television and sports; more vital than food and diet. People on the street furiously debate the authorship of Shakespeare's plays. Vending machines named Will Speak dispense speeches from the Bard for a small fee. Bookworms are bio-engineered. Book cops do battle with philistine bibliophobes. Syntax-slaughtering grammasites run amok inside classics. LiteraTecs, a literary detective squad, monitors book crimes. Classic works of literature are turned into reality book shows – *Pride and Prejudice* becomes 'The

Bennets'. And a giant philistine corporation is turning the world of books into theme parks for tourists.

The Thursday series is full of book references and recognizable characters from famous books, and is not only an amusing and irreverent romp through the classics, but also a celebration of storytelling itself. In the first book, *The Eyre Affair* (rejected 76 times before Penguin finally signed him on), Thursday is forced to alter the ending of Jane Eyre! Isn't the idea that a reader can enter a book, interact with characters and even change the ending irresistible to a book lover?

That characters have lives of their own to live after we shut a book is the delightful premise that Fforde works with. His books come with DVD-like extras: deleted scenes, the making of, and many special features. How could a book, you ask, possibly contain this? The extras are stored in Fforde's richly imagined and very expansive website where a password (usually the name of a character from the book in question) usually leads you to all these added DVD-like features.

Other kinds of inter-textual whimsy runs riot through his books: the endpapers carry bookplates, illustrations, and even advertisements (holiday character-exchange programmes: Rhett Butler and Scarlett inviting you to Tara for the weekend). The Jurisfiction Unit is a policing agency within the BookWorld that advertises for readers wishing to be inside books.

In *The Well of Lost Plots*, Thursday Next is a pregnant single mother hiding inside the plots of unpublished novels. This unusual but snug refuge is threatened when the authorities decide to control the number of plots. When this book was presented at the Hay festival, the festival director said the book 'has the true Wodehousian joy of brilliant verbal playfulness, and seems genuinely and outrageously original. It's a happy marriage of delightful intelligence and complete lunacy.'

Fforde's plots contain more bibliophile japery: Hamlet has disappeared from his play in *Something Rotten*. To save her lover, Thursday must chase after an enemy inside Poe's poem 'The Raven'. Readers must watch out for PageRunners – 'the name given to describe any character that is out of his or her book and moves through the backstory (or more rarely the plot) of another book.'

He is also the author of the wildly inventive Nursery Crime novels (*The Big Over Easy*, *The Fourth Bear*), another bookish series that some of his fans feel are not as snappy as their favourite Thursday Next books. His latest book, *Shades of Gray*, (published in December 2009), is a complete departure from his biblioadventures. Jasper Fforde's imagination seems to me effervescent and bottomless. The Thursday Next series is best summed up by one critic who referred to it as 'a hitchhiker's guide to the library'.

Apart From the Text: Book History in India

In 1995, a box of very old and brittle Hindi and Urdu pamphlets at the Heidelberg University library was about to be discarded when Ulrike Stark, a researcher of modern Hindi literature, realized she was looking at something very valuable. They were the few surviving remnants of a booklet printed more than a century ago by the Naval Kishore Press of Lucknow (1858), one of the most successful publishers in 19th-century North India, and the largest Indian-owned printing press in the subcontinent at that time. Stark, who wanted to go beyond looking at literary texts, felt she had found the subject she had been searching for: the history of the book in India.

'The history of the book in India is a history largely untold,' noted Stark in *An Empire of Books* (Permanent Black, 2007) her book on early print culture in India. And it may have remained that way if it hadn't been for a small but growing band of intrepid scholar-bibliographers of the book in India who are well on their way to changing that. Abhijit Gupta and Swapan Chakravorty are the editors of two anthologies on book history in India: *Print Areas* (2004) and *Movable Type* (2008, Permanent Black).

In their introduction to the first volume, the editors note, 'Despite being a country with a long, rich and complex book culture, India does not have a comprehensive history of its books. *Print Areas* is the first attempt to write such a history and brings together the work of leading contemporary historians of the book in India'. There are a range of essays here by such book historians as Priya Joshi, Rimi Chatterjee, Francesca Orsini, Siddhartha Ghosh, Veena Naregal, and Anindita

Ghosh. Essays dealing with the histories of Macmillan and Oxford University Press, bibliographical notes on the first edition of a book of nonsense verse, Benares as a centre of publishing, and the impact of popular books in Bengal.

Before these volumes came along, there had been little focus in academia, let alone journalism, on Indian book culture and book history. And as a bibliophile interested in a book's bibliographical details, I am grateful for these pioneer book historians who traveled beyond literary analysis to investigating our own hidden and neglected book history. It could not have been easy to research and write our book history – you can imagine how difficult it must have been to find early primary and archival sources. There are several books on the history of books in the West, but in South Asia book history is just beginning.

Among the protagonists of the book – authors, editors, publishers – is also the printer. But most of us forget that, and the printer (and typesetter), equal heroes of the book, often go unheralded. And it is the printer who is the real subject of the book historian. Though we readily recognize that print culture contributed to India's modernity, scholars and journalists have focused more on Indian newspaper and periodical press history than the story of how the book came to India. What has all this, though, to do with the common reader – that is, you and I? The book historian's interest in print culture is professional, but why should a reader, even a serious reader, take an interest in book history?

The interest begins unselfconsciously: from reflecting on what is inside a book – its content – you begin thinking about the book as an object. You grow curious about the year a book was printed, then you begin noticing other things such as the binding, typography, jacket wrapper, and who printed it. Suddenly, you want to know what a book in India from the 19th century looked and felt (and even smelled) like. What kinds of books were printed then? And who read them? In fact, how did this whole publishing thing get started in India? Like the book historian, you, too, go from being reader to bibliophile to bibliographer of the book.

Movable Type, the companion volume to *Print Areas* offers more fascinating examples of India's encounter with books. A.R. Venkatachalapthy's essay, for instance, is on the making of a Tamil encyclopaedia. (His fascination with printing began as early as when he was six!) 'My forthcoming book from Permanent Black,' he told me, 'is called *The Province of the Book: Print Culture in Colonial Tamil Nadu*. It looks at the period from about the 1850s to the outbreak of World War II. It is concerned with how Tamil publishing was largely sustained by forms of traditional patronage (of zamindars, religious monasteries and caste leaders) which broke down at the beginning of the twentieth century.

'A limited market emerged through the birth of an educated middle class. While I talk of structures of publishing I also look at the emergence of new literary genres, especially the novel, which helped to bring in the middle class within the ambit of reading and books. I also have chapters on popular publishing (of chapbooks and ballads) and on how the colonial state tried to ineffectively police book publishing. I have a chapter on how new reading practices, especially the mode of silent reading (as opposed to reading aloud) arose in colonial Tamil Nadu.'

I asked Rukun Advani, Permanent Black's publisher, how they came to recognize the significance of publishing book history and the answer, though not the one I had expected, was still inspiring:

'I don't think Anuradha Roy or I foresaw the importance of book history at all. We only try to judge whether a specific academic, or bunch of academics, studying any area connected with South Asian history, culture, and politics happens to be of very high calibre or not. If it seems to us that the individual or group approaching Permanent Black has the intellectual, moral, political, and personal qualities we respect, we try to publish their work (provided we're not overcommitted).

'I suppose we had some inkling that book history would burgeon in our region since there was quite a lot of it in the West and very little here, but the central fact for us was that people such as Vasudha Dalmia, Francesca Orsini, Swapan Chakravorty, Abhijit Gupta, Sukanta Chaudhuri, Venkatachalapathy and Ulrike Stark were all focusing on this area and asking us if we'd publish them. If this bunch of people had been focusing instead on changes in the breeding habits of the rosy pelican during global warming, we'd probably have had an inkling of this as a breakthrough in the historical ethology of South Asian ornithology and published them equally happily.'

What is just as exciting as these emerging book histories of India is that at Jadavpur University, Chakravorty and Gupta teach a course in book history!

At the university is a School of Cultural Texts and Records which, among many interdisciplinary things, teaches students to prepare bibliographies, bibliographical catalogues, book search engines, edit manuscripts and printed texts, to investigate the history of publishing and printing, collecting all sorts of ephemera and street literature (*heto* books – pulp peddled on trains and buses) and archiving documents and manuscripts of modern writers.

I asked Abhijit Gupta what had brought him to bibliography when his colleagues in the English departments around the country had stayed closer to literary criticism and theory. 'My interest in printing and publishing began during my first job, a nearly two-year stint as a subeditor in the newsroom of *The Statesman*. My time working as a journalist gave me an opportunity to reflect on mainstream English studies and what I had learnt in my five years as a student. I knew I was bored with the traditional emphasis on textual hermeneutics, and was much more interested in the material processes which resulted in the creation and consumption of texts. Being in a newsroom was particularly revealing, for here the interface between materiality and the text was evident at every point. As a result, I became more interested in the process rather than the product.

'I have been working for the last six years on a database of all Bengali books printed between 1801-1947, with full bibliographical description, title-page transcription and location details in the major libraries in Bengal and UK. Work on the first phase 1801-67 has recently been completed and the second stage 1868-1914 is in an advanced stage. From this data, I hope to be able to write a History of the Book in Bengal in the next five years'.

When Gupta began his doctoral research at Cambridge in the early '90s, he wasn't even aware of the term 'book history'. In 1997 he attended the first proper 'book history' conference, and learnt of the Society for the History of Authorship, Reading and Publishing (SHARP), the apex body of international book history. Two years later, when he joined Jadavpur University as a lecturer, he was gratified to find a postgraduate course in Book History already in place, begun by his erstwhile teacher Swapan Chakravorty, who was one of the world's experts on Renaissance drama and Thomas Middleton.

During his D. Phil at Oxford, Chakravorty had studied under the legendary Don McKenzie and this is likely to have been an influence behind setting up a book history course. Book history at Jadavpur was further strengthened when they were joined by Rimi B. Chatterjee in 2003 whose history of the OUP in India went on to win SHARP's book history prize in 2007. Other than starting a series in book history in India (a new volume titled *New Word Order: Essays in the Transnational Histories of the Book* is slated to come out in 2010) they held two conferences: the first 'Towards Book History in India' in 2002, and then two back-to-back conferences in 2006, 'New Word Order' and 'Print and Palimpsest', the first part of SHARP's regional conferences. It was at this time that Sukanta Chaudhuri set up the School of Cultural Texts and Records in 2003, and that has now become a major centre for the creating of resources in book history and textual studies.

In *An Empire of Books: The Naval Kishore Press and the Diffusion of the Printed Word in Colonial India*, Ulrike Stark (who now teaches at the department of South Asian Languages and Civilizations, University of Chicago) looks at how commercial book publishing happened. Her aim is to 'shed light on the social, cultural, and material aspects of book production... and to investigate the impact of the commercial book trade on the diffusion of knowledge, and on the processes of intellectual formation, modernization, and cultural renaissance in North India.'

A more intriguing aspect of the book is one that Ulrike Stark herself celebrates – that pioneer publishers such as

Naval Kishore were 'not just savvy businessmen but men deeply engaged in the intellectual and literary life of their time'. That they did not publish for profit alone. That book printing and publishing in 19th-century India was a 'venture as much entrepreneurial as intellectual'.

They were not just 'early industrialists but intellectual path breakers'; publishing for them was 'a vocation, not a business.' Stark names the great icons of early Indian publishing: Fardunji Sorabji Marzban in Bombay, Munshi Harsukh Rai in Lahore, Maulvi Abdul Rahman Khan in Kanpur and Mustafa Khan and Munshi Naval Kishore in Lucknow. They had 'a sense of the publisher's cultural mission in society'. They published to revitalize India's literary heritage and to contribute to 'Indian modernity through the diffusion of education and knowledge.'

These early print houses become vibrant meeting places for intellectuals and writers. It is this 'dual nature of the publishing house as modern capitalist enterprise *and* an important site of scholarly pursuits that the book seeks to explore.' In a very interesting footnote, Stark calls our attention to how 'virtually nothing is known about female participation in the early North Indian publishing trade, perhaps the sole exception being that of Mallika, the cultured young Bengali protégé and companion of Bharatendu Harishchandra', who goes on to set up a small publishing house and bookshop for her.

Munshi Naval Kishore (1836-95), says Stark, is the book's central character. Khvaja Abbas Ahmad, she notes, characterized him as a 'Muslim pundit and Hindu maulvi'. In his lifetime he published 5000 titles, of which 2000 were in Urdu. 'To narrate his life,' she notes, 'is to narrate the story of an Indian Hindu who participated in the revival of Hindu traditions while acting as one of the foremost promoters of Islamic learning and preservers of Arabic and Indo Persian literary heritage in the subcontinent…'

He published literary works, cheap novels, religious tracts, medical and astrological manuals, song books, legal forms and almanacs. Using the Naval Kishore Press, Stark looks at the transition from oral and manuscript culture to print culture. She is quick to warn the reader that this is not the focus or the concern of the book; neither are readership and reading practices in India. Early in the book she notes that we often forget that India had had a rich and long tradition of manuscript culture. But manuscripts were becoming hard to come by for many reasons. 'The step from the rare and costly manuscripts,' she tells us, 'to the mass produced printed book – costing barely one tenth of the manuscript, if not less, and available through a rapidly expanding network of distribution sites and agents – was indeed revolutionary.'

Elsewhere, Stark observes that 'the history of public libraries in India remains unwritten'. There were hardly any public libraries that people could use, she informs us. The few early circulating libraries were for Europeans and a few rich, educated Indians. Again, in a fascinating footnote she tells of the first ever full-fledged public library in India which was set up in Calcutta in 1818. This happened to be the private holdings of the college library of Fort William that being made available to the public. 'For the first time a collection of 8341 printed books and almost 3000 manuscripts was made accessible not only to Europeans but to literary men in general in India.'

I was curious to know what the experience of writing such a book had been for Stark, and she spoke of the difficulty of finding source material. 'Book history in India is a relatively new and fascinating field of inquiry, which offers tremendous scope for pioneering work.

However, the South Asian book historian faces particular challenges. The lack of primary sources was the greatest difficulty I faced when researching the Naval Kishore Press. But for a few stray documents nothing has survived of the publishers' archive. I was working without the very documents that a book historian usually relies on and that constitute his most importance source, that is, a publishers' account books and ledgers, business correspondence and private papers. The regular coverage of the firm's business activities in British colonial records could only partly fill this lacuna.' Francesca Orsini's *Print and Pleasure* (November 2009), the newest book history title from PB, also tells the story behind the boom in commercial publishing in 19th-century North India. How did the new technology of printing and the enterprise of Indian publishers make the book a familiar object and a necessary part of people's leisure in a largely illiterate society? What genres became popular in print? Who read them and how were they read? The work of all the book historians on print culture I've spoken of is invaluable to anyone who is interested in India's early intellectual, literary and (not so literary) history, and is curious, even in the slightest bit, about the history of the book in India.

From the introduction of print to India in the year 1556 to the first book in an Indian language, *Doctrina Christam* (1557), a Tamil translation of a Portuguese catechism, to a book of Bengali Nonsense Verse, is a long, exciting and dramatic journey for the book in India to make, and our book scholars, immersing themselves in bibliographical minutiae (the history of documents, the physical book as object) have evoked this book-obsessed world with clarity, devotion and absorbing scholarship.

WRITERS

Thomas Merton on a Frequent-Flier Pass: Pico Iyer
Through the Looking Glass of Books: Amitava Kumar
Turning the Wheel: Pankaj Mishra
One Robe, One Bowl: Ryokan
The Glass Family: J.D. Salinger
A Genius for Suspense: Ira Levin
Reverend & Mrs Panicker's Paying Guest: Conan Doyle (or, The Non-Canonical Sherlock Holmes)
The Movie, Not the Book: Ayn Rand
The Edgy Enthusiast: Ron Rosenbaum
Opposites Attract Him: Craig Seligman
The Second Lolita: Michael Maar
The Haunted Videotape: Suzuki-Nakata

Thomas Merton on a Frequent-Flier Pass: Pico Iyer

Pico Iyer lives in a small, austere apartment in rural Japan. He checks e-mail but doesn't surf the net. When he is not writing and travelling, he spends part of the year in a Benedictine hermitage, mostly in silence. He has never owned a cell phone, a Discman or an iPod. Often, in the evenings, he will turn out the lights in his flat and listen to U2 or Van Morrison or Sigur Ross or Leonard Cohen in the dark.

'As for choices,' he once told me, 'I think I came to Japan to explore the beauty of limitation. The richness of the empty room, the luxury of a life without car and television and newspaper, the liberation of a life lived in very tight margins. I cry out with delight at the passage of the day – the leaves, the light, the sudden sun on my walls – precisely because it is as tightly bounded as a haiku. No culture has so mastered the richness of tight limits as Japan.'

He has tried as a journalist to live in (what he terms) 'just autumn radiance'. What I find moving about the way Iyer lives and works and travels is that he is neither reclusive nor worldly. I can think of no better contemporary example of a famous writer living the Middle Way that the Buddha spoke of. It would be tricky for anybody to negotiate life between extremes and live so mindfully but especially so for an accomplished, well-travelled and celebrated author. And yet I can't think of another writer who has made journeying and living on the razor's edge so appealing and fulfilling.

A worldly monk, an unworldly writer. Pico Iyer

is Thomas Merton on a frequent-flier pass. A writer recording the world in all its dark grace. Here is an author whose work, in its published form, is seen by his readers even before he has laid eyes on it. Once Iyer sends his work out into the world – whether a book or an essay – he withdraws from finding out what became of it. And even when the book or the essay is published, he may not know of it for months.

Two instances: Once, browsing on the Net to find out what Iyer had essayed recently, I came across an introduction he had written to *A Wanderer in the Perfect City*, essays by *New Yorker* writer Lawrence Weschler. I wrote to Iyer saying how magically he had captured what the essays were doing, and he wrote back saying he had written that introduction six months ago and since had no idea what had become of it.

I chanced on another essay by him in *Rereadings: Seventeen Writers Revisit Books They Love* (edited by Anne Fadiman) in a bookshop, only to discover that Iyer, in his austere apartment near Kyoto, was yet to see the book.

He is best known as a travel writer but more recently the journeys he has taken his readers on have been inner journeys. When he visited Tibet in 1985, for instance, he tried to give the reader every sound and smell and sight in a place that almost no one had seen or could hope to see; returning to Tibet for the third time in 2002, knowing that most of his readers could see places in remotest Tibet on the Internet or the Discovery Channel, he tried to give them what they couldn't get on screens, 'the inner Tibet, the debates it sets up within our hearts and imaginations, the Tibet that plays out in parables.'

The journeys of the spirit he writes of are not those twee, self-help writings but difficult, clarifying journeys narrated with luminous detail, irony, and compassion.

And in a prose that is always uncompromisingly radiant and intense.

For some time now, Iyer's essays have been steadily advancing a remarkable kind of writing: the literary spiritual essay. Whether it is the poet of longing, Leonard Cohen, he is writing about, the towering genius of theatre director Peter Brook, hope and light in poor countries, the transcendent in the films of Terrence Malick, or the healing paradoxes of the Dalai Lama's life, the real subject of the essays is the invisible, inner world: imagination, the subconscious, the soul.

His literary heroes, W.G. Sebald, Peter Matthiessen, James Wood, Derek Walcott, Emerson, Keats, Lawrence, le Carré, Maugham, Melville, Greene, Robert Stone, and Annie Dillard are all chroniclers of the spirit. The theme in his essays and books has now become more and more about 'the dissolving of Self, what happens when we lose our bearings, how the world looks different when we don't see ourselves at its centre. To explore beyond the self, deeper than the self, more permanent than the self.'

His fictional world is also an echo of this. His novel *Abandon*, for instance, is the best contemporary love story I've read: it belongs to the small, beautiful tradition of the mystical love story. Reading it, you are reminded of other stories about God amidst lovers. I thought of *Shadowlands* straightaway – the story of C.S. Lewis and his love, Joy Grisham – and of another little known, astonishing book titled *A Severe Mercy* by Sheldon Vanauken: the story of Van and Davy, two American scholars sworn to true love, who, while studying at Oxford, meet C.S. Lewis and find their lives radiantly changed.

In both these stories, God is a very real third presence in the lives of the lovers. In Iyer's book the mystical is present in the Sufi poems and tales that mean so much to John and Camilla, the lovers in the book. The transcendent is also gently present in the California landscape that the lovers often trod. In the mystical love story, human love is often an allegory for divine love; with the reverse being true as well – the metaphor of the Lover and the Beloved. And so, unfolding are always two love stories for the price of one. The way men and women come together here is mystical and mysterious, while the devotee's longing for her God is familiarly, tenderly, achingly human.

Our love is a shadow of divine love, pointing to Love as a home or a city that we long for and are in exile from. (For C.S. Lewis this is to live in the shadowlands.) Preparing for his seminar paper, John McMillan, the reclusive scholar-hero of *Abandon*, notes: 'like all mystics, Sufis are singers of a homesickness that is a kind of hope; all of us are exiles in the world, they tell us, longing to get back to the place that is our rightful home.' Elsewhere he writes, 'The soul is an abandoned girl, lost in the wilderness, and crying out for the home that she has lost. The cry of the Sufi, is quite simply, the cry of abandoned love.'

One of the difficult tasks that he sets up for himself (and accomplishes brilliantly and movingly) is to write about Sufism in a way that will not sound like something from a New Age self-help book or a quote from a greeting card (John wonders if Rumi has not supplanted Rilke and the Dalai Lama as the reigning king of greeting cards). In innumerable passages he is able to evoke, in sentence after beautiful sentence, the mystery at the heart of Sufism.

In the words of another character in the book – a more traditional Iranian Sufi scholar: 'You do not come to the Sufi way... through your heart... You come to it through grief... Our hearts are broken open, and then we know real loneliness... We say yes to affliction, and in affliction find our faith.'

When John and Camilla fall in love, it feels like two people in exile returning home. They love each other in their solitude, in their loneliness. They are drawn by the other's sadness. What is so attractive about their romance is that so much of it is unspoken and silent. Neither will speak of the things that consume them. They are perhaps two of the most convincing, interesting lovers in contemporary fiction. It is amazing what Pico Iyer has pulled off here: as the lovers go deeper into each other, you feel the depths. The electrifying intimacy he creates between them will put most other love stories to shame.

You are taken so utterly into their experience that one loses all distance. When John first meets Camilla he isn't even drawn to her. Her constant chattering feels like an intrusion on his usual silence. But it isn't long before he discovers that her chattering hides much. That her silence is deeper than his. More troubled but also more mysterious. Camilla slowly takes on such mystery that, along with John, the reader longs for her sudden appearance at his door at those unearthly hours she comes knocking – usually 3 a.m.

When these two lovers want to comfort one another, they tell each other Sufi tales; and when they want to celebrate, they don't go to a California beach resort – they head to a monastery. This passage is just after they've checked into the monastery: '…the little cell they entered was furnished with starlight and silence. Its two simple beds were pressed against opposite walls, and above each of them, on the wall, was a cross. A lectern sat by the window through which the stars, the desert came.'

Camilla has many secrets but there are two that will partly solve the riddle that is Camilla. John discovers the first one quite by chance in a newspaper obituary. That moment is a twist worthy of the best mystery thriller. The solution to the second riddle comes towards the end – a word game linked to the fugitive Sufi manuscript John has been pursuing – and the revelation here is one of the most satisfying, surprising and touching discoveries in recent fiction. Their love is so fragile, so wounded, you often find yourself holding your breath for them, praying that everything will be okay. No reader was gladder than I when the lovers make it, and their love comes shining through.

'If I were to summarize my writing,' Iyer told me, 'it might be: it's relatively easy to live a life of clarity and peace if you take yourself on retreat to a mountaintop. But how do we bring the fruits of that stillness and clarity into the rush of the modern world and the need to be a real human being living in a world of change and flux?

'Writing for me is like a kind of scribbling in the air that tries to undo itself as it goes along; it's the best way I know – like prayer, I suppose – trying to transport us to those places where we have nothing to say and have to accept that we are beyond the reach of our thoughts. Those places where love and worship converge. Travel is for me just a way of talking about transformation.'

Iyer tries to root himself in the invisible – in the values and friendships and enthusiasms, the handful of books and tapes and ideas, that he takes everywhere he goes. 'The beauty of writing,' he notes, 'is the paradox of writing: that it uses words (and the self) to try to get to those places where both give out.'

Our commitment to movement, Iyer seems to be saying, is only as valuable as our commitment to stillness and vice versa. For Iyer, being too much in the world is as dangerous as being too far out of it. He is always trying, as Merton did, to keep himself honest by keeping both impulses alive in him. I am grateful for a writer like him, for sharing his journeys – both outer and inner – with us and for the example of his life, his writing and his concerns.

More than any contemporary writer today, he can instruct us on what Eliot meant when he wrote, 'Teach us to care and not to care. Teach us to sit still.' For all these reasons and more, Pico Iyer is a clarifying, transfiguring voice for our times, and my literary hero.

Through the Looking Glass of Books: Amitava Kumar

On an impulse, I decided to read Amitava Kumar's *Bombay, London, New York* again. I read it in a hurry when it first came out in 2002, noting with pleasure that it was, among many other things, the first really good book on reading written by an Indian. Reading it again, I discovered with excitement that it is not only still the best Indian book about how and why we read but also an original, riveting work of non-fiction. *Bombay, London, New York* is a meditation on the self, the home and the world as experienced in books – a sort of 'Amitava Through the Looking Glass of Books'.

While the theme of Diaspora runs memorably through his work, Kumar uses it to explore what home means in poignant, complex ways. 'What I am always going back to is the moment when I was going away,' he notes. 'The movement I am most conscious of now is the movement of memory, shuttling between places. One place is home, the other the world.' The different journeys Amitava Kumar makes in the book – actual and from memory – are insightful, deeply moving and clarifying for both the reader at home and the reader abroad. His perspectives are tough minded, unsentimental, nuanced.

For instance, in the chapter 'Travelling Light', he writes that what he is asking for is not that we turn our backs on the past but, 'Rather, the point is to ascertain what our narratives of travel are going to be… what I'd like to know more about are the day to day struggles, successes, failures, and confusions of the ones who leave home to seek better fortune elsewhere. And equally crucial, what I want to see are accounts of what is suffered as well as celebrated in the most ordinary of ways by those who do not leave, those who stay behind, whether because they want to or simply because it cannot be otherwise... What if we were to replace all the hypocritical, self-mythologizing accounts of expatriate fiction... with imaginative maps of toils and tales of small, unnoticed triumphs?'

The book's structure is beguiling: moving back and forth in suspenseful and surprising ways from personal narrative to marginalia on contemporary Indian fiction to cultural and political criticism. The photographs (by the author) that accompany the book are lovely – both the pictures themselves and the idea to use them that way. (One photograph in it – two young, striking looking South Asian women taking a cigarette break on a stoop – is something you almost want to own. It feels like a favourite still from a favourite movie.) The epilogue titled 'Indian Restaurant', an account of an older, burnt-out academic, Shastriji, befriending a younger Kumar at an American university, reads like a wonderful chapter from a novel you don't want to see end.

I have a favourite passage in the book: a visit Kumar makes to the Khudabaksh library in Patna, his hometown. With my fondness for descriptions of the holding and handling of books, I found myself seduced. The library, the author tells us, is perhaps the richest manuscript library on Islam in India, and it is full of hidden treasures, such as 22,000 handwritten books, out of which at least 7,000 are rare manuscripts. The old, gentle librarian with his shaky right hand shows Kumar a 'priceless book of poems by the Persian Hafiz' that was 'presented by the Mogul ruler Humayun to the emperor of Iran... The librarian's dark finger hovers over the lines that the emperor had inscribed. The page is filigreed in gold, the bare portions stained with age. I want to touch the page myself. I ask the librarian's permission, and he says yes, I gently place my index finger where the emperor has signed his name.'

Kumar, the author of *Evidence of Suspicion* (2010), has a fine way of filtering literature, politics, and culture in a kind of personal writing that he brings with intelligent economy into his writing (his website, www.amitavakumar.com is a fine example of this). What is invaluable is how he draws your attention to other significant writing, to the work of others. What is also especially remarkable about his writing is the way he puts himself on the line over and over again in a way few Indian writers would in their work. He writes in the tradition of the best personal essayists such as Philip Lopate, Joan Didion and Vivian Gornick, who write about the self and the world with a sense of discovery and intrepid candour.

Amitava takes himself as the starting point and then goes on to examine his relationship with the world with even rarer, brutal, moving honesty. And yet the personal details in his books don't amount to self-absorption or self-promotion: more remarkably, his presence in the narrative, because of the risks he takes, feels self-effacing, illuminating, heroic.

TURNING THE WHEEL: PANKAJ MISHRA

OVER THE YEARS since Pankaj Mishra's *An End to Suffering* was first published, I have found myself returning to it again and again, rereading it with great pleasure and absorption. I feel certain now that it is one of the best contemporary literary non-fiction Indian books, and a rich addition to Buddhist literature. *An End to Suffering: The Buddha in the World* is also Pankaj Mishra's masterpiece. And I'd wager it is the work closest to his heart. This is that rare book that touches a reader deeply, personally. There must be readers all over the world for whom this book has become a personal favourite; a book they completely inhabit.

I embraced it for its beautiful, shimmering prose, those solitary, book-haunted spells in Mashobra (exact, honest autobiographical details that serve the narrative perfectly), its gripping narrative of the Buddha's life, the complex and lucid way it criss-crosses and unravels history, philosophy, scholarship and the alluring, intimate breath of its travel narrative through ancient and present-day Buddhist India.

I was particularly drawn to two aspects of the book, both autobiographical: the romance of Mishra the reader aspiring to be a writer, and Mishra the seeker. Three-fourths into the book, he allows these details to intersect. One day, the author suddenly catches himself feeling empty though he has fulfilled his early ambitions to be a well-travelled, successful and famous writer.

By the end of the book, and many years later, he has found some answers to what this sense of *dukkha* in his life (and in the life of all sentient beings) means in Buddhism. And he begins writing *An End to Suffering*, a long-held book project on the Buddha he has been hoping to write but has been putting off because he had not, until then, found it urgent and personal enough to begin.

I find this admission – full of a rare candour and an even rarer humility – moving. The journey for Mishra, however, began 10 years earlier when he left college and moved in 1992 'to a small Himalayan village called Mashobra'. Reading the Mashobra section of the book, I often found myself under the spell of the time he spent there, a picture of stillness and contemplation that you can reach out and touch.

I discovered with a thrill that I could identify with him when he wrote: 'For years, I had felt a small thrill at the sight of the sentence, "I read all morning." The simple words spoke of the purest and most rewarding kind of leisure. It was what I did now: I read all morning…'

Elsewhere he writes, '…I would finally be able to begin fulfilling an old and increasingly desperate ambition. I had wanted to be a writer for as long as I could remember. I could not see myself being anything else.' Once he settles into Mr Sharma's cottage, he begins travelling 'to the inner Himalayas, the Buddhist-dominated regions of Kinnaur and Spiti.'

Throughout, Mishra's prose is, sentence by sentence, hard-won and beautiful. He went on these long journeys, he writes, 'attracted by nothing more than a vague promise of some great happiness awaiting me at the other end'. 'The bluish air trembled with temple bells' and 'Moths knocked softly against the oil-stained glass of the lantern'.

It is in Mashobra that the idea to write a book on the Buddha first emerges. 'It seems odd now: that someone like myself, who knew so little of the world, and who longed, in one secret but tumultuous corner of his heart, for love, fame, travel, adventures in far-off lands, should also have been thinking of a figure who stood in such contrast to these desires: a man born two and a half millennia ago, who taught that everything in the world was impermanent and that happiness lay in seeing that the self, from which all longings emanated, was incoherent and a source of suffering and delusion.'

It is only several years and a couple of books later that this search turns from intellectual to spiritual. 'I can't recall,' he notes, 'a spiritual crisis leading me to the Buddha. But then I didn't know myself well; the crisis may have occurred without my being aware of it. In my early twenties, I lived anxiously from one day to the next, hoping for a salvation I could not yet define.' But a decade later one afternoon in London he feels a sense of crisis. 'But on that afternoon in London, a few weeks after my return from Pakistan, when I thought again of the Buddha, I had become aware too of the futilities of my own life... and I couldn't always suppress the quiet panic at the thought that the intellectual and spiritual vagrancy I had come to know was all I had to look forward to, no matter how much I knew or travelled.'

It is in the last few pages of this many-layered 400-page book that Mishra reveals that he could now see the Buddha as 'a true contemporary'; 'an acute psychologist' who had seen that the mind, where suffering arises from, is also the only place where suffering ends. 'I now saw him in my own world, amid its great violence and confusion, holding out the possibility of knowledge and redemption – the awareness, suddenly liberating, with which I finally began to write about the Buddha.'

Make no mistake: though the author says that in his 'grasping selves' and his 'nexuses of desires' he could not find 'as much as a trace of humility, or compassion', the act of writing *An End to Suffering* is an act of loving kindness, humility and courage. It is Mishra the writer turning the wheel of the Buddha-dharma in the way only he knows. I was persuaded by its literary beauty as well as the author's own (self-effacingly stated) *dukkha* and enlightenment.

I can't think of very many books on Buddhism that are as literary and transforming as this book. What come to mind are Peter Matthiessen's Zen journals, *Nine-Headed Dragon River*, Pico Iyer's *The Open Road*, Rudolph Wurlitzer's *Hard Travel to Sacred Places*, Karen Armstrong's *Buddha*, Sherab Chodzin Kohn's *The Awakened One*, Stephen Batchelor's *Verses from the Centre*, and George Crane's *Bones of a Master*. Mishra's book is the rarest of things in contemporary non-fiction: a masterpiece of literary spiritual writing.

One Robe, One Bowl: Ryokan

Ryokan was an 18th century hermit-poet who lived in poverty and simplicity, contemplating the Way. From his hermitage deep in the mountains, he begged for food in nearby villages. He spent his time listening to the rain and leaves falling, playing with children and animals and writing Zen poetry. One night, returning to his little hermitage after a day of begging for food, he found a robber had stolen even his meagre possessions – a mat, a begging bowl and a washcloth. Immediately, he sat down and wrote this: *'The thief left it there/on the windowsill/the shining moon.'*

I think I first came across this Zen poem in a collection years ago, and though I was very moved, I did not bother to learn who had written it. In 2007 I stumbled on a Ryokan anthology, *One Robe, One Bowl: The Zen Poetry of Ryokan* (translated beautifully and with radiant simplicity by John Stevens) and ten pages or so into it, came upon the poem again. 'So it is by Ryokan!' I thought excitedly because, by then, I had read a dozen poems from the anthology and had found them the most remarkable spiritual poetry I had read in many years.

His poems record his joy and loneliness in living the life of a Soto Zen monk – practising zazen, knowing solitude, silence and deep stillness. There are two emotions that run through his poems: joy in having abandoned the world and the deep loneliness that accompanies it.

'At night, deep in the mountains I sit in zazen. The affairs of men never reach here. In the stillness I sit on a cushion across from the empty window. The incense has been swallowed up by the endless night; My robe has become a garment of white

dew. Unable to sleep, I walk into the garden; Suddenly, above the highest peak, the round moon appears.'

In another poem, he writes: *'If your heart is pure, then all things in your world are pure. Abandon this fleeting world, abandon yourself, Then the moon and flowers will guide you along the Way.'* These same poems, touchingly, also record the loneliness and hardship of a hermit-monk's life. *'I sit quietly, listening to the falling leaves. A lonely hut, a life of renunciation. The past has faded, things are no longer remembered. My sleeve is wet with tears.'*

The last line, with its sudden confession of tears, moves me more that I can say. Ryokan's family was wealthy and cultured, steeped in literature and religion. At 18 he surprised his family by becoming a monk. After many years in the monastery, he travelled as a pilgrim, meeting different Zen masters. When he was 40, he dedicated himself to a life of seclusion deep in the mountains. He was often seen during spring and summer in the nearby villages, begging for food or playing with children. In winter, he was confined to his hut. He felt his loneliness most during those long winter nights. *'Loneliness, and the night is only half over. There are no obstacles in my heart. But still I lack a true companion.'*

There are many stories, says Stevens in his introduction, about the way Ryokan forgot the world and abandoned himself to the moment. A friend visiting Ryokan found him deep in zazen. He waited for hours before the hermit greeted him. They went in and talked late into the evening, at which time Ryokan felt they must drink and talk. He asked his friend to wait a few minutes while he fetched some sake from outside the hermitage. When the monk had not returned even after an hour, his friend went looking for him and found Ryokan just a hundred yards from the hermitage gazing at the full moon.

The friend exclaimed that he had been waiting and waiting, thinking something terrible had happened to the hermit. To which Ryokan answered: 'You have come just in time! Isn't the moon splendid?' But what about the sake? 'The sake? Oh, the sake? Please forgive me, I forgot all about it.'

Ryokan, Stevens tells us, never preached, never judged. He gave away whatever he had, was kind to trees and flowers and was tender even to objects. *'Picking violets by the side of the road, I forgot my begging bowl. How sad you must be, my poor little bowl! I forgot my bowl again! Please nobody pick it up, My lonely little bowl.'*

When he was 69 and ill, he met Teishin, a 29-year-old Buddhist nun, who would go on to become his most famous and best disciple. 'They seem to have fallen in love almost immediately,' records John Stevens, 'they delighted in each other's company, composing poems and talking about literature and religion for hours. She was with him when he died on January 6, 1831. Four years later, in 1835, Teishin published a collection of Ryokan's poems titled *Hasu no tsuyu* (Dewdrops on a lotus leaf). Teishin devoted herself to Ryokan's memory until her death in 1872.'

The poems that repeatedly draw me to *One Robe, One Bowl* are the poems that speak of Ryokan's joy in forgetting himself and being enlightened by all things around him. *'My bowl is fragrant from the rice of a thousand homes; My heart has renounced the sovereignty of riches and worldly fame. Quietly cherishing the memory of ancient Buddhas, I walk to the village for another day of begging.'* Hundreds of years since they were first written, Ryokan's poems still feel immediate, speaking to us in the gentlest of voices of the radiant beauty of knowing simplicity, emptiness and joy along the Way.

The Glass Family: J.D. Salinger

On the day J.D. Salinger died, a friend called to say she wished Salinger had published more. 'His refusal to dialogue feels authoritarian,' she said. There was that; but it was only one aspect of his silence and invisibility, I wanted to tell her. Like many who worshipped daily at the altar of his work and life, I have tried to listen to that silence; dialogue with it. I would say his reclusiveness made more conversation and engagement possible by provoking us, seducing us.

The lingering sadness now isn't from the thought that there won't be new work to look forward to – because there are all those yet to be published Glass stories in the safe – but that it's the end of a kind of silence we had begun taking refuge in. Salinger's solitude, silence, and refusal to publish only drew us closer to him: how could we not find his long (50 years!) emblematic resistance to publicity, adulation, success and money instructive, comforting, and very nearly a sanctuary?

The artist as hermit; the artist as seer; the artist as renunciate – where silence and vocation and contemplation isn't retreat from the world but an intense, passionate and creative engagement with it. Salinger was a stunning instance of a great writer who found more fulfilment and joy in writing for himself than in writing for a public. He said: 'There is a marvellous peace in not publishing. I love to write. But I write just for myself and my own pleasure.'

There's an unavowed aspect to this Salinger statement that's often missed: yes, he wrote for himself but also (and always) for a *particular reader* – You. Yes, yes, *you*. 'You'll deny it up and down, I fear, but I'm really in no position to take your word for it... I look on my old fair-weather friend the general reader as my last deeply contemporary confidant.' Hadn't Buddy Glass told us this a long time ago in *Seymour: An Introduction*?

'I privately say to you, old friend (unto you, really, I'm afraid), please accept from me this unpretentious bouquet of very early-blooming parentheses: (((( )))).' And from between and within these floral parentheses he has always, always been talking to us; who after all do you imagine Holden has been shooting the breeze with these many years? 'Don't ever tell anybody anything. If you do, you start missing everybody.' That's the very last thing Holden told us.

But his creator, who has always kept a 'steady and sober regard for the amenities of such a relationship'– that is, the private, intimate and secret conversation between writer and reader – could not, over and over again, resist taking us into his confidence in the Glass stories. So, there was always that dialogic quality to his stories. But to talk back to Salinger would destroy not just the private universe that Buddy Glass and we share inside the Glass stories, it would also shatter Salinger's own immersion in it. To do so would be stepping outside 'the casino proper of my fiction', S would say.

And this is what legions of fans could not resist doing: mistakenly calling on the author, when they should, like Salinger, have been content with hanging out with Franny, Zooey, Buddy, Seymour, Bessie, Boo-Boo, Charlotte, Holden, Esme, De Daumier Smith, the Matron of Honour and the mute, grinning bride's father's uncle with the lighted cigar. Because 'how terrible it is when you say I love you and the person at the other end shouts back What?'

On every page of the Glass stories this Zen Buddhist-Vedantin-Homeopath adept's other self, writer Buddy Glass, is acutely aware of the reader; actually listening *for* a reader: 'Oh, you out there – with your enviable golden silence,' he calls out to us mid-paragraph. 'Oddly, the joys and satisfactions of working on the Glass family peculiarly increase and deepen for me with the years,' he confessed. 'I have several new Glass stories coming along – waxing, dilating – each in its own way, but I suspect the less said about them, in mixed company, the better.'

See: that's the hesitation, the shyness – mixed company. He'd rather talk to you 'the old confidant', 'the bird lover' ('those little beings of pure spirit') the 'amateur reader who reads and runs'. 'God, how I still love private readers,' he said to an old friend once. 'It's what we all used to be.' It is friendship and love he was offering us. Didn't Buddy say, 'My current offering isn't a mystical story, or a religiously mystifying story, at all. I *say* it is a compound, or multiple, love story, pure and complicated.'

Salinger never stopped talking to us. What he did really was to continue doing what that other dear old Tiger that sleeps, Seymour, said a writer must do: 'Give me a story that makes me unreasonably vigilant.' And that's as good a definition of the Glass stories – published and unpublished – as any. The enchanting and brilliant companionship of the Glass stories will never cease to make us kinder and happier. (Ah, and a story like 'De Daumier Smith's Blue Period' – you read that and you simply know that 'his writing was his, and his alone.')

I don't think there ever will be a voice like J.D. Salinger's in literature, nor is there anything in it as original, beautiful and tender as the Glass stories. Writing was his religion. In my head I have carried on a conversation with Salinger's imagination through the four Glass novellas ever since I first read them in college. The stories we hear he had been working on (in his filing system, said his daughter Margaret, he has 'red dots on stories that are ready to go, should he die') are very likely stories that continue the miniature saga of the Glass family.

I sincerely believe that even here, in these unpublished stories, Salinger did not abandon his old fair-weather friends, his readers: that while working fourteen straight hours every day for five decades in that studio garage in Cornish with no intention to publish, deepening and embellishing the world of the Glass family, he kept his old confidants by his side, those bird lovers, still listening to him with that 'enviable, golden silence'.

A Genius for Suspense: Ira Levin

And what, exactly, is Ira Levin's notion of suspense?

It's the comic suspense that results from paranoia. It works on the deliciously paranoid theme that no one is who they seem to be. It's the suspense that arises from ambiguity which is at the core of every Levin thriller. Are those dotty old people in the apartment next door actually modern-day witches or just nosy, over-friendly neighbours? Is the handsome, rich bachelor upstairs (whom the heroine is falling in love with) an electronic gadget geek or a psychopathic voyeur? Can an entire town of husbands be secretly plotting to replace their wives with Barbie dolls or do they just have very devoted wives?

The mechanics of Levin's suspense was shaped by two key novels about ambiguity and paranoia from the 1940s and '50s: Cornell Woolrich's *The Bride Wore Black* and Jack Finney's *Invasion of the Body Snatchers*. But Levin put his own original spin on it: diabolical plotting, a knowing, sophisticated urban wit, and suspense so fine you could cut your skin on it.

A Kiss Before Dying, his first book, written when Levin was only 22, is a virtual textbook in the craft of suspense. All his novels are a marvel of plotting: from *Rosemary's Baby*, *The Stepford Wives*, *This Perfect Day*, *The Boys from Brazil* and *Sliver* to his last – a sequel – *Son of Rosemary*. One of the many pleasures of reading Levin is that his books are not wordy and overwritten: they are slim (no more than 250 pages) and the prose is stripped down, cinematic, precise.

A good instance of how Levin structures suspense can

be seen in *Kiss*. The book is in three parts. All through part one the identity of the killer is concealed from you. That, of course, is standard. Levin's original touch was to *narrate the story from the killer's point of view*. The killer is always simply referred to as 'he'. 'His plans had been running so beautifully, so goddamned beautifully, and now *she* was going to smash them all', is the first line of the book. The situation, you soon realize, is simply this: lying in bed with his girlfriend, 'he' is contemplating ways to murder her.

Now, I'm perfectly aware that Agatha Christie also got her killer to narrate one of her books (I'm not saying which – why ruin it for those who haven't yet read it?) but that was in first person, while Levin's intentions are different. This device pays off brilliantly in the second part. When the murder investigation begins, the heroine discovers there were three young men on campus that had dated the victim through the semester. One of them is probably the killer. The problem with finding out whodunit is that they all seem to share some of 'his' characteristics. Levin has craftily strewn enough details about 'him' in part one to make you think that all of them could be 'him'.

For most mystery writers the whodunit aspect is their plot's climax; Levin tosses off the killer's identity midway through the book because he has more suspense up his sleeve. Whodunit is only one of the pleasures afforded by *A Kiss Before Dying* – Levin means to toy with us: 'it's him', we declare to ourselves. A little later we say, 'no, no, this must be him', and a little later, 'this *has* to be him.' But we are wrong, completely wrong. The moment of revelation is more potent than anything dreamt by Hitchcock.

It is with *Rosemary's Baby* that Levin hits upon what was to become his trademark suspense: paranoia. A young, pregnant New York housewife begins to feel that their apartment neighbours – an old couple – are plotting against her. Is she paranoid or is there really a conspiracy against her? It is Levin's masterpiece. Its graphic cinematic quality is often mistakenly attributed by critics to Levin's long experience with plays and television scripts, but it lies in Levin's early ambition to be an illustrator.

It's the kind of book you have to read a second time – indeed, several times – to see how the author did it. (In the movie version, Roman Polanski got all the spooky nuances and the comic undertone of Ira Levin's great horror novel just right.)

One of the true pleasures of reading Levin's thrillers is their re-readability. This tantalizing sense of a seesawing paranoia is equally effective in *The Stepford Wives*: is the independent, creative New York housewife imagining that her new, dull, suburban neighbouring housewives are not human but mechanical dolls fabricated by their clever husbands? Or will she, too, eventually, become a Stepford wife?

Levin's achievement is that such satire does not deflate the horror but enhances it. For instance, he uses wit and irony here to tweak the horror. He takes that old wonderful *Invasion of the Body Snatchers* idea of duplicates and gives it a neat, contemporary feminist twist.

Proof of Levin's genius lies in the book's climax: when the terrified, paranoid heroine demands that the Stepford husbands prove that their Stepford wives are human – creatures of flesh and blood – by asking one of the wives to cut herself with a knife so she can see a little blood, Levin ends the scene just before the knife presses the flesh. Levin knows suspense can never be literal. It is far more suspenseful, far more terrifying to keep wondering, to leave our imagination to it.

'The Stepford Wife' is now part of pop culture myth and refers to any woman who has changed into a zombie, into a toy thing for men to play with. In his brilliantly suggestive way, Levin leaves the conclusion open-ended.

Sliver is *Kiss* meets *Rosemary's Baby*. It toys with the reader about the identity of the killer in the fiendish way *Kiss* does, and surrounds the book with the eerie, claustrophobic mood of paranoia that *Rosemary's Baby* had by setting it in a Manhattan high-rise apartment. His *Deathtrap* is one of the most electrifying, diabolical suspense plays ever written for the stage. *Son of Rosemary* is vintage Levin and though it may not match *Rosemary's Baby*, it still is, as contemporary thrillers go, in a class by itself.

Rosemary wakes up from a coma after 27 years and finds out... well, it would be a shame to reveal even a page of the book's utterly delicious plot with its even more delicious final twist. Levin slyly slips in several in-jokes and references to *Rosemary's Baby* that only fans of the book will be quick to catch. That instrument of terrifying revelation from the original – the Scrabble board – plays a part here again but this time it is used as a comic set-piece; Levin knows fully well what our expectations would be, so he reverses them.

The word Rosemary is looking so hard to unravel using her Scrabble – Roast Mules – is a neat red herring. But red herring though it may be, none of the characters has solved it even by the end of the book. Levin leaves it to us to figure it out with this postscript: 'The solution to the puzzle is honest and pleasing. Save your postage.'

Levin wrote sparingly – one book in five years. While his work has been highly influential, few writers have actually dared to imitate him – either because they don't have his brilliance, wit and sleight of hand or because suspense that is so subtle, so sophisticated, doesn't sell anymore.

Levin's thrillers are not about 'whodunit' but 'who'll-do-it'. Suspense, not shock, is what Levin is after. He is more interested in the process of suspense, its nuances. Characters and situations remain eerily ambiguous till the end. Most suspense novelists are content with a single layer of suspense in their plots.

Levin's genius was to shade the plot with several layers of suspense that can leave you (pleasurably) in knots. He showed us why suspense is superior to surprise. He made suspense an emotion you could actually experience. He turned it into art.

CODA

I had begun to feel that my obsession with Levin must end in meeting the man in person, at which time I would get my first edition of *Rosemary's Baby* (which I bid for and won on eBay) signed and inscribed, and tell him – perhaps even show him – how much I admired his work.

In June 2005, I was in New York for a few weeks and decided to grab this chance to make contact. Ira Levin's phone was, predictably, unlisted. When I could not turn up any contact information for Levin on the Net, I called his publishers who told me that Mr Levin was a shy person, did not usually meet fans, and liked his privacy. Besides, he was busy working on a new book. I persisted, saying this was my only chance, and that I had come all the way from India to meet him (which was partially true). Perhaps just to get rid of me, the PR person informed me that the best she could do was forward him a message from me, which she asked to be emailed to her.

I quickly wrote out a note for Levin via the PR person,

careful not to sound like an obsessive fan. Perhaps I should have. I did not hear from her for two weeks.

When I finally called her, she told me that Mr Levin thanked me but did not as a rule meet fans. I felt sure that she had not passed on the message or if she had, Levin had not got a chance to read it. Or was she perhaps telling the truth? I had only a couple of days left to return to Bangalore. All I really wanted at this stage was to at least get my books signed.

I knew Levin lived somewhere in the Carnegie Hill district (where he had set *Sliver*) of Manhattan. 'The Mysterious Bookshop' and 'Murder Ink', two of the city's best mystery stores where Levin was known to give readings and sign books, were my only hope to get the actual address.

I had no luck at 'The Mysterious Bookshop' (the clerk told me archly that she knew his phone number and address but would not give it). I begged the friendlier staff at 'Murder Ink' (now, alas, shut down) to tell me where he lived, and taking pity on me, the staff wrote down the address for me but not the phone number. An hour later I found myself before his elegant apartment building. I stood dithering for at least half an hour by the door buzzer, feeling strongly like an intruder. I turned away from the door and started to leave.

At the end of the street, and heading for his apartment, was Levin carrying a small bag of groceries.

I recognized him at once from all the book jacket photos I had. He was walking towards me. I knew I would look foolish if I were to say everything I had been meaning to tell him – this is what I would do I quickly decided: just hand him my first edition *of Rosemary's Baby*, request him to sign it and keep moving. As he drew closer, I got the book ready. But in that instant I knew I could not do it

– it felt too much like an invasion of an author's privacy. I simply stood watching as he passed me. And then he turned the key at the door, and was gone.

Ira Levin died on November 14, 2007. In August 2007, on www.alibris.com, I located a copy of *Sliver* that Levin had actually signed. It was not inexpensive to acquire, and it now sits on my shelf next to my first edition of *Rosemary's Baby*, which, of course, will remain unsigned.

Reverend & Mrs Panicker's Paying Guest: Conan Doyle (or, The Non-Canonical Sherlock Holmes)

I CAME LATE to Sherlock Holmes. The whirring whodunit mechanics of Agatha Christie and the flamboyant ingenuity of Hercule Poirot's grey cells acted as effective red herrings early in my mystery-reading life, leading me away from the two usual suspects – Conan Doyle and Holmes. I wanted plot and cleverness and Christie supplied that; Doyle and Holmes provided elegance and style, but I didn't see that until I saw Jeremy Brett!

Brett's wildly stylish and yet precise interpretation of Sherlock Holmes in the Granada television series was mesmerizing, addictive fun. His intense, stylized performance that didn't shy away from the detective's drug dependency – and the meticulous, atmospheric production of the series – made Doyle's originality and intellect come alive. (My favourite Watson was the later one played by the gentle Edward Hardwicke. Now we have Sacha Baron Cohen, alias Borat, playing the gentle doctor, with Will Ferrell as Sherlock in one, and in the other, Robert Downey as the great detective, reinvented as a macho type cop with Jude Law as the good doctor – such outré Holmes pastiches worry purists.)

Anyway, so it was Brett and the television series that led me finally to the Sherlock Holmes stories, and to the realization that Doyle and Holmes were far superior company to Christie and Poirot. Since the time Doyle made Sherlock Holmes disappear in *The Final Problem* and later resurrected him, contemporary mystery writers have been paying their own homage to Doyle and Holmes by featuring the great detective in original stories, novels and essays. These take the form of Holmes pastiches to imaginary versions of Sherlock Holmes' life after retirement, to the long-lost adventures of the detective.

A critic from *Publishers' Weekly* observed that 'Writing a Sherlock Holmes tale is for popular writers equivalent to playing Hamlet for male actors: a challenge that few refuse and many regret.' Nevertheless, the fantasy these pastiches fulfil are not just for Sherlockians (who very often scrutinize – more than read them – for mistakes; though the efforts of the newer pastiches should please them because they reflect a deep knowledge of 'Holmesiana') but for all of us who yearn for more cases that break the canon by taking the great detective from Victorian London and placing him in the modern world with newer and more baffling problems to solve.

An outstanding example close to home being Jamyang Norbu's *The Mandala of Sherlock Holmes*, the detective's long-lost adventure in Tibet. Also, two overlooked, very desi Holmes tributes: Vithal Rajan's *Holmes of the Raj* (Writer's Workshop, 2006) and Neelum Saran Gour's *Messrs Dickens, Doyle and Wodehouse Pvt. Ltd* (Halcyon Books, 2005).

In Gour's *Messrs*, several characters from Dickens are the clients of Sherlock Holmes, with Jeeves serving as butler! Rajan's stories are set in colonial India, where Holmes and Watson cross paths with Tagore, Vivekananda, Ramanujan, Annie Besant, and Jinnah. And watch a cricket match in Bombay! In passing, they expose the true identity of Jack the Ripper, send Professor Moriarty to an ashram, and foil General Dyer's attempt on Annie Besant's life. Reviewing these books, the late Meenakshi Mukherjee noted, 'It is one of the ironies of history that Sir Arthur Conan Doyle who embodied so completely the Victorian value system and faith in the British Empire should now live on in postcolonial India as the subject of affectionate parody and tribute.'

Revisionism and refashioning is the order of the day, and the Holmes stories in contemporary fiction have seen plenty of pastiche making. One of the earliest, of course, was Nicholas Meyer's *The Seven Percent Solution* – where Holmes is treated for his drug addiction by Freud! In an interview to *Bookforum*, Leslie S. Klinger, a world authority on Doyle and Holmes and the editor of *The New Annotated Sherlock Holmes*, speculated that such fervent pastiche-making could be because Doyle told us so little about the detective, leaving it to us to fill in the blanks.

'There are a lot of blank pages in the biography,' noted Klinger. 'The very nature of a Victorian male leaves a great deal to explore, because the standard code of conduct was that you didn't talk about your personal life.' He points out that we know little about the detective's family life. He also wonders if we 'should take Holmes at his word that he abhors romance?' Newer entries in the Holmes mystique: *Dust and Shadows: An Account of the Ripper Killings by Dr. John H. Watson* (2009) by Lyndsay Faye, has the Baker Street detective solving the case of Jack the Ripper.

In Michael Chabon's *The Final Solution*, Sherlock Holmes is not named – throughout the novel he is simply referred to as 'the old man'. After retirement, Holmes has moved from London to Sussex, where he spends his days keeping bees. Holmes is now 89, and rooms in a house run by the wife of a Malayali pastor, The Reverend K.T. Panicker of the Church of England. Rev. Kumbhampoika Thomas Panicker is a high-church Anglican vicar who has lost his faith, and is riddled with doubts. He looks to this old lodger for clarity.

When a mysterious mute boy turns up with a remarkable parrot that utters numbers in German, the detective is once again compelled to pick up his magnifying glass and go to work. Concluding the case, the old man ponders on the meaning of detection: 'The application of creative intelligence to a problem, the finding of a solution at once dogged, elegant, and wild, this had always seemed to him to be the essential business of human beings – the discovery of the sense and causality amid the false leads, the noise, the trackless brambles of life.'

Mitch Cullins' Sherlock Holmes is a frail, forgetful but still brilliant 93 in *A Slight Trick of the Mind*, reminiscing about a recent trip to Japan. Both Watson and Mycroft are dead, and Holmes spends his time bee-keeping and writing letters. Laurie King's Mary Russell mystery series imagines a romance for Holmes: Mary meets Holmes in his bee-keeping days, becomes his apprentice, marries him and they travel the world together, embarking on new cases. King's *The Game* is set in India. Mark Frost, author of *The List of Seven*, and *The 6 Messiahs* and co-creator of the cult TV series, *Twin Peaks*, has a series where Arthur Conan Doyle himself is the detective. In Caleb Carr's *The Italian Secretary*, Holmes pursues a case with supernatural overtones reminiscent of *The Hound of Baskervilles* and *The Adventure of the Sussex Vampire*.

The literary estate of Doyle authorized a book of stories to commemorate the 100th anniversary of the first appearance in print of Sherlock Holmes. Sixteen of the best contemporary mystery writers from around the world were commissioned to come up with new stories to fit a new canon. One of the best stories in this anthology, 'The Doctor's Case', by Stephen King, has Dr Watson solving the case!

A pastiche of an entirely different order is the ingenious work of the French culture critic and psychoanalyst, Pierre Bayard, author of *How to Talk About Books You Haven't Read*, *Who Killed Roger Ackroyd* and *Sherlock Holmes Was Wrong*. Bayard proposes a new method of reading literature that he calls 'Detective Criticism'. Here a reader should read in a method that is 'more rigorous than even the detectives in literature and the writers who create them, and thus to work out solutions that are more satisfying to the soul.' The main premise of Detective Criticism is that the killer unmasked by the author is not the true murderer. As in life, the true culprits allow secondary characters to take the rap, eluding justice.

By using DC, which is essentially suspicious by nature, the text is re-investigated, the author questioned, the real criminal brought to light, and the names of the innocent cleared. Thus Bayard demonstrates that Roger Ackroyd was not killed by the book's famous killer but by Agatha Christie, and Sherlock Holmes did not satisfactorily solve the case of *The Hound of the Baskervilles*, proving that even his creator, Conan Doyle, could be wrong.

In David Grann's *The Devil and Sherlock Holmes*, the mythology of the great detective now acquires a real-life modern legend in the true story of a great Holmes scholar and his mysterious death. Grann, the bestselling author of *The Lost City of Z*, is a fearless, imaginative reporter who painstakingly follows the footsteps of his subjects. In Z he followed the explorer Percy Harrison Fawcett into the thick of the Amazonian jungle, encountering hardship and danger, risking his very life. In this anthology of various true tales of murder, madness and obsession, he attempts to solve a sinister mystery surrounding the legacy of Arthur Conan Doyle that has all the characteristics of one of Dr Watson's casebooks.

Richard Lancelyn Green, the world's foremost expert on Sherlock Holmes, is murdered just when he finally solves the case of the missing Conan Doyle papers. Over two decades he had been looking for a trove of letters, diary entries and manuscripts written by Doyle which had vanished. If they ever turned up they would be worth nearly four million dollars. But some believed the whereabouts of the papers remained hidden because they carried a deadly curse, not unlike the one from *The Hound of the Baskervilles*. Those who had pursued had either died suddenly or mysteriously. (Doyle's own son, Adrian, for instance, who once had these papers, died rather suddenly.)

The papers had disappeared soon after Doyle's death in 1930. Scholars were desperate to find it also because access to such material would finally create a definitive biography of Doyle. Green's great ambition was just that. After years of searching Green had a break that led him to the doorstep of Doyle's youngest child, Jean Conan Doyle. She showed him some boxes and let him peek inside and Green noted that they certainly seemed like the missing archive. But she was unable to let him examine it further because it had come under family dispute. She did tell him, however, that she wished to bequeath all of it to the British Library. When she died in 1997, Green waited for the papers to surface but nothing happened.

He waited and waited for years and nothing showed up. Then, in March 2004 Green opened the London *Sunday Times* to see the lost archive had turned up at a Christie's auction house and was to be sold for millions of dollars. If this happened it would go into the libraries of private collectors scattered around the world and scholars may never have access to them. Green immediately set about alerting various Sherlockians, the Sherlock

Holmes Society of London, members of the Baker Street Irregulars, and the Doyleans, the more orthodox Doyle scholars. Together they found a way to block the auction. A month later Green told friends that he was being followed, and felt his life might be in danger. One night, soon after, Green disappeared.

The police found his body on his bed in his apartment with a cord wrapped around his neck. Around him were Sherlock Holmes books and posters. Even his closest friends were baffled and concluded his death was 'a complete and utter mystery'. Fascinated by this unsolved mystery, Grann sets off to solve it.

My own little favourite reworking of Sherlockania is Stephen Kendrick's novel *Nightwatch: A Long Lost Adventure in which Sherlock Holmes meets Father Brown*. The mystery is set in 1902: Holmes, Mycroft and Watson are invited to the World's Parliament of Religions convention. Present are scholars and clerics from various faiths – Roman Catholic, Anglican, Eastern Orthodox, Buddhist, Jewish, Hindu and Muslim – who have gathered to find a common ground.

The host, an important clergyman, is murdered, and by dawn Holmes has already solved the case. But – and this is the beautiful twist here – in a quiet epilogue we learn that Holmes solved only part of the mystery: G.K. Chesterton's Father Brown, who was also invited to the convention, offers the real solution in his self-effacing, humble manner.

Kendrick, a Universalist cleric himself, knows his Church history and his Conan Doyle. His other Holmes book is unique in Holmesiana – *Holy Clues: The Gospel According to Sherlock Holmes* is a meditation on how the great detective's methods can throw light on spiritual mysteries. 'After all, if the sleuth can discover the darkest and most guarded and protected stories within the human heart,' writes Kendrick, 'can that of God's inscrutable will be far behind?'

Gilbert Adair, though, is the most devilishly entertaining, stylishly clever and wittily erudite post-postmodern maker of pastiches. As he himself said once, if he likes a book, he will simply rewrite it. It's his way of parodying, celebrating and critiquing it. (*Death in Venice* becomes *Love and Death on Long Island*.) In *The Act of Roger Murgatroyd* and *The Mysterious Affair of Style* he took on Agatha Christie. His new book, *And Then There Was No One* brings Christie, Conan Doyle and Adair together to face-off. Yes, Adair is the narrator of the book and a character in it.

When the book begins, Adair has just finished his latest postmodern riff: 'The Unpublished Case-Book of Sherlock Holmes', a collection of apocryphal Holmes stories (such as 'The Giant Rat of Sumatra'). On the strength of this he's invited to a Sherlock Holmes festival taking place in Switzerland. On the list of guests he notices Umberto Eco is an invitee; next to his name it says: (unconfirmed), and disappointingly enough Eco doesn't turn up because of an illness in the family.

After he reads from his book to the audience gathered there, he fields many questions ('What is the difference between bookshops in Switzerland and bookshops in Britain? Adair: Your bookshops sells fifty types of books and one type of coffee, while ours sell fifty types of coffee and one type of book.') and it is at this point that one of his characters from the earlier Christie pastiches – his heroine, in fact, the crime novelist Evadne Mount – turns up at the book reading and demands to know why he would waste his time on pastiches since postmodern playfulness and self-referential novels are all a thing of the past? Why won't he invent his own detective? Why borrow a famous one?

Sherlock Holmes pastiches are cheap and commonplace, she reminds her creator. The bookshops are swarming with them, linking Holmes to Jack the Ripper, Sigmund Freud, and every type of modern-day villain. 'All of them tosh, I call him the bogus Holmes – Schlock Holmes, ha ha!' Eventually, there's a murder and Adair and his heroine will have to solve it. But not before Adair finishes answering his heroine on why he persists in pastiche-making.

The story Adair reads out at the festival is a full-fledged 30-page Holmes pastiche that he invents for the book. At the end of the story, Watson as usual sits down to record the case but Sherlock asks him to desist for personal reasons. Watson replies that he will write the case but with the stipulation that it be opened and read only a hundred years from now. Holmes laughs. 'A hundred years? 2011? Oh, how you do exaggerate, Watson! I can assure you that in 2011 the name of Sherlock Holmes will have been consigned to the most complete and utter oblivion.' Watson tells us that his friend is usually right but notes down as the last entry in his casebook: 'In this instance, however, I fancy he might be mistaken.'

The Movie, Not the Book: Ayn Rand

Ayn Rand completed the screenplay for *The Fountainhead* in June 1948. When the film was completed in '49, many friends recalled how euphoric she sounded. Ayn wrote: 'For the first time in Hollywood history the script was shot verbatim, word for word as written.' She was happy that not a single word of her script had been cut. But twelve years later she confessed that the whole thing had been a miserable experience.

There had been frequent arguments on the sets with King Vidor, the director, over ideological and stylistic aspects. Once she walked in to find Vidor shooting a shortened version of the notoriously long courtroom speech Howard Roark makes at his trial. She stormed out in rage shouting that she would take her name off the film completely. Warner Bros, terrified that the cult of readers the book had gathered, would stay away from the film, ordered that no cuts could be made from her script.

On the opening night of the film, Rand discovered one crucial Roark line ('I wished to come here and say that I am a man who does not exist for others') had been cut after all, but no one had dared tell her beforehand. In the end, the movie had not been a hit, commercially or critically, with the *New York Times* critic labelling it 'high-priced twaddle'.

In her deeply researched and compellingly written biography, *Ayn Rand and the World She Made*, Anne C. Heller throws light on why Rand put on a happy front and pretended to like the film for the first few years. It had always been the grand flaw in her character, observes Heller – the inability to see or admit that she was not as perfect as her characters. In this instance, not willing to concede, even to herself, that she may have written a flawed script.

The experience also ended her romance with Hollywood, Heller tells us, making her swear that she would never work in films again, and would never allow her future work to be turned into movies. 'Though dramatically set and beautifully shot, the movie was stiff,' concludes Rand's biographer.

Unlike probably all the acolytes of *The Fountainhead* who read it when they were in their teens, Anne C. Heller devoured the book (and Ayn Rand) in her forties and became 'a strong admirer, albeit one with many questions and reservations... Like Dickens, Rand's art is the art of melodrama. At heart, she was a 19th-century novelist illuminating 20th-century social conflicts...'

Heller *gets The Fountainhead* and its author in a way no literary writer before her has, but surprisingly (not unlike Ayn Rand herself) misses seeing that the movie is actually magnificent. It hasn't dated one bit, and stylistically it still feels so modern and cool – something I can't say about the book anymore.

King Vidor's *The Fountainhead* is one of the most underrated American films from that period. It's a classic romance. As good as anything Hollywood ever made, with all the characters brilliant and driven and conflicted. But because the book is saddled with so much puzzling philosophy, the movie has never gotten its due. Vidor (1894-1982) was, for forty years, obsessed about the theme of life as a battle in his films. (It's available now in a remastered version on DVD. Also available finally is that long out of print Italian version of *We the Living* starring Alida Valli restored and reissued as a brand new DVD in September 2009.)

Watching *The Fountainhead* today, you can see that it was clearly ahead of its time: stylish, crisp, ultra-modern with some beautifully stark black-and-white cinematography. All the philosophy has been pared down to a few scenes – it is unbelievable how minimalist, spare and ruthless Rand has been with her own book: she understood the mechanics of Hollywood storytelling so well. And those unforgettable characters played with such heady abandon by Gary Cooper as Roark and Patricia Neal as Dominique Francon.

Cooper's great face *is* Roark, and though Neal's face may not be what we imagined as Dominique's, she becomes Ms Francon before our very eyes as the movie progresses. In the minds of many fans, Neal's haughty, sexy performance *was* Ayn Rand. (Heller notes that Ayn once said that Dominique was 'myself in a bad mood' and all the research for the psychology of the character of Roark was herself.)

After all these years, just when you thought you'd gotten over all that Howard-Dominique foolishness, the movie knocks you silly with their improbable romance. And you get a high from watching these tormented romantics taking on the world. Boy, that Wynand-Dominique-Roark triangle! I mean, what melodrama, what dialogue, what emotion. (The movie ought to be very close to Indian hearts; think of it as a black-and-white Bollywood epic without the songs.)

An intriguing movie on the life of Ayn Rand is *The Passion of Ayn Rand* (there's also an uncritical bio-pic titled *Ayn Rand: A Sense of Life*) with Helen Mirren playing the derided author. The film looks at her as a character rather than as a mouthpiece for a philosophy. Based on Barbara Branden's book of the same name, the film is a fictional recreation of the last controversial years of Rand's life, tracing the tangled 15-year-long love affair between the author and Nathaniel Branden, her handsome, much younger protégé. She was 49 and he was 24.

Amazingly, the affair was conducted with the consent of Nathaniel's wife, Barbara, and Ayn's husband, Frank O'Connor. In Nathaniel, Ayn felt she had at last found her intellectual heir. But this strange quadrangle was doomed from the start. After it ended, Ayn Rand retreated and turned even more reclusive.

In an interview that accompanies the film, Helen Mirren – still Britain's sexiest, smartest older actress – says she grabbed the chance to play Rand because here was 'a woman with the size, grandeur and flaws of a Shakespearean character'. Mirren pulls off something unusual and fantastic here: along with all the anger, intelligence and passion, she also shows Rand's vulnerability.

I wish Heller would re-evaluate the film, just as she has the book. She had a clear advantage in approaching it for the first time as an adult, not as a vulnerable young reader. It is both rare and odd to find adults picking up *The Fountainhead* to read so late in their reading life. They are usually warned off by its veteran but disgruntled readers that it is not something grown-ups ought to read, as if it only belongs to an adolescent's curriculum.

Her biography is balanced, clear-eyed, and toughminded with several illuminating and brilliant chapters. It is also interesting for the kind of hidden biographical details she unearthed: as a school girl in Russia one of Ayn's closest friends was Olga Nabokov, the writer's sister. Heller demonstrates why that legend about the author plucking her name from the Rand-Remington typewriter she owned is only a myth: in 1926 the Rand-Remington had not come into the marketplace. How she came by that name will always remain a mystery.

But we learn from Heller – and again for the first time – the story behind her first name. Ayin ('an affectionate Jewish diminutive for bright eyes') is how her father called her when she was a child in Russia. And Ayinotchka, Heller notes, 'is a perfect Russian inflected endearment for a little girl with bright, bold, hypnotizing eyes'.

Heller respects what Ayn achieved as a struggling Russian refuge, and calls our attention to her courage and self determination. She sees Ayn Rand as 'Gallant, driven, brilliant, brash, cruel, as accomplished as her heroes, and ultimately self-destructive, she has to be understood to be believed'. What she particularly celebrates is Ayn's gift for writing; the 'solitary, self-made literary genius' she willed herself into.

I have always liked her natural gift for plotting and storytelling, the scale of her melodrama, her outré characters, and most of all, her absolute, uncompromising, deadly romanticism. But I was never too crazy about her philosophy. Because of the years of embarrassment of once having turned *The Fountainhead* into a private bible (you were quite certain then that the world was divided into those who liked Any Rand and those who didn't), readers nowadays rarely admit to being affected by it.

Until the very end Rand believed that 'romantic love is a response to your highest values'. Make that a capital R. In her sparkling and bracing essay on Rand ('Twilight of the Goddess' from *Passionate Minds: Women Rewriting the World*) Claudia Roth Pierpont points out that Ayn Rand herself claimed she was compelled to write political books but what she really wanted to write were romance and adventure stories – like the ones from all those Hollywood movies she was crazy about, growing up in Petrograd.

When I read this, it immediately made sense: I knew

now why the romance of *The Fountainhead* had stayed with me, while the philosophy had faded. Ayn Rand's heart had really been there – in that romantic manifesto. And the movie, in spite of that infamously long Roark-Cooper courtroom speech, is the essential Ayn Rand.

At the end of her life, Pierpont informs us, she *did* begin such a novel, but her illness kept her from finishing it. She returned the advance to her publishers. It was about a woman who falls madly in love with a man who rejects her and she suffers terribly for it. It was the only novel she was interested in writing after *Atlas Shrugged*.

And it would end, Pierpont tells us, with her hero at last realizing the 'qualities of the woman who has worshipped him with such passionate intensity, and returns her love. He begs her to forgive him for all the pain he caused her. The last line of Rand's only work to be liberated from politics is the woman's simple but consoling reply: '"What pain?" she asked.'

THE EDGY ENTHUSIAST: RON ROSENBAUM

IT TURNS OUT that Ron Rosenbaum, the Shakespeare of investigative journalism, is the best-kept secret in narrative non-fiction writing. Perhaps that is as it should be – because what he writes about are secret societies, clandestine subcultures, conspiracy theories, obscure writers of genius and their secret subtexts, unsolved mysteries (that he often comes close to solving), cultural paradoxes and historical enigmas. He pursues the elusive and the complicated with great clarity. He calls the subject of his intense investigations, 'edgy enthusiasms'.

I've seldom encountered cultural journalism of such high order: original, provocative thinking combined with great prose. The writing is opinionated, brilliant, intensely (almost diabolically) researched, funny, deeply intelligent, and restlessly probing. His essays (always satisfyingly lengthy and intriguing) read like beautifully written spy stories. A good place to begin reading him is his monumental, seductive, generous anthology (800 pages, 57 speculative essays) titled *The Secret Parts of Fortune: Three Decades of Intense Investigations and Edgy Enthusiasms*. This is a collection of compelling, thoughtful non-fiction; intellectual adventure stories that somehow manage to be philosophical, comical and suspenseful.

His edgy enthusiasms include: the first ever story to reveal the occult rituals of Skulls and Bones, the legendary Yale secret society that has produced spies and presidents, the secrets of the Little Blue Box, the classic story (another first) about the birth of hacker culture, the unsolved murder of JFK's mistress, the secrets of The Dead Sea Scrolls and the scholarly infighting behind it, the underground realms of 'unorthodox' cancer-cure clinics in Mexico, the identity of the unreliable narrator in Nabokov's *Pale Fire*, Starbucks's Orwellian New Age culture, Oliver Stone versus Quentin Tarantino, revealing America's least-known great writer, explaining Hitler, the spiritual self-loathing of Martin Amis, cats versus dogs, the mysterious suicide of identical twin gynaecologists, Thomas Pynchon's true identity, and (my all-time favourite piece) the hidden life of America's most haunted and haunting writer, Jerome David Salinger.

What Rosenbaum is drawn to is the seductiveness of the hidden. He explains this as 'the primal, almost theological, root of the hide-and-seek impulse in human beings… The glory of man is to fantasize about the hidden.' His journalism, he says, is the 'journalism that asks the same questions literature does.' He feels journalists must investigate ideas as thoroughly as they do politics and crime. He makes his obsessions our obsessions. He's no ordinary journalist — I sometimes feel he is like some towering Talmudic scholar of the contemporary world, making exegetical interpretations of its mysteries, its unknowableness.

The best explanation offered for Salinger's silence, his retreat from the world, is Rosenbaum's essay 'The Catcher in the Driveway'. Determined to at least discover where Salinger lives and leave him a letter, Rosenbaum stands outside Salinger's driveway, near his mailbox, pondering S's baffling silence. 'It is the work of renunciation and determination and expensive litigation… the silence is in itself an eloquent work of art. It is the Great Wall of Silence J.D. Salinger has built around himself.'

The silence of a writer, he goes on to add a little later, may not be too different from the silence of God. Another reclusive genius writer (long out of print) he discovers for us is Charles Portis, best known, unfortunately, as the author of *True Grit*. But his true masterpieces, according to Rosenbaum, are *Masters of Atlantis* and *The Dog of the South*. Portis is a 'maddeningly under-appreciated American writer,' he notes, 'perhaps the least known great writer alive in America. Perhaps the most original, indescribable *sui generis* talent overlooked by literary culture in America.'

His new work, *The Shakespeare Wars: Clashing Scholars, Public Fiascoes, Palace Coups* is, he explains, 'a kind of guide – leading the reader, like Virgil in Dante, down into the scholarly inferno, hoping to illuminate some of the genuine intellectual (and visceral) delights, the tormenting conflicts, the unbearable pleasures to be found therein.'

Rosenbaum has constantly alluded in his previous essays, books and column to his fierce passion for Shakespeare. This is a book that has been on his mind (and soul) for a long time, and in his introduction (addictively digressive and personal) recounts how he came to be Shakespeare-smitten. It began with an extraordinary 1970 staging of *A Midsummer Night's Dream* by Peter Brook. He writes that this production changed an entire generation of Shakespearean players and directors. 'I'd never experienced anything of such radiant clarity... It was a lifelong love potion.'

Until that moment, Rosenbaum had not been a Shakespearean obsessive. But seeing Brook's staging of the *Dream* marked his 'outsider's odyssey into the innermost citadels of scholarship'. He writes that he would walk 'around the city listening to Shakespeare tapes on a Walkman.' (I haven't seen Peter Brook's legendary production – nor can I ever hope to see it – but because I have seen his *Mahabharata*, I can fully understand why

Rosenbaum was so affected: Jean Claude Carriere and Brook's film version of the epic is, for me, the definitive one. I return to it again and again.)

For *The Shakespeare Wars*, Rosenbaum researched and interviewed the foremost living scholars, theatre directors and actors. The book contains summaries of the work of important critics, asides on his encounters with the poems and plays, and scholarly and critical issues that are being 'warred' over. Debates over the authentic way to pronounce and deliver lines, deconstructionists/ new historicists versus critics who write for a lay public, moderate versus fanatical hunters of verbal ambiguities, and the importance of the early 17th-century spellings.

One Shakespeare scholar Rosenbaum visits argues for reprinting the plays without updating the spelling of their words. When the modernized line from *Hamlet* 'the air bites shrewdly' is replaced with the original spelling 'the air bites Shroudly' the reader can suddenly and clearly see death looming. The battle that he gives fullest coverage to (in a 30,000-word chapter) is over textual variants: The squabbles, for instance, among editors of *Hamlet* on sources for the definitive text. A 'good' and a 'bad' quarto and the trimmed version that appears in the complete Folio published in 1623, eight years after Shakespeare's death. Are the variants among these editions the result of compositors' errors or are they Shakespeare's own revisions? The debate over King Lear variants and the decision to print two versions of the text in the Oxford edition. And an 'Enfolded Hamlet' project that digitizes the play so that all the variants can be read at once.

The biggest fiasco Rosenbaum reports on is the one rigged by an American professor claiming that a 'Funeral Elegy' signed 'W.S.' had to be by *the* W.S. because his computer told him so. The professor later retracted this but by then publishers had already included this 'new work' in their collected editions.

Rosenbaum shows here that he can dish Shakespeare with the best of the academics. In particular, I enjoyed the blow-by-blow account of feuds between rival scholars (he gamely attacks Harold Bloom for arguing that Shakespeare 'invented the human' personality) and Rosenbaum's own interjections that keep the book from becoming one more pedantic Shakespeare study or another fashionably opaque postmodern project.

To return to *The Secret Parts of Fortune*: even his lighter pieces here offer insight, wit, complexity, pleasure. 'Stumpy Versus Lucille: The Great Pet Debate' is about cats versus dogs, in particular about his marmalade-coloured cat, Stumpy. One of the sweetest tributes you'll see is on the inside jacket of the book cover: a tiny photograph of Stumpy under 'About The Author' with this note: 'Aware of the controversy over authors posing with their pets on book jackets, he has not posed with his soulful cat, Stumpy, whose comic genius is described on pages 702–7 of this volume.' Reading Ron Rosenbaum (to borrow his own take on Portis) is one of the great pure pleasures available in contemporary journalism.

Opposites Attract Him: Craig Seligman

I'VE FANTASIZED ABOUT a book like this but never thought somebody would write it: criticism as autobiography! What Craig Seligman has done in *Sontag and Kael* is to write his own intellectual autobiography by closely reading the life and work of Susan Sontag and Pauline Kael – two of America's most influential culture critics – and telling us what they have meant to him. He basically sets up a 'three-cornered quarrel' and invites us to argue with him.

One of the classic critical texts some decades ago was George Steiner's *Tolstoy or Dostoevsky?* that attempted to see who the greater writer was (and if I'm not wrong, by the end, Fyodor edges out Leo) but it's interesting that Seligman's title is Sontag *and* Kael, not Sontag *or* Kael. It's a marvellous premise for a book: put two great critics side by side not to see who is better but to illuminate each other, to examine two very different but valid critical styles. 'Opposites attract me,' says Seligman, and feels that he doesn't have to choose between them, that he can find pleasure in both kinds of writing.

And he nearly succeeds. Nearly – because he wears his bias for Kael on his sleeve right through the book. On page one he confesses: 'I revere Sontag, I love Kael.' He tried hard to not have a villain in the book but Sontag 'kept making it hard' for him. Kael is likeable, Sontag is lofty, distant. His constant warmth for Kael throughout the book is easily explained: Seligman knew Kael as a friend for twenty-three years but he has never met Sontag, and doesn't wish to.

I, too, read Sontag and Kael in college and was

instantly drawn to the latter. Not simply because she wrote on cinema but because she was so entertaining, so stylish, so personal. But reading Seligman, I found myself surprisingly rooting for Sontag. I feel now that I need more Sontag and less Kael in my life! I find Sontag more absorbing now; her writing is the kind of writing that is interesting sentence by sentence. Towards the end, Seligman grudgingly admits Sontag as the greater writer but he is quick to add: 'And what does the greater writer mean, anyway? It certainly doesn't mean the *better* writer.' Huh?

But I think I see his point: something about Kael's writing being consistently exciting – every essay, every review – and thus making her the better writer, while Sontag's individual essays build to a crescendo, her greatness to be found in her spectacular body of work, whose scope and range and amplitude was – is – magnificent. Sontag's subject was everything (Kael too was trying to write about everything through the movies): from aesthetics to pornography to silence. Sontag once said that she could only write about the things she loved and admired; it felt distasteful to her to be negative, to write about things she didn't care about.

Seligman draws our attention to this, to point out that Sontag saw herself as a critic who commented on art, not evaluated, while Kael felt happy evaluating. I like the later Sontag even better, the Sontag of *Where the Stress Falls*, where she gets down to specifics and away from larger arguments, looking at writers and books she cares deeply about. Seligman doesn't like the later Sontags precisely because they lack polemics. Sontag, who like Kael is no more now, herself had moved on to fiction (*The Volcano Lover*, *In America*), feeling 'narrative lasts more than ideas'. It is her fiction, she said, that she liked more now than her criticism!

Whether it is the early polemical essays or the later portrait essays, Sontag has never wavered from her purpose: 'to defend the idea of seriousness – true seriousness.' Kael hated seriousness in art, championed the vulgar and trashy in cinema. Kael was subjective, Sontag left herself out of her writing. She wrote slowly, precisely, agonizingly (fanatically spending an hour on just one word), Kael wrote quickly, confidently, recklessly.

For Seligman, Kael's writing glitters, Sontag's 'sentences give off a soft glow'. They 'glimmer with a subdued but very beautiful light. He remarks on the 'lunar beauty of her prose', and gives as an example, her definition of beauty: 'a gladness of the senses'.

A book critic for *The New Yorker* and *Salon*, Seligman's pleasure and excitement in this whole project – placing Sontag and Kael next to each other as perfect foils in their approaches, their purposes and their personalities – is evident on every page, every line.

Reading their work closely, he makes this astonishing discovery: 'writing is not a conduit to thinking, writing *is* thinking.' The one obligation a critic has, says Seligman, is to get it right. And Sontag and Kael, each in their way, got it right. So does Seligman.

The Second Lolita: Michael Maar

Can a work of scholarship be Borgesian? That is, labyrinthine, tantalizing and open to mystery? A work of fiction, yes, but a slender thesis? In 1916 a book of short stories called *The Accursed Giaconda* was published. It was written by a man named Heinze Von Lichberg. The ninth story in it was about a cultivated man of middle age who travels abroad, takes a room as a lodger, and falls in love with the daughter of the house. The girl is a child. On simply looking at her he is lost; her charm enslaves him. They become intimate. The story was titled 'Lolita'. And this was 40 years before Nabokov's famous novel. How to explain this? Had Nabokov plagiarized the plot and the title? Or was it sheer coincidence? Or is there a third explanation?

The Two Lolitas, a true story, is like something Borges could have imagined. And the tale itself, as explored by the German critic Michael Maar, unravels with the kind of scholarly mischief the blind Argentinean would have envied. The book, translated by Perry Anderson, is but 63 pages and can be read (as I very nearly did) in one sitting. What is the mystery about the second Lolita? Lichberg, we learn from Maar, was a German journalist who lived in Berlin. His book, *The Accursed Giaconda*, was lost in obscurity.

But Nabokov, a very young man at that time, had lived in Berlin for a while, and could have chanced on it. N's name for her heroine was initially Juanita Dark – how, then, did he come to call her Lolita? When Humbert sees Lo he records: 'the same frail, honey-hued shoulders, same silky supple back, the same chestnut head of hair'.

When Lichberg's narrator sees his Lolita, he says, 'her body was boyishly slim and supple, and her voice full and dark.' Forty or more years before the more famous Lolita! Maar is forced to ask: 'Had the author of the imperishable *Lolita*, the black swan of modern fiction, known of the ugly duckling that was its predecessor?'

The critic offers three possibilities: 1) N had no idea of Lichberg's Lolita, and it was one of those mysterious coincidences. 2) N had read it but then forgot about it, a case of literary 'cryptoamnesia', and 3) N knew it, consciously cribbed from it, but in the fashion of a quotation: taking light literature and making deep literature out of it.

Now, the first possibility of pure contingency: Maar asks, 'Why should it not simply be a splendid, mysterious and even faintly comical example of the way life displays patterns that look deliberate yet are only the caprices of coincidence? In a certain sense that would be a classic Nabokovian theme.' But the critic dismisses it and moves on to the second.

2. N could have come across the story, seen that it was very much like what he was fashioning and so forgot about it entirely. He notes that the history of literature is not without examples of 'cryptomnesia'. Apparently Nabokov would read two or three books a day and forget them. The plot of Lolita had prefigured in his work several times. There is a pre-Lolita character in his 'A Nursery Tale' (1926). He had created a child-woman here, narrated by an old poet – a pre-figuration of Humbert. In his *The Gift*, a secondary character actually discusses the plot of Lolita. And in *The Enchanter*, the story is fully present, in a shortened form. Thus Lichberg's story was buried deep in his literary psyche, manifesting itself in various forms until it became the novel we know now so well.

But no. Interesting, but no. What interests Michael Maar is the third tale in the Lolita labyrinth. N knew the tale well, admired it and used the plot as a quotation. This wasn't plagiarism (though Thomas Mann called it 'higher cribbing'): you take from a lower source and turn it into something else. 'Literature,' Maar informs us, 'has always been a huge crucible, in which familiar themes are continually recast.' Maar then takes us through a series of revelations that qualify as top-notch literary detective footnote work. Like some literary Dan Brown, Nabokov had placed several veiled references to the original source – what Maar terms as the Ur-Lolita – in his life and work. Maar's literary sleuthing led him to the clues that reveal the way this ur-text and its obscure author pop up in N's work.

The critic discovers an even earlier pre-Lolita appearance in the character of Annabella from a play by Nabokov titled *The Waltz Invention*. Here there is an ominous male pair called Waltz, and in German the name for waltz is Walzer. In Lichberg's *Lolita* there are two brothers who go by the name of Walzer! This is not all, says Maar: in Lichberg's *The Accursed Giaconda* there is a story called 'Atomit'. It contains, to our astonishment, nothing less than the plot of – *The Waltz Invention!* And finally, finally, in Nabokov's *Ada* there is a story called 'Lolita', whose author is not N but a man whose name ends in Osberg – only a slight variation on Lichberg, surely? In a footnote N himself says Osberg is an anagram. To be read as Borges? wonders Maar.

What seems of final interest in this twisty literary mystery is that in both cases, the narrators are, by the end of their encounters with their respective Lolitas, initiated into art. 'The great novel's famous ending: he who survives Lolita becomes through her an artist,' Maar reminds us. So, too, in Lichberg's story: the professor-narrator becomes a poet in his retelling of his erotic compulsions with 'this immortal daemon disguised as a female child'.

In Michael Maar's new work, *Speak, Nabokov*, published to coincide with the posthumous *The Original of Laura*, the critic once again demonstrates how N rigged and boobytrapped his work with all sorts of clues about his life. Maar uncovers more mysteries here – but this time his subject is the author himself, pursuing more hidden clues and themes buried in the novels to offer a surprising new portrait of Nabokov, one that is different from what we've known from previous biographies and memoirs. Someone even darker, more mystical and tormented. With just two slender books of beguiling literary criticism, Michael Maar proves his impeccable credentials as the most captivating literary detective working today.

The Haunted Videotape: Suzuki-Nakata

You've heard of the Curse of the Videotape, surely? The one where if you don't watch at least one videotape a week, you'll die within seven days or your DVD/Blu-Ray player will go bust (which amounts to the same thing if you're a movie addict). Like you, I, too, rather foolishly thought that this was just the premise of a book and movie (where people die after watching this very sinister, grainy, unlabelled videotape).

But now I'm beginning to become really nervous that if I forget videotapes and VCRs and make a total switch to DVDs, the Curse of the Videotape will haunt me, too. And beware all of you who have also forgotten videotapes, the same curse may visit you.

There are several significant variations between Koji Suzuki's book, *Ringu* (1991) and Hideo Nakata's 1998 film, but for me what is striking is that both agree that the solution to dodging the curse of the killer videotape is to make a copy of the video and pass it on to someone else. And if they don't want to die within a week, they, too, must see the video, make a copy, and press it on others.

Conversation in Suzuki's *The Ring* (republished in English with a dizzy cover by Chip Kidd) typically revolves around the subject:

'They have a video deck, don't they?'

'Yes.'

'Beta or VHS?'

'VHS.'

'Good… Once you have seen it you have to make at least two copies, and show them to at least two different people.'

'Everybody who had seen the video had been subconsciously infected with this virus.'

However, for Suzuki lifting the curse of the killer videotape has more to do with finding ways to help a ghostly virus mutate forms using a videotape as a medium. For Suzuki the videotape and the VCR is the Devil in disguise; for director Nakata videotapes and VCRs are not accursed but part of our shared movie past. His *Ringu* is probably the first genre film to take note of, and comment on, the death of videotape culture.

Ostensibly, a chilling and eerie ghost story, but if you watch it attentively, you can't miss the subtext about the end of VCR culture. More people, I suppose, are familiar with the Hollywood remake, *The Ring*, adapted by Ehren Kruger and directed by Gore Verbinski, than the J-horror original.

Consider the plot: Naomi Watts plays a journalist investigating rumours of teenagers dying because they watched a haunted videotape. Supposedly, after you watch it, the phone rings and a child's voice says: 'You'll die in seven days.' She hunts for the tape and finds it. It's sitting pretty innocently on a shelf of original, pre-recorded videotapes. It's the only unlabelled one.

She slides it into a VCR and presses 'Start'. The whole tape lasts for just a few minutes. It begins with the hiss of static of an empty screen. And then in grainy black and white tones, a menagerie of seductive to nightmarish images: a woman in a mirror, a man at a window, a ladder against a wall, a centipede crawling from beneath a table and 'the ring', a circle of light resembling the corona of a solar eclipse.

(This eerie-looking ring – a dark, round circle – takes different forms: it's the orb of the sun setting, the shadowy crescent of the moon, and different circular objects in the film, including the round stone lid that covers an old well.) The images aren't really frightening as much as creepy. The kind of unsettling, indescribable non-narrative montage that Buñuel first came up with in *Un Chien Andalou* and that you continue to see in avant garde films).

The phone rings. Naomi jumps in fright. 'You'll die in seven days,' hisses the voice at the other end. Eventually, she gets her ex-husband – a videogeek – to look at the tape. Foolishly, he watches it, too. Later they take it to a studio with has more high-end VCRs and watch it frame by frame. They freeze-frame it, zoom in on close-ups, fast forward, rewind, pause and at one point, even struggle to track the tape. But it is in trying to track the jumping tape that they spot a clue hidden in the corner of the frame.

That clue – of a lighthouse – ultimately leads them to the heart of the mystery and its solution. Part of the solution, if you recall, to lifting the curse of this killer videotape is that you must make a copy of this tape, and then pass it on. What an odd, even amusingly self-conscious dénouement in what is essentially a ghost story (and a truly frightening one at that).

As in David Cronenberg's *Videodrome*, videotapes become living objects, taking on a life of their own, becoming viruses. At one point in the movie, the heroine dashes this videotape to the ground, screaming: 'What do you want from me? Tell me! Tell me!' Well, what IT wants is not to die, not to be forgotten, not to become history. Not to be replaced and taken over by the DVD!

By forcing every person to watch a videotape, this killer videotape in *The Ring* is making sure that videotapes will not be condemned to oblivion; (and by extension: records, spools, cassettes and everything analog) that such primitive analog magic will not die. Videotapes and VCRs revolutionized movie-watching. You could even say that they were responsible for making a film culture possible. Because you could own (and rent) films and watch them over and over again at home, it made movie buffs and film scholars out of us, giving us the film education we needed.

They let all of us get deeper into movies. Our simple tools were 'rewind', 'fast forward', 'stop' and 'play'. Where would an entire film generation be without videotapes? Hideo Nakata is obviously the child of the videotape generation – which would be the late '70s and the '80s. Nakata dreamed up this wonderful way of fusing a contemporary fable of urban paranoia – a videotape that haunts – with a folkloric Japanese ghost story.

(Nakata has supplied us with the single most frightening scene in recent horror films when he has this woman in a white kimono walk out of the television screen and into the living room. You can't see her face because it's covered by her flowing black hair. All you see is one large white eyeball through her hair. It's scarier than anything CGI can do for you.)

The cycle of *Ringu* films share a recurring theme: your survival is linked to the survival of videotapes. A point of view that could only have been created by a generation of filmmakers brought up on videotapes. *Ringu* makes a fetish out of the videotape and VCR: there are loving close-ups of the VCR in action. Different VCRs are shown, including that old, sturdy top-loading one which is a relic now. One character gets into the bathtub hugging a VCR and kills himself by electrocution.

The Japanese version ends with a close-up of a videotape that says: 'Copy'. The beauty of *The Ring* is that you don't have to get the subtext or even really notice it – it is a satisfying horror film in itself. It just becomes more fun and layered when you catch the subtext. I once screened *The Ring* to some college students, and afterwards replayed parts of it, going over the scenes that illuminate this subtext. When I wrapped up, I could see some had bought it, but there were many who looked unconvinced. There was nothing more I could say. The projector light was still on, and the screen was a bright blank. I leaned forward to press eject on the player to retrieve the DVD disc.

And in that moment understood fully the extent to which Nakata had conceived the reference; saw in a flash what the ring really referred to, what it had stood for all along. In a dash of inspiration, I whipped out the disc, held it against the projector light, and asked them: 'Now do you believe me?' I think I heard a few gasps: from where they were sitting, behind the light, there was no mistaking it: it was the round, dark, ominous ring we had seen over and over in the film.

Hideo Nakata underlined it further in the extras section of the *Ringu* DVD. When you insert the disk into your DVD player or computer, the TV screen fills with static. Then the menu springs up and you see 'Play Movie' and 'Extra Features'. I pressed 'Enter' on 'Extra Features' and one of the options that comes up is that you can view just the killer videotape (called *Sadako's Video*), separately.

I pressed 'Enter' on *Sadako's Video* and this is what came up next: 'Warning: The distributors are not responsible for damage that might occur to your DVD player or PC on playback of the following sequence. By selecting the "I Agree" button, you can view the video, by selecting "I Decline', you can return to the menu.'

Amused, I was about to press 'I Agree' when I paused. What if...? After all, I'd just bought my DVD player. My fingers hovered over the remote for some time, and then I said, 'Oh, what the hell' and hit 'I Agree'.

Ring, ring.

You pick up the phone nervously, because you've heard that new urban legend too.

'You'll die in a week,' whispers the voice on the phone.

Unless?

'Unless you read a *printed book* and pass it on.' (Or your Kindle will go bust.)

That's right. It's the sequel: *The Curse of the Haunted Book*.

Ruined by Reading

Reading in Bed
Rereading
The Good Parts Version
(or 80% Austen, 20% Zombie Mayhem)
Unwired, Offline, and Off-screen

Reading in Bed

I felt guilty about reading in bed until I discovered that many serious readers do their best reading in bed. While I enjoy the sight of someone reading stooped over a desk, I myself have never been tempted. I was warned of bad posture, squandering time and spoiling my sight. But the chair still did not beckon. School was the last place I used the desk to read; forced these days to read a book that way in a public library, I find myself, almost unknown to me, slowly sliding down my chair until I have slumped to the point of lying in it.

Summer, monsoon or unwintery winter, the inveterate Indian reader must cuddle up and read. The cosy reader isn't just a cherished image but a true story. Our favourite place to read is the bed. It is here that we seem to read with perfect hermetic concentration.

There are rituals that accompany reading in bed and none is more common than the putting on and taking off of spectacles. In perhaps what is easily the most fascinating book written on the subject – *A History of Reading* – author Alberto Manguel devotes an entire chapter called 'The Book Fool' to the different kinds of spectacles worn (and looks sported) by bookworms through the ages.

Lying in bed and reading also makes me more contemplative. Reading sitting upright or at a desk, I become focused, keen to get to the task at hand – say, reading at least fifty pages straight through – and I seldom pause to reflect. Twisted and tangled up in bed, I keep putting the book down, pause and wonder, and then read on. And one of the things that often haunts me when reading in bed is how cosy and safe it feels to be with a book when very possibly it is a dangerous thing. Reading, I mean. Risky, even.

With some books you are not the same person after you have closed it. Readers know this. Which is why a serious reader will wantonly pursue subversive books – she likes the danger, likes being damaged and wounded – and book junkies mainlining on bestsellers will keep away from anything too intense – such as an unhappy ending. Why do we read at all, though? In bed or elsewhere? Besides the usual answer – that we read for pleasure and for instruction – are there other subterranean reasons?

Could there be a more personal, private reason why we read what we read? For instance, there are those who read because they are infatuated with someone – they must read the same books as the one they are infatuated with. 'We read to know that we are not alone,' said C.S. Lewis once. The books we read make us part of a larger (invisible) community of readers. Could the opposite be true as well? That our reading makes us lonely. Wrapped up in a book, we shut the world out, cutting ourselves off from those who cannot share in our private world.

I remember being lonely in college because no one I met had read the writers I liked. Desperate attempts at getting others to read my favourite books only alienated me even more. But then, I have also known those who read only in solitude. It doesn't matter to them if others care for the things they read. To me such self-containment seems daring, enviable, puzzling. In *Changing My Mind*, Zadie Smith notes, 'Nowadays I know the true reason I read is to feel less alone, to make a connection with a consciousness other than my own.'

I read less and less these days. 'Don't we all?' chorus my friends when I tell them that. Reading has become a form of discipline for me. Something I must mindfully do every day (in bed, naturally); and not let myself be swamped or distracted by easier or less rewarding tasks. I know many devoted readers (pardon me, but I hate 'voracious'; 'voracious' is a word used by non-readers to describe readers) who don't read in that crazy fashion they used to anymore. And they feel more than a twinge of regret that they watch more movies or chat longer on the phone than getting back to a book they started.

We are readers in exile; reading has become a nostalgic act, a home we long to return to. For every exiled reader, there are readers who have never left the world of books. I rejoice when I meet these venerable ones. Books still mean everything to them. Other things – love, marriage, work, children, television, keeping house, eating out – has not taken the place of books. There's nothing nostalgic about the way they read. It's as natural as breathing for them.

I have become suddenly aware that curling up with a book (in a bed or elsewhere) is one of the few solitary pleasures left to me. These days I read not so much for literary reasons as much as personal enjoyment. Surely what we read is what we are or what we are becoming – or desire to become? Reading has taken me from a sense of myself to a reading of all life, and then returned me to my solitude. And that is why, though it might make me lonesome sometimes, it's too precious to give up doing – especially in bed.

Rereading

A TRUE READER, I have always thought, is one who rereads. To know one book well than to know many peripherally seems like something worth pursuing. It can take the form of revisiting a favourite book or just rereading a favourite passage. It helps to have a bad memory. I often have to reread (or re-see a movie) because I've forgotten the details of the plot (fiction) or the argument (non-fiction). I have friends who recall a book so well that it's useless for them to go back to it. Once, one of them recalled what had taken place in a scene in *The Great Gatsby* fifteen years after she had read the book. I had read the book several times and still couldn't remember the details.

I know at least one friend who reads every book so closely the first time around that she doesn't have to revisit them – and yet she does! If a book is a place you can inhabit, then she lives among these books, making a home in them.

In his hunger to possess books he admired, one friend copied down, sentence by sentence into a notebook, entire chapters from a favourite book. When I asked him why he did this, he replied that it might teach him how the author did it, like trying to learn a magic trick by repeating it. Friends making train journeys tell me they prefer taking along a book they've already read. Like an intimate companion.

'Curiously enough,' Nabokov noted once, 'one cannot read a book: one can only re-read it. A good reader, a major reader, an active and creative reader is a re-reader.'

Increasingly, it seems to me that what a committed reader has with a book is a relationship. And, like most relationships, it is sustaining, volatile, vulnerable. I know that I have found an entire community among books.

The question is – does the book remain the same book the second time around? Are we even the same readers when we revisit these books? I'm sure many of you have marvelled at how the same book expands before you, surprising and humbling you with how much you missed seeing on the first reading. Did we change or has the book changed? It seems to me that our experience alters the book even as the book alters our experience.

You return to a once loved book only to discover the enchantment is gone. How do you deal with this, and is there any way to reclaim the experience? The best answer to this dilemma is Laura Miller's answer in *The Magician's Book*. It's a book about her deep reading of *The Chronicles of Narnia* and its creator, C.S. Lewis. Rereading the series as an adult, Miller found many things problematic about it. And then, she says, something Philip Pullman told her offered a new way of rereading, of making a second encounter.

Pullman said that the original innocence and grace of the first reading is always and forever lost to us. What we can do, rather than dismiss the experience of a first enchanted reading is to plunge further into the book, until another grace replaces it, the grace of experience. It's as if you are entering the book now from a back door, notes Miller. Since you can't regain the grace you've lost, since there is no going back, go *through* that (i.e. an even closer reading as if it were a second door) and acquire the other grace, 'the conscious grace, the taught, the learned grace of a dancer'; honest and tempered now by knowledge and experience.

This will be a truer picture of you, of 'who we are, more human'. If a reader devotes time and energy to learning how to do this, she will once again reach a point where she can read the book better than she ever did before. This back entrance still leads to paradise, but a different version of paradise. Of all the books on reading that I have read, Laura Miller's *The Magician's Book: A Skeptic's Adventures in Narnia* is the most beautiful and illuminating.

And then there are times when you are simply not ready for a book. You can approach it as many times as you like but it will shut you out. Once you know something about life (or about books) that you didn't know before, then the book opens out to you. I hear people say: 'My first reading is to get the plot, the story, out of the way, so on a second reading I can look at more important things like character and detail and style.'

But I think we always return because we are hungry for the same story, the same plot. Only this time we choose to hear the story differently: emphasizing another part of the story, listening more closely to another aspect of the plot. In the best stories, character, style and vision always emerge from plot.

Rereading brings a rush of memory – not just of the book at hand or an evocation of a time and place but of being: happiness or heartbreak. Revisiting a book from your past is like revisiting yourself – returning through a book to the kind of person you were then. It can be a terrifying and gratifying experience.

In *Rereadings*, edited by Ann Fadiman, 17 contemporary writers revisit books they love. Pico Iyer on D.H. Lawrence's *The Virgin and the Gypsy*, David Samuels on Salinger's *Franny and Zooey*, Vijay Seshadri on Walt Whitman's *Song of Myself* and Allegra Goodman on Jane Austen's *Pride and Prejudice* are some of the rereadings that feature here.

What informs all the essays is a very personal recollection of how they read a particular book then and how they read it now. What they have to say about themselves – their prejudices, love affairs, political views, family life, literary ambition or childhood – is just as valuable and interesting as their commentary on the book itself.

Philip Lopate, who has always championed the contemporary personal essay, reveals what he was really after as an adolescent – worldliness. Not for him, he says, the detachment of a *Catcher in the Rye*. He was seeking disenchantment, and if the price was giving up innocence, so be it!

'Marginal Notes on the Inner Lives of People with Cluttered Apartments' is a record of the various readings David Samuels gave *Franny and Zooey* over the years. At various points his loyalties, likes and dislikes keep shifting from character to character. As a teenager he didn't get the end, much less Franny's obsession with *The Way of the Pilgrim*. As an adult when he finally did, he thought it unconvincing.

All his early readings are as a reader, and his last two are as a writer, where he comes to a full and real appreciation of what Salinger had accomplished: all those perfect moments, rich, funny and wise, and the 'dreamlike specificity' of his prose. When he says at the end, 'I'm still grateful for this book. This is what I mean to say,' it sums up the sentiments of all of us who admire the Glass family stories.

Before Pico Iyer discusses the novel at hand, he serves us with a delightful primer on the different, colour-coded paperback Penguin Modern Classics in existence when he was a young reader. In the nearly monastic English boarding school he studied in, those grey Penguin paperbacks with European writers were symbols and tokens of a worldliness that were forbidden to these schoolboys. Those orange paperbacks didn't count because they smacked too much of the local.

(In college, I remember students doing the same: bumming Penguins off their classmates like cigarettes. *The Outsider*, *The Trial*, *A Portrait of the Artist as a Young Man*, *Nausea* were passed from hand to hand like contraband. Once I ran into an old college friend who happened to be carrying *The Old Man and the Sea* with him. He brandished it in front me, establishing his literary pedigree. I said I didn't particularly like it – and he said defensively and with a little shock, 'But it's a Penguin classic, boss!')

Vijay Seshadri's excitement over his rereadings and sudden personal insights into Whitman's *Song of Myself* is infectious, even electrifying as he tries to explain to his young students that the poem isn't about the poet's narcissism but a St. Paul-like cry about the triumph over death. What holds your fascination here (apart from his elegant prose) is Seshadri's impassioned energy to repeatedly get to the heart of the poem.

Sven Birkerts was sixteen when he fell abjectly in love with a tall blonde girl he calls K. It was during this lovelorn summer that he chanced on Knut Hamsun's *Pan*, which to his young mind felt like 'nothing if not the most numbingly pure distillation of a young heart's passion…' This little book transported him to a deep sadness from which he felt he would never recover. He gains from the book his 'first earned wisdom, that life touched by the genius of love was ultimately not to be endured'.

And now as an adult and a writer, preparing to write an essay on the book, Birkerts begins to read a marked up copy. He is certain that it would not affect him now, and is surprised to find that against the memory of his first reading he is still powerless. He notes, 'We do not survive the dream of love, not at that pitch... We grow wise and find balance – or perish.'

As the editor of the literary journal *The American Scholar*, Fadiman had the wisdom to commission writers to review not just the latest releases but classics as well. As a veteran re-reader she instinctively knew serious readers would take more pleasure in reading about old books than new. In her perceptive foreword, she lists the essential differences between reading and rereading: that reading has more velocity, rereading has more depth.

Reading shuts out the world to offer you just the story, while rereading brings the world closer to evaluate the story. Reading is fun, rereading more cynical. But what is remarkable about rereading is that it contains all the things the first reading contained.

Fadiman seems to have penetrated to the very heart of rereading when she remarks that reading a good book for the first time when you are young is like being with a lover, while reading the same book later feels like a friend. 'This may sound like a demotion,' she notes, 'but after all, it is old friends, not old lovers, to whom you are most likely to turn when you need comfort. Fatigue, grief and illness call for familiarity, not innovation.'

The Good Parts Version
(or 80% Austen, 20% Zombie Mayhem)

A CULT BOOK that my friends and I re-read in college (it's a little embarrassing now to say which one, but some may recognize it) had a gimmick in it that tickled us no end. The plot, the author informed you right at the start, was a retelling of a famous adventure book about pirates, swordfights and true love. Except the author was going to tell us only the 'good parts' version. That was his term for it: the good parts, which meant cutting to the chase, keeping all the action in and leaving out the boring bits. This inspired us to play a little literary game of our own which we (naturally) called the Good Parts Version: each of us would pick a hefty classic and show the others what a good parts version of the story would read like.

Such as leaving out all the chapters about whaling in *Moby Dick*, the pages and pages of agrarian reforms in *Anna Karenina*, thick descriptions in the books of Eliot, Thackeray, James, nearly all of *Ulysses* except a few chapters, all the drawing room customs and rituals from Austen, and several characters from Dickens while keeping only Alyosha's story in *The Brothers Karamazov*. (Some of us went as far as doing this with film, re-recording our favourite movies on VHS with only the good parts left in). I was pleasantly surprised, then, to discover that some publishers have been quietly bringing out compact versions of classics. The idea, they say, is not to cut as much as weed out. They promise that the books will be 'sympathetically edited'.

An abridged classic is nothing new, but these publishers would like adult readers to consider the compact version as a worthwhile edition to read and own. (Tweaking classics took an interesting turn in 2009 with Quirk Books' *Pride and Prejudice and Zombies* where the Bennet girls, trained in the art of judo, fight the Undead, filling the book with 80 percent Austen and 20 percent 'ultraviolent zombie mayhem'. Up next is *Sense and Sensibility and Sea Monsters*.) I think a lot of contemporary novels can benefit from slimmer editions. After all, we do enjoy movie adaptations of classics that reduce the book to half its length. A compact version of all Thomas Pynchon and James Michener novels, for instance, will make it possible for us to finish the book that we started and put down. I'm not sure I would be tempted to read Stephen King even if he was trimmed down to fifty pages, but I'm certain his overwritten novels could use the axe. (And I'm quite sure there is a lot of non-fiction out there that could be more to the point).

Long after my friends had abandoned the 'good parts version' game, I continued amusing myself with it, except this time I picked on contemporary fiction. Modern classics and bestsellers I've always taken to be sacrosanct and untouchable such as *Remembrance of Things Past*, *One Hundred Years of Solitude*, *The Lord of the Rings*, *Atlas Shrugged*, *The French Lieutenant's Woman*, *Gravity's Rainbow*, and *Midnight's Children*– I worked out a good parts version of all these books.

I also realized that it's not just fat books that need paring down, but thin ones too. I would certainly welcome compact versions of these modern books, and urge those who've given up on reading literature to give these a try. They just might find the length inviting enough to begin, say, *Lolita*, and actually finish it. If they really admired the 'good parts version', they can always go back and read the complete text.

There are, however, some books that should stay bulky. Because that's their purpose. I'm thinking of the same book you are thinking of: *A Suitable Boy*. Seth wrote it with an intention to draw readers back to one of those leisurely 19th-century narratives. The idea is to let you immerse yourself in the story and not hurry. The reader's wish halfway through the book for it to move faster won't work here, defeating the purpose of beginning a novel like this one. He wants you to take as much pleasure reading it as he had in writing it. Charles Palliser offered the same sort of reading experience in *The Quincunx*.

A colleague never tires of telling me of how suspicious she is of books that are gripping and move too quickly. 'I want a book that I can wallow in,' is her lament. How often do you hear that? I sort of understand that, though. It reminds me of something I read in a Pauline Kael movie review once. I forget which movie she was talking about, but at some point she digresses to tell us that the highs in a book can really be experienced as highs only after a lengthy period of flat sections, where little happens. As an example she points to Levin's transformation in *Anna Karenina*. He goes off to live with the farmers and then we get some 40 or so pages of agrarian reforms. The reader is tempted to skip it and get to something eventful. But Tolstoy is in no hurry.

If you stick with the agrarian reforms though, you'll suddenly encounter at the end of it, Levin's radiant moment of transformation. And, says Kael, it feels radiant and gives a reader such a buzz *because* you patiently waded through all those even, uneventful passages. Like life – an exhilarating moment after a flat period, made all the more interesting because life had been so mundane until then. So, that's your reward for letting the book take you where it wants: it suddenly lights up.

Unwired, Offline, and Off-screen

Can the fetishistic bibliophile really stop worrying and learn to love the e-book? As the e-book war heats up between the three big players in the market – Amazon/Kindle, Apple/iPad and Google Books – we are now told that it's not just the printed book that will eventually vanish because of the digital book but the brick and mortar bookstore and the traditional publisher as well. One scenario Amazon projects is writers selling their books directly to them, cutting out the publisher. Publishers have looked to bookstores to sell books, and with direct e-book marketing you can eliminate both – or so goes the thinking of some e-book sellers. (You have to wonder about the fate of the printing press).

Several major publishers are looking instead at an alternative 'Agency Model' for e-books where they become the sellers and online venders act as agents for a fee. Ken Auletta, in his lucid and compellingly researched piece in the *New Yorker* on e-book pricing, quotes Carolyn Reidy of Simon & Schuster: 'In the digital world, it is possible for authors to publish without publishers. It is therefore incumbent on us to prove our worth to authors every day.' Auletta quotes other publishers who point out that publishing is not just about selling but finding and cultivating authors. Book editors speak of the importance of editing and nurturing writers.

What is emerging as a clearer and truer scenario is that the printed book and the digital book will and must co-exist. After all, even after Blu-Ray and high definition TV, people are still stepping out of their houses to see movies in theatres, aren't they? Movie theatres and videos

– they're great together. Physical bookstores and online bookstores, good combo; nice to have them both. The book and Kindle, if not happily married at least a smart live-in couple.

Some books are simply not available in an e-book format, like the books of J.D. Salinger who has not allowed his work to be digitized. On the other hand, a book like *J.D. The Plot to Steal J.D. Salinger's Manuscripts*, a political and literary farce about a professor's obsession with the unpublished manuscripts of Salinger is available *only* as a Kindle book. And if you are a Salinger devotee, you won't hesitate to put aside the printed book you're reading to make way for an exclusive (and scandalous) e-book where Salinger figures as a character.

In his new book, *Worlds Made By Words*, book historian Anthony Grafton notes that e-books 'will illuminate rather than eliminate the unique books and prints and manuscripts that only the library can put in front of you... where sunlight gleams on varnished tables, as it has more than a century, and knowledge is still embodied in millions of dusty, crumbling, smelly, irreplaceable manuscripts and books.'

I think the case for the printed book is simple and clear: while e-readers like the Nook, the Kindle, and iPad make the reading enterprise faster, cheaper, interactive, more convenient *and* keep the complex pleasures of reading intact, they are not, uh, how do I put it...*books*? Where's the dust jacket? Where's the design? And why do you need to charge it up?

The printed book just feels like the definitive *book-reading* experience. If there is a hierarchy of modes of book-reading, then I vote we privilege the cloth and paper book (just like the preferred mode to see a movie is in a theatre on the big screen, not on video). And if there's a hierarchy for a mode of reading essays or reviews or reports, then there's no argument that the e-reader comes first. (I love the way reading articles and essays and reviews and blogs online or through an e-device hyperlinks you on and on through doors that fling open to related reading. Often I feel like I'm running through someone's fabulous bookshelf or a well stocked bookstore.)

But like any new technology, e-devices can turn obsolete or change. On the other hand, even a very old book remains – give or take some foxing – the same book. You can open it anytime and read it, and it won't require batteries. Unwired, offline, and off-screen.

An exchange between culture critics Sven Birkerts and Matthew Battles in the March 2009 issue of *The Atlantic Monthly* – one resisting the Kindle, the other defending it – demonstrates how two book scholars can still feel two ways about the same thing:

Waiting for a poetry reading to begin, Birkerts overhears a conversation in progress: someone in the room can't remember a line from a Wallace Stevens poem, and her neighbour 'Blackberrys' the quote, and in a few seconds supplies the line. All present are duly impressed except Birkerts, who wonders if the Kindle has become to literature what Wikipedia is to information: 'a one-stop outlet, a speedy and irresistibly efficient leveler of context'. That is, the poet Wallace Stevens had been taken out of his historical flesh and blood literary context, and his poetry turned into a piece of information.

Battles noting Birkert's dismay observes that Blackberrying or Kindling Stevens instantly doesn't deprive him of his historical and literary context – only forgetting him can do that. And if young people, say his fourteen-year-old son, can 'call up' a poem on his Blackberry in a matter of seconds, then a difficult poet like Wallace Stevens, always in danger of not being read enough, will actually find new readers. 'Such liberation of access,' he notes, 'can only enrich and deepen the historical imagination – extending its nourishment to new audiences.'

Book historian Robert Darnton notes that the Gutenberg galaxy will expand 'thanks to a new source of energy, the electronic book, which will act as a supplement to, not a substitute for, Gutenberg's great machine.' The digital book industry is also racing to reassure us: CaféScribe, a French online publisher, hopes to satisfy the traditional reader by providing customers a sticker that 'will give off a fusty, bookish smell when it is attached to their computers'; Kindle's screen uses e-paper so you won't miss white-cream paper, and tablet PCs have the dimensions and shape of books.

In *The Case for Books: Past, Present, and Future*, Darnton describes at least one complex way the digital book enhances reading. 'An "e-book"... can contain many layers... Readers can download the text and skim through the topmost layer... if they come upon something that especially interests them, they can click down a layer to a supplementary essay or appendix. They can continue deeper through the book...'

From a long use of the printed book in our lives we know its aesthetics. In time, I feel that the e-book will acquire its own history, aesthetics and culture. If, for instance, the printed book is one of the few solitary experiences left to us, then the interactive e-book will be the one that offers community, companionship. I can carry 1000 books in my pocket – that's something, and not to be scorned at; a whole portable library. Add all those books – out of print and in print – Google is making available and I won't even have to pay very much for it. And I don't ever have to fear I'll run short of reading material. I can amuse myself reading almost anything under the planet.

But I can't physically browse through a mountain of books. And as a longtime reader of the printed book, I'll tell you exactly what else I'll miss from an e-book: a particular memory of reading a book, that *specific copy*, in a certain way; when you return to re-read a book, the act of reading from the same *well thumbed* copy. Of lending *that edition* to a friend. The smell of old ink – and not just a generic book smell but the familiar smell of *that* copy. Writing in the margins, bookmarking and shelving *that copy*.

The familiar, even sensual ritual of feeling paper as you turn a page. Nicholson Baker once spoke of how your thumb and index finger know when they have turned two pages accidentally by the familiar thickness of something you've known by touch since a child. This is why the printed book becomes the quintessential reading experience. It's so intimate, this turning of the page unconsciously, says Baker, that you and the book are one.

Interestingly, the *kind* of object a book is becomes clearer with e-books and Vooks. Suddenly the form, the texture, the feel of the book in your hand that you'd never given much thought to, becomes something to wonder about – even question. (That's our experience with records, with vinyl – which are, not surprisingly, coming back.) Before reading devices and digital books, it is the collector and the bibliographer who mostly paid attention to the physicality of books but now even the casual reader is talking about things like the sensation of touching and smelling and looking at paper. At Princeton University they put a whole course on Kindle, and more than one student spoke of missing reading from textbooks.

Another instance of why the materiality of books carries with it something more than just that: In putting together a few pieces on the world of the used bookstore, Nikki Tranter, editor of the magazine *PopMatters*, observed: 'The secondhand book is more than merely a bargain for the book lover. It's a cross-cultural, inter-generational link between readers. A torch-race, of sorts, with batons passed in all directions, from the collector to the student, the casual reader to the obsessive… the secondhand book can be art, as valuable for its subject matter as its personal history.'

We are also known – and like to be known – by the books we read, the books we own. The book in our – or someone else's – hand, say, in a train says something about us to the other. So to with someone's book collection on a bookshelf: this is who I am, or what I'd like to be. A Kindle in someone's hand doesn't kindle very much.

The initial skepticism of many traditional bibliophiles is from an old but lingering confusion that e-books signal the decline of reading. We forget that reading itself is in no danger; whether on the page or screen, what remains constant is the experience of reading itself. In the end, reading makes all forms its own and what culture critic Gabriel Zaid said in *So Many Books* puts it in perspective and nicely settles the debate: 'The freedom and happiness experienced in reading are addictive, and the strength of the tradition lies in that experience, which ultimately turns all innovations to its own ends.'

Loved and Lost

The Unlived Life: A Literature of Failure
Writers of the No
Elected Silence
Lost Books

THE UNLIVED LIFE: A LITERATURE OF FAILURE

FAILURE IS PERHAPS not the most common theme in literature. There are just a handful of novels, plays, and short stories on the subject of the unlived life. (It's a theme rare in cinema, too.) Searching for a literature of failure, I came up with Chekhov's *Uncle Vanya*, Isak Dinesen's *Babette's Feast*, Frederick Exley's *A Fan's Notes*, Malcolm Lowry's *Under the Volcano*, John O'Hara's *Appointment in Samarra*, John O'Brien's *Leaving Las Vegas*, Terrence Rattigan's *The Browning Version*, Gilbert Adair's *Love and Death on Long Island* and Fernando Pessoa's *The Book of Disquiet*.

Once in a way there is the odd book that visits conditions close to failure, like the 2005 anthology *Mortification: Writers' Stories of Their Public Shame*, a collection of seventy specially commissioned contributions by several contemporary writers, 'true stories of public indignity celebrating defeat and humiliation'.

Novelists and filmmakers seem reluctant to explore failure and its attendant emotions and baggage: self-pity, lovelessness, regret, addiction (sexual or substance abuse), boredom, a death wish, and self-destruction. I'd like to look at one novel, *Love and Death on Long Island*, one novella, *Babette's Feast*, and two plays, *The Browning Version* and *Uncle Vanya*, and their wrenching film adaptations about unlived lives.

Terrence Rattigan's play, *The Browning Version*, is about a failed schoolteacher. Andrew Crocker Harris, a teacher of Latin and Greek, discovers in his last year that he has failed to inspire his students. Over the years

Crocker Harris has buried his identity in his devotion to the classics.

In the play's most unforgettable moment, Tupelo, the only student who likes the curmudgeonly Latin teacher, gives him a farewell present – a lovingly inscribed ('God looks down kindly upon a gentle Master') version of Robert Browning's translation of 'Agamemnon', and the teacher cries softly like 'a well that's been dried up for 40 years.' The British director Mike Figgis has an honest, spare film adaptation (there's also a 1951 classic version with Michael Redgrave as Crocker Harris) of the play with Albert Finney (at his quietly furious best) as the failed teacher.

Most stories of this genre – gifted, struggling teacher inspiring students – eventually have rousing scenes of self-congratulatory classroom sessions and an emotionally overblown climax with the teacher finally triumphing (like that piece of fakery, *Dead Poets Society*). Not here, though: the only triumph at the end is Harris acknowledging to the entire school assembled to bid him farewell, that he has become a failure. The triumph is personal – he's had the courage to see that. Every time you think the story is going to do some heartstring-wringing, it piles up one more humiliation and defeat for its hero. And there's nothing even romantic about his failure – it's just ordinary failure.

There exits also a stunning filmed version of *Uncle Vanya* called, simply, *Vanya on 42nd Street*. This small masterpiece has mostly gone unnoticed, even by film aficionados. Adapted by Andre Gregory and David Mamet and directed by Louis Malle, the production (filmed inside a rundown movie theatre) obliterates the distinctions between the artifice of theatre and life – the actors perform in their street clothes, with the audience a few feet from them. And as the film opens, the actors drift in chitchatting and before we realize it, the chitchat has turned into Chekhov. (Though the actors make it all look seamless and spontaneous, they spent three years rehearsing.) We leave the character of Vanya at the end, despairing that love and success will never be his. His great anguish is: how can he live out, day by day, the next bleak and empty thirty years of a failed life?

His gentle, heart-broken niece, Sonia – sitting by his side, sorrowing, because she has just found out (after years of longing and wondering) that the wonderful man she loved does not love her back – has this sudden, luminous, transcendent revelation: 'What can we do? We must live our lives. Yes, we shall live, Uncle Vanya. We shall live through the long procession of days before us, and through the long evenings; we shall patiently bear the trials that fate imposes on us… and when our last hour comes we shall meet it humbly, and there, beyond the grave, we shall say that we have suffered and wept, that our life was bitter, and God will take pity on us and we will live a life of radiant joy and beauty.

'And we will look back on this life of unhappiness with tenderness. And we'll smile. And we shall rest to the songs of the angels, in a firmament arrayed in jewels, and we'll look down on and we'll see evil, all the evil in the world and all our sufferings bathed in a perfect mercy. And our lives grown sweet as a caress. And we shall rest. I have faith, Uncle, fervent, passionate faith. My poor, poor Uncle Vanya, you have never known what happiness was, but wait, Uncle only wait. We shall rest. We shall rest.'

It is *Uncle Vanya* (more than any other work by this Russian master) that shows us why Harold Bloom called Chekhov 'the indispensable artist of the unlived life'.

(August 2009 saw the debut of director Sophie Barthes' perfect little metaphysical comedy *Cold Souls* which returns us to Uncle Vanya. Actor Paul Giamatti playing himself is struggling with the character he's playing – Uncle Vanya. In wanting to interpret him correctly, he has his soul extracted and becomes soulless and plays Vanya as an optimist. Unable to live so shallowly, he borrows the soul of a Russian poet for a week and experiences the unlived life. This is Woody Allen meets Chekhov meets Louis Malle.)

Love and Death on Long Island, an overlooked, unsung British gem about lost chances is flawless in every way. And John Hurt's performance here is not only his greatest, it must also rank with all the great English performances because it is, at once, a caricature and the apogee of Englishness but with a twist. Hurt's raspy voiced English recluse is a fine comic performance.

In this sly, contemporary update of *Death in Venice* (it's also a neat twist on *Lolita* by the way) based on Gilbert Adair's cult novel, an older man falls in love with a younger man. Giles De'Ath (Hurt) is a reclusive academic who finds himself one day near a multiplex showing the new E.M. Forster adaptation. Once inside the movie house, he's puzzled to see American teenagers in bikinis and cars romping near the beach.

'This isn't E.M. Forster,' he growls to himself. It slowly dawns on him: he's walked into the wrong screen. He's about to walk out when he is transfixed by one of the actors on screen (played by Jason Priestley) and stays for the whole picture, which happens to be something called *Hotpants College II*. He discovers the boy's name is Ronnie Bostock and decides to come out of hiding and seek the boy out even if he must leave London and travel to Long Island.

In this teen idol, the older academic sees a contemporary embodiment of the Romantic ideals he has devoted his life and scholarship to. He is quick to tell us what this obsession is not: 'As a classicist... I know nothing more shaming and tedious in literature... than the maudlin neo-Hellenist cult of the ephebe, with middle-aged men like Wilde and Gide tastefully salivating over sleeping youths and making mawkish comparisons with asphodels and eglantines.'

In once answering the famous Proust questionnaire – What is the thing that most depresses you in life? – he answered, 'The unequal distribution of beauty.' And so we see this classicist (who scorns even high culture) in wanting to learn more about Bostock, immersing himself into pop culture: soap operas, fan-zines, VCRs, B-movies, science fiction, Stephen King and finally a trip to the land of Philistinism itself, America, home of his beloved. It's the meeting of high culture and popular culture and the result is hilarious and heartbreaking.

Stand-out scenes: De'Ath telling the cab driver who has just pointed to his 'thank you for not smoking' sign, saying, puffing away, 'Well I am smoking and so don't expect to be thanked.' De'Ath finally alone with Bostock, confessing what he feels: 'In years past, I told him, there had risen almost a tradition of such romantic friendships, and I mentioned Cocteau and Radiguet, Verlaine and Rimbaud.'

Priestly, a mediocre actor having to actually play a mediocre actor, surprises us with a complex piece of acting, particularly in this key scene when Hurt confesses his love for him.

I've read the Adair novel and can report that the film, for once, is even better: there's not a scene or line or moment that is false, wasted or not in place. First time Brit director Richard Kwietniowski's adaptation of lost chances and lost loves is astute, knowing and wise. It's also economical, brilliant, funny and oddly moving.

Another parable about the unlived life that I return to again and again is Isak Dinesen's *Babette's Feast*. Dinesen, author of *Out of Africa*, wrote this long short story in English when she was 65 years old. Having read it probably nine times over the years, I am as broken up by it as I was the first time. *Babette's Feast* is a spiritual parable about the hidden rewards of the unlived life.

The story concerns Martine and Filippa, two beautiful, gifted, devout sisters who belong to an austere Lutheran sect led by their pious father in a remote Danish village. These simple, saintly sisters are admired for their beauty and their talents: a soldier, passing by falls in love with Martine, only to discover that though she is in love herself, she will not come away with him but stay and serve God. A renowned opera singer from Paris, who happens to be passing by, hears Filippa sing like an angel in the local church and dreams of making her a diva but he too discovers that as much as she loves singing, she will sing only for God.

Years pass and the Dean (the leader of the sect and their father) dies. Soon, the congregation begins to become cantankerous, quarrelsome, bitter, unchristian – except the sisters, who remain faithful to their father's words. Many more years pass; they grow old and one stormy night a woman appears on their doorstep, asking for shelter and work. The letter of introduction she carries with her simply says, 'Babette can cook'. She begins cooking their frugal meals and the sisters show her how, not realizing that Babette was once a great cook in

Paris, a culinary genius. The sisters become troubled at how bitter the congregation is becoming and invite them all for a dinner in honour of their Pastor, hoping it will bring them together.

Now it comes to pass that Babette wins 10,000 francs from an old lottery ticket she had. She insists that the dinner will be not only cooked by her but hosted by her as well – a real Parisian gourmet dinner. But the sect thinks that such pleasures are from the devil and vow to not be seduced by it: this they will do, not by not eating it but by pretending it is tasteless. The soldier, now a famous General, is visiting his old aunt and so he is invited too. As the splendid meal progresses with its many fine, vintage wines, it is the General alone who speaks rapturously of the meal, astonished that in this remote, obscure, austere place he can come across such a feast. He tries to get the others to talk about it but they reply something about how the weather is fine this year too.

But the meal is having its effect and we see these quarrelsome lot turn kind and forgiving, Abruptly the General, unable to stand it any longer, stands up and says a toast, concluding with 'For today mercy and truth have had a lover, and righteousness and bliss have kissed one another!'

It is the General's words that show us and the dinner guests that it is this feast that has brought them to this 'unimaginable forgiveness' and this same sinful indulgence they are so worried about, 'is a sign of God's magnificent love and grace'. The dinner guests forgive one another and even embrace as they leave. The sisters smile, go into the kitchen to find out, to their disbelief, that Babette has spent every penny on the dinner. 'Now you'll be poor for the rest of your life,' says Martine. 'An artist is never poor,' replies Babette.

The life they had renounced (love, art, the world) in their youth, had never really been taken away from them. But this is not the end! Filippa, the one with the angelic voice, assures Babette, 'In Paradise you will be the great artist that God meant you to be! Ah! (she added, the tears streaming down her cheeks) Ah, how you will delight the angels!' And so Isak Dinesen's *Babette's Feast* turns out to be not only a parable about the unlived life but a story about how art transforms us.

All these stories illustrate that art illuminates life in a very special way when its subject is failure, not success. Success seems the boring subject of commercial art, failure is far more interesting. Failure, paradoxically, is more compelling and complex than success. There's a sameness and universality to success; the theme of failure (to me at least) in literature seems more personal, more individual than success. Is it perhaps because we truly *live* in our failures?

Writers of the No

TO WRITE ABOUT not writing – that's the theme of *Bartleby and Co.*, a Spanish novel by Enrique Vila-Matas. Vila-Matas's hero is a humpbacked clerk who feigns melancholy at the office, goes on medical leave, and sits down to meditate on all those writers who, for one reason or the other, gave up writing. This slender, beautiful and honest work is about invisible writers and their phantom books.

The theme of hermetic writers who stopped publishing or who simply were unable to write any longer has long held a fascination for me because it's really about the theme of abandonment, renunciation, and silence in literature. Vila-Matas's invisible writer reminds me of something Evan Shipman tells Hemingway in *A Moveable Feast*: 'We need more true mystery in our lives, Hem. The completely unambitious writer and the really good unpublished poem are the things we lack most at this time.'

Bartleby & Co. (translated by Jonathan Dunne, New Directions) is written as a series of 86 footnotes, cataloguing known, less known and sometimes entirely invisible (not fictional) writers and artists who are all 'Bartlebys'. The book's strange hero identifies himself with Herman Melville's clerk, Bartleby, who simply puts down his pen one day saying, 'I'd prefer not to.' The humpbacked narrator also once wrote an acclaimed novel about the impossibility of love, and has never written since. And now, after 25 years, he is writing again to examine other silent writers – 'writers of the No', as he likes to call them. Some never published at all. Some even killed themselves in order to never write again. For our hero, such a writer our hero, such a writer of invisible books is a true writer!

Who are these Bartlebys, these writers of the No? Of those we know there is Melville himself; Rimbaud who said no to writing at the age of nineteen. J.D., of course, who still writes the Glass stories but does not publish, the mysterious B. Traven, Beckett and Borges whose work grew slimmer and slimmer, Kafka who was invisible in his lifetime, and Fernando Pessoa with his *Book of Disquiet*.

Many I was hearing of for the first time: the Mexican novelist Juan Rulfo, the Swiss writer Robert Walser, whose work is said to consist of voluminous illegible scribbling, and who preferred the madhouse to his desk and pen, the Spanish poet Ferrer Lerin, and Hugo von Hofmannsthal and his *Letter of Lord Chandos* that our hero calls an 'emblematic text in the art of refusal'. And then there is that most invisible and silent of authors, the one who never wrote – God.

As the book progresses (that is, if footnotes can ever progress) we learn just a little more about our hero, our 'tracker of Bartlebys': 'I never had much luck with women, I have a pitiful hump, which I am resigned to,' he tells us at the beginning. He is also sick of his job, has no friends or family, feels overwhelmingly isolated, and is often anguished and alone. A being 'inhabited by a profound denial of the world', and yet 'possessing a very demanding literary conscience'.

He is compelled to write again, and begins this diary in the form of footnotes, which itself resembles a labyrinth. The 86 footnotes are 'fragments, chance finds, the sudden recollection of books, lives, texts or simply individual sentences that gradually enlarge the dimensions of the labyrinth'. This way our hero sets up a dialogue between these hermetic writers. In asking why these writers stopped writing and publishing, our hero answers that they wanted 'to let their silence do the talking instead'. The uncompleted, the suspended, the only imagined book becomes purer than what is completed and published. If they write, they write only for themselves. Many of these writers refused to write more because it became an act of vanity for them.

The paradox that Vila-Matas wants us to relish is that this deep meditation on not writing, not performing, not going public, is the text that is completed and published. It becomes this Spanish Bartleby's last act: footnotes on invisible writers and their phantom texts. With this, our humpbacked narrator – literature's radical non-hero – sums up on behalf of all the Bartlebys: 'The great book that… we were really destined to write… we shall never be able to write or read now. But that book, let it be clear, exists, it is held in suspension in the history of the art of the No.'

Elected Silence

Every time I look at my bootleg *Calvin and Hobbes* t-shirt, I'm tempted to wear it. But I restrain myself – barely. I stopped wearing it when I learnt that Bill Watterson had fought to keep his characters from turning up on products. Another of my guilty pleasures is to have read from cover to cover all those unauthorized J.D. Salinger biographies, knowing he would disapprove. But I couldn't help myself – I had to know. The more reclusive, unworldly, shy and silent an artist is, the more enchanted I become. These are the people who most want to be left alone in our celebrity-crazed culture and they are the ones we won't leave alone. Or can't. Perhaps we don't even know how.

'Salinger's silence is a kind of remedy for the disease of noise we all suffer from,' says culture critic Ron Rosenbaum. But I find myself torn between wanting to respect that silence and wanting to get close to it. The reclusive artist seems to know something about fame, money and greed that I don't. Salinger is, of course, literature's most famous recluse but not the only one.

Outside of literature, there is Greta Garbo, who, when Hollywood's biggest stars were clamouring to be in the films of Woody Allen, coolly turned down his invitation to come out of seclusion and do a cameo in *Zelig*. She apparently didn't even answer his letter. And in Suchitra Sen we have our own Garbo-like recluse. And then there's Karnan, the mysterious and intriguing Tamil film director from the 1970s, maker of those very kitschy Indian westerns (and the inspiration for *Quick Gun Murugan*), who is said to be living a reclusive life in Chennai. Leonard Cohen, who, after having given up making albums and becoming a lay Buddhist monk, has surprised the world with making albums again.

The film-maker Terence Malick (he can be contacted only at a phone booth in a small American town by prior arrangement) who also came out of seclusion to make *The Thin Red Line*, his first film in 21 years; Debra Winger who, in her prime, bid goodbye to Hollywood and its phoniness. The comic strip artists – most famously, Bill Watterson (*Calvin and Hobbes*) and Gary Trufeau (*Doonsbury*) – and less famously, Patrick McDonnell and his wonderful, little-known comic strip, *Mutts*. Like Watterson and Trufeau, MacDonnel has refused to let his characters from *Mutts* (mainly Earl the dog and his cat buddy, Mooch) turn up on calendars, cards and t-shirts.

I am particularly moved by Watterson and Salinger. Watterson was giving up millions of dollars when he refused to product merchandise *Calvin and Hobbes*. But it isn't their attitude to money that fascinates me (there has been, after all, a long history of kings and millionaires renouncing) as much as their attitude to art – their work, their vocation. To me, this seems more an aesthetic choice than a spiritual one: the pleasure of staying with your art, working on it, perfecting it.

In the *Tenth Anniversary Calvin and Hobbes* collection Watterson wrote of his efforts to keep the strip personal. Watterson strongly believed that once a cartoonist licenses his characters, endorsing them as celebrities, the characters lose their soul and the cartoonist his integrity. And then the work loses its deeper significance. 'My strip is about private realities,' he noted, 'the magic of imagination, and the special-ness of certain friendships.' Salinger and Watterson were very eager to be published when they began. When they discovered how much their art would be compromised by success, they retreated.

There seems to be, though, more than one kind of recluse.

William Wharton and Thomas Pynchon have never wanted fame and recognition from the start and have remained anonymous. Thomas Harris is not so much a recluse as someone who values his privacy greatly: he makes an appearance only when needed. Harper Lee simply went back to quietly practising law in her small town. DeLillo, once publicity shy, has now decided to sample a bit of the world by agreeing to do book promotions.

Leonard Cohen and Debra Winger, who had made such a long retreat from the world of showbiz, have surprised us with new work, while Patrick McDonnell continues to practise his art with sweet detachment. Whatever the nature of their reclusiveness, all of them have learnt to maintain a tightrope balance between the world, the self and their art. In one of his novels, DeLillo says, 'The withheld work of art is the only eloquence left.' There's a purity, an integrity, a sense of mystery and beauty to such retreat from the world to art to silence – what the Trappist monk Thomas Merton once called 'elected silence'.

We respect it and yet want to break this Wall of Silence – wanting, hoping, that their secret devotion to their work and their unworldliness will rub off on us.

Lost Books

THERE ARE MANY versions of lostness: The book that disappears from a house during a divorce. A writer committing suicide after finishing his work, and a reader exhuming it from a second-hand bookstore. A book that a writer only hears about which infects his imagination so much that he spends years looking for it. And then steals it. What about a favourite book that has been not just overlooked and under-read, but completely lost to us? A little known book (or books) that we admired so much, we find ourselves urging friends to discover it. Except it doesn't exist anymore. Borges once noted that 'a certain class of objects, very rare' can be 'brought into being by hope.'

And this is exactly what the writers in *Lost Classics* accomplish: they bring into being, simply by their devotion and hope, books that were lost, and return them to our secret bookshelves. The editors of this unusual books on books anthology, Michael Ondaatje, Michael Redhill, Esta Spalding and Linda Spalding, invite 73 contemporary authors to evoke books loved and lost, unavailable, stolen or extinct.

Githa Hariharan picks *All About H. Hatterr*, a book she discovered in 1974, 'emerging from the safe portals of Bombay University's Sophia College... my friends and I took to ransacking the lost-and-found bookstalls... and then I came across a strange and wonderful book.' Pico Iyer's choice is *The Saddest Pleasure* by Moritz Thomsen, a strange travel book that is, in effect, 'a journey towards extinction'.

'Curiously, it is a book I haven't read,' says Laird Hunt

of Lafcadio Hearn's *Some Chinese Ghosts*. 'I saw a copy once: a dark blue, leather bound Modern Library edition that sat unread on my girlfriend's uncle's shelf. It was all I could do (i.e. my girlfriend said, No!) not to steal it.' Since then Hunt has been searching used bookstores for the book but has never found it. But he feels strongly that 'somewhere out there, *Some Chinese Ghosts*, the one that I had hoped for, exists. I just have to put my hands on it again.'

John Irving swears by Richard Hawley's *The Headmaster's Papers*; first published in 1983 and now available only with the small independent publisher who brought it out. 'This is an epistolary novel so heartbreaking that no one is likely to surpass its emotional effects in a letter form,' writes Irving. It is entirely composed of one suffering headmaster's letters to friends, students, parents and his own son.

Murray Bail introducing his lost book, *The Fish Can Sing* by Halldor Laxness, writes that the first sentence placed it above the ordinary at once: 'A wise man once said that next to losing its mother, there is nothing more healthy for a child than to lose its father.' This Icelandic novel has been out of print for nearly thirty years. Christian Bök writes of an otherworldly encyclopaedia called *Codex Seraphinianus* by Luigi Serafini which contains descriptions of 'eyeball eggshells hatching into eyeglasses; serpent shoelaces latching onto ankleflesh, an automobile melting into white stick gum…'

The Salt Ecstasies is a breathtakingly beautiful collection of poems by a little-known American poet called James White. Jim Moore who brings it to our notice, tells us that White, who died in 1981, lived alone and with very little money in a modest apartment. He knew he was dying and wrote these 22 poems on death. *Classics Revisited* by Kenneth Rexroth is seldom mentioned by today's academic critics, points out Brian Brett. A pity since this is the most 'delicious outline of a literary canon' he has ever read. The essays are 'cheeky, loopy, opinionated and diverse.' Rexroth on the style of 'Julius Caesar': 'The simple nouns and verbs carom off each other like billiard balls.' And his legendary remark on the prose of Tacitus: 'a style like a tray of dental instruments.'

Margaret Atwood picks an out-of-print Swedish novel first published in 1905 called *Doctor Glass* by Hjalmar Söderberg. She notes that it was a short but astonishing book about sex and death that a friend ferreted out of a second-hand bookshop. *Capital of Pain* is a book of surrealist poetry by Paul Éluard that has been virtually forgotten even by poetry lovers. 'It's a tall, narrow white book that never fits on my shelves properly,' writes Natalee Caple and quotes: 'I no longer move silk over the ice / I am ill flowers and pebbles / I love him most inscrutable to the clouds.'

The book ends with a 'Lost List', which tells you how and where you can find these lost books – if they are in print or out of print. The essays in *Lost Classics* are brief, precise, elegant. Many of them are not more than two pages; some are just a page. But all of them summon up a book, once loved and lost, carefully, faithfully and with true longing.

Is the history of the book also the history of loss? Books lost, damaged, stolen, and never written? What is famously known is Kafka asking his literary executor to burn all his books, the Alexandrian library on fire, and Gogol burning the second half of *Dead Souls*.

What is less known is *Sandiston*, a novel about hypochondriacs that Jane Austen never completed; Shakespeare's 'Love's Labour Won' (perhaps a sequel to you-know-which-play) which has been missing; *Speak, America*, a second volume Nabokov had planned to his memoir *Speak, Memory* but never wrote; Malcolm Lowry's only manuscript copy of *Ultramarine*, which was stolen from his publisher's car and then had to be reassembled from his wastepaper basket; Socrates's version of *Aesop's Fables* and Homer's first work, *Margites*, (a comic epic poem about a fool, who, 'knew many things, but all badly') – both destroyed; some nearly thousand pages of Burrough's *Naked Lunch* that Algerian street boys stole from his hotel room and sold on the streets; and *Double Exposure*, a second novel that Sylvia Plath had been writing about her marriage that has been lost.

Stuart Kelly, the author of *The Book of Lost Books: An Incomplete History of All the Great Books You'll Never Read* is a compulsive reader and a compulsive collector. He is what I call a 'completist': a collector who is obsessed with completing his or her collection. For Kelly it began as a teenager when he had to have every Agatha Christie title in every edition, and once he discovered literature, every Penguin Classic he could buy. In the process he discovered, to his dismay, that there are several books by classical and modern writers that are lost forever – destroyed, missing, stolen, or conceived and abandoned.

Only seven of Sophocles's plays have survived out of 133 lost, only 18 of more than 90 by Euripides remain. And Aeschylus? Eight known, 73 missing! The 90-odd chapters of *The Book of Lost Books* are really wide-ranging mini-essays on the stories of books we don't possess, and tantalizingly researched biographies of their authors. The next question is – so what? What if all these books are lost? You can mourn them only if you really care enough about them. And Stuart Kelly does. His impassioned book is not another book of lists – like those deep sea divers, he is a deep reader who has travelled down to the very bottom of literature to bring up what is there and what is not there. Imagine the reading of this man!

You can report a book lost only if you have first read prodigiously – all of Austen, all of the Hellenic dramas, all of Shakespeare, all the modern masters, most of world literature and all the obscure writers in between. What Kelly writes about is not only not common knowledge but news to literary scholars as well. This is why *The Book of Lost Books* has become one of the best-reviewed books about books (one critic calls it 'a formidable piece of bibliographical belletrism', another 'a Borgesian library of books') since its publication.

Not all loss, Kelly discovered, is tragic. T.E. Lawrence mislaid his manuscript of *Seven Pillars of Wisdom* at a railway station and by his own admission his second draft was 'shorter, snappier and more truthful'. Hemingway lost all of his early unpublished writing when his trunk was stolen en route to Switzerland in 1922 – but this forced him to write new stories in a new style – that spare, unaffected prose he is now famous for. Around individual essays that look at a particular lost book, Kelly spins intriguing asides and digressions: Dylan Thomas lost the manuscript of *Under Milk Wood* three times and found it three times – the last was in a pub; Dostoevsky had a sequel planned to *The Brothers Karamazov* in which Alyosha, writes Dostoevsky, 'leaves the monastery and becomes an anarchist. And my pure Alyosha will kill the Tsar!'

Strangest of all: Mikhail Bakhtin, while exiled in Kazakhstan, 'used his work on Dostoevsky as cigarette papers, after having smoked a copy of the Bible'. He writes of how vulnerable books are to destruction – from the material used to make them – paper – to the deliberate destruction of literature at the hands of fascists, religious zealots and spouses. But then he also wonders, 'Is becoming lost the worst that can happen to a book? A lost book is susceptible to a degree of wish fulfilment. The lost book… becomes infinitely more alluring simply because it can be perfect only in the imagination.'

There is something nostalgic and wistful about books becoming actually lost – because we can't imagine such a thing today when every book published is preserved and backed up and Google-linked. My one little disappointment with the book is that in his survey of lost books, Kelly sticks largely to reporting on the Western canon. The wide-ranging reader that he is, he should follow this book with a report of what has been lost to us in other literatures.

Bookstores

The Bookwoman of Madison Avenue
The Bibliophile's Dream-Bookshop
At the Museum of Books
Strictly Books
The Ultimate Bookshop
The Book in the Movie
Shakespeare & Co.
The Lame Duck

THE BOOKWOMAN OF MADISON AVENUE

'SO, WHAT ARE the high spots in the bookstore now?' I asked Bibi. And realized at once how foolish the question was in a room full of high spots: fine bindings and rare books. 'Let me show you,' she said, getting up. I followed her to a glass-fronted bookcase which she unlocked with a key that looked as antiquarian as the surroundings, and carefully brought out an exquisitely bound book. 'Fitzgerald's *Omar Khayyam*,' she said softly, 'and look, jewelled binding. By Paul Riviere, London, 1879. Adorned with 86 semi precious stones. A completely one of a kind binding.' The asking price, I noticed, was $35,000.

I was inside Imperial Fine Books, owned and run by Bibi Mohamed, one of very few high-end book dealers of Indian origin in the world of fine books. And certainly the only Indian woman in the rare book business in New York, very possibly the country. Imperial Fine Books, located on upscale Madison Avenue in midtown Manhattan, is the leading specialist in leatherbound sets and fine bindings. 'Come have a look at this Kipling set, there's something special about it,' said Bibi, and was off to another corner of the bookstore, key in hand.

She slid a volume out and opened to the title page, and placed her finger opposite the frontispiece: it was *signed* by Kipling. She handed it to me. It occurred to me that this copy had been touched by Kipling, probably held by him. And now I was holding it. The moment was electric.

'My God, you have signed editions, too?'

'A few,' she said, smiling, and was already walking

away to another part of the bookstore. 'Come.'

It was the complete works of Arthur Conan Doyle, *signed by the author*. 1930, bound in tan morocco, all edges gilt, raised bands with marbled endpapers. I had to take it off her hands and hold it, running my finger across that signed half title. The price? $26,500.

'Not too long ago we had a copy of *The Fountainhead*, signed and inscribed by Ayn Rand.'

Being inside Imperial Fine Books really feels like being in one of those finely appointed libraries you see on a fancy postcard or a magazine advertisement or a movie set. Leatherbound books from floor to ceiling, antique furniture around the room, and plush sofas to sink into and look at the books. I was hesitant to handle the books, allowing Bibi to show me around, but now I felt I had to look around on my own and asked her if I could. 'Sure, I have some letters to catch up on anyway. We can talk later. Let me know if you want to see anything from the locked cases.'

Just the books on the bookshelf will be fine, thank you. I mean, why ask for more when on the open shelves were entire sets of Dickens, Emerson, Tolstoy, Balzac, Hazlitt, Wordsworth, Browning, Conrad, Hardy, Melville and a few high spots like first editions of *Alice in Wonderland*, *The Jungle Book*, and A.A. Milne's *Pooh* books. I handled the books gingerly at first and when I grew more confident, inspected them more carefully. (At some point, I had even begun to pretend that I was in my personal library – I was only missing the evening jacket and pipe.)

Many book collectors and rare book dealers consider leatherbounds more decorative than valuable, preferring unsophisticated (unrestored) bindings and first editions with dust jackets. Lacking jackets, the leatherbounds look elegant and stately but uniform. Though, if you look carefully, you'll see the dazzling craftsmanship of gold tooling, raised bands, and multicoloured labels, offsetting the sameness of leatherbound spines.

And in a bookshop full of fine bindings, leatherbounds are the very picture of cosy antiquarian bookishness. I spent a little more time looking at modern editions: leather sets of the entire run of Fleming's Bond books. It was oddly gratifying to see *Goldfinger* retooled in leather. The last time I read from a Bond book it was a tattered paperback. I noticed that the average cost of one volume here started at $1,500 and went up to $50,000 for a set. There were also a few modern editions for less. Fortunately, or perhaps less fortunately, I was here merely to look, not buy, and to find out more about Imperial Fine Books. 'Who are you?' I asked Bibi, 'And how did you create such a fine bookstore?'

'I'm originally from British Guyana, and many generations before my family came from India. My father is a Muslim, my mother was a Hindu. Life was especially difficult for my parents there. They came away to America. We lived in the Bronx, in a poor neighbourhood. My father had been an accountant in Guyana, but here, to begin with, he worked in a gas station, and my mother was a cashier in a store. I did well in school, and as a reward was asked if I'd like to intern in a bookstore.

'I gladly accepted. It was not just any bookstore but at J.N. Bartfield Fine and Rare Books. Working there, I began to learn the antiquarian book trade, which is very different from retail and used bookselling. In the evenings and weekends I began to slowly buy my own books, whatever I thought was interesting and valuable in the fine books market, with an eye to one day selling books myself. The only place I could store them in was the basement of my parent's apartment.'

'So Imperial Fine Books began in a *basement?*'

'You could say it did! Because I made my first sale there.'

'But these weren't used books you were selling but expensive bindings – how did you find customers in a town known for fine bookshops?'

'There was a certain serendipity to my first customer: I was on an Amtrack train, and opposite me was a gentleman who asked me out of the blue what I did for a living and I told him I dealt with fine books. He gave me his card and said he had just bought a house and wanted the library furnished and asked me if I'd like to do it. This was like a sign for me– I had just the books he wanted in my basement and with my first sale became a consultant for wealthy homes in New York looking to build a personal library full of fine bindings.'

From a basement in the Bronx to this elite upstairs gallery on Madison Avenue – an immigrant success story in the world of fine books unlike any I had heard. Located at 790 Madison Avenue, 2nd Floor, New York, Imperial Fine Books celebrated its twentieth anniversary in 2009 with special exhibitions of various fine bindings.. Bibi is now a member of the Antiquarian Booksellers Association of America and the International League of Antiquarian Booksellers.

I noticed a small pile of books on a table with loose binding, looking very out of place there, needing repair, and pointed them out to Bibi. 'They are there to be custom bound, something we undertake along with bookbinding and restoration.'

How does it exactly work, I asked her. She took out a book that had already been beautifully bound. It happened to be *The Great Gatsby*. 'This is a first edition but it lacked that scarce dust jacket. Now as the owner of this book you can do two things: get a facsimile jacket made or custom bind it. A customer brought this to us in poor condition, and we rebound it for her in full green morocco. We also specialize in Cosway bindings – these are books whose leather covers have been cut to reveal oval miniature portraits in the style of the 19th century English painter Richard Cosway.'

Mohamed had told me earlier that she had just returned from the London book fair and I asked her what she had bought. 'It wasn't very successful but I was happy to get hold of these.' She pointed to a set of books on the table between us, and I picked up one of them. 'History of India, Romesh C. Dutt. 9 volumes in all, profusely illustrated as you can see. Bound in 3/4 red morocco, marbled boards, top edges gilt. And put out in 1906 by none other than the Grolier Society!'

And the price? '$2,500 – the Grolier books are collectibles.'

In the rare book trade, a dealer is usually called a bookman, and it's rare to spot a bookwoman. Bibi Mohamed has been a bookwoman in the fine books business for twenty-five years now, and I was curious, before I left the bookshop, to find out what the experience had meant to her.

'I can't forget the time I outbid Sotheby's for a collection of Cosway bindings signed by C.B. Currie, and the day I acquired a magnificent jewelled binding by Sangorski & Sutcliffe of Wordsworth poems, adorned with 140 precious stones. What I've enjoyed most is putting whole libraries together. It's been a privilege to be surrounded by such fine books, and to commune with them on a daily basis. I've been lucky, but also feel a sense of destiny that I was meant to do this.'

The Bibliophile's Dream-Bookshop

It's the bookshop that every bibliophile secretly fantasizes about, and occasionally encounters in a Jorge Luis Borges story. An entire bookstore full of just books about books. Reader, I'm here to tell you that this is no *ficcione*: such a dream bookshop exists. You will find it in the historic colonial town of Old New Castle in a three-storied Opera House built in 1879 where two floors house, in an almost labyrinthine fashion, shelf upon shelf upon shelf of books on books. Oak Knoll Books has the largest inventory in the world of books on books. Its publishing imprint, Oak Knoll Press, tops even this Borgesian fantasy by being a fine press devoted exclusively to publishing books about books. I stumbled on Oak Knoll in 2009 when I began noticing that nearly every great book about books I was reading was either something that was bought from their bookstore or published by them.

The Z call number stack is the place where university libraries keep their books on books. Nearly every other book you pull out here is bound to be from Oak Knoll. Browsing in the Z stacks is exactly how I found Oak Knoll. For a time I thought they probably just have a special interest in this genre, but soon it became apparent that there was a method to their bibliographic madness. I became feverish with excitement. Could it be that Oak Knoll was just all about books about books and nothing else? Was there actually somewhere in the world an Umberto Eco-ish-Borgesian bookseller and publisher crazy – fabulously crazy – enough to give his life over to books on books? Not long after I started wondering, I found myself in this dream bookstore shaking hands with the owner, Robert Fleck.

I told Fleck how awed I felt to be here finally, after being limited to just viewing his bookstore on their website and through catalogues. He was a little taken aback (he wasn't expecting me at all, I had simply turned up out of the blue) at my zealot's enthusiasm for Oak Knoll when I said it was the bibliographical paradise all bibliophiles dream of. This is where, I exclaimed, old books about books go to live, not die. He laughed and told me I was prejudiced because I liked books about books. He was too rushed for time to give me a tour, but I was happy to explore on my own. Two spacious floors with wall to wall shelves crammed with books up to very high ceilings. That's how most good bookstores look (or should look), but the difference here, though, was that these were *all* books on books.

My standard question on entering a new bookstore is: 'Where are your books about books section?' And what I'm routinely used to (if I don't draw a complete blank) is being directed to one small shelf space. But now that I was looking at thousands of books on books I couldn't comprehend it. Who would have thought there were this many books written about books? I thought I knew the genre well, but even just a few hours spent browsing here made me realize I knew nothing at all. For every single title I recognized here, I didn't know hundreds. My familiarity was limited to popular books on collectors and collecting; here, however, were hundreds of scholarly titles and antiquarian accounts on the subject. And thousands of books on book arts: print culture, book history, bibliography, libraries, book design and binding, typography, private press, illustration, calligraphy, bookplates, and papermaking.

How had such a bookstore (which now felt something

not just right out of Borges and Eco and Pérez-Reverte, but out of Carlos Ruiz Zafon's *The Shadow of the Wind* as well) come into existence? I turned to Bob Fleck for some answers. Though a chemical engineer by training in the 70s, Fleck found himself increasingly drawn to the antiquarian book trade. An impassioned collector of books about books, he noticed there wasn't a single bookstore anywhere specializing in stocking book arts. In 1976 he took the plunge and opened Oak Knoll Books, making it a one-stop shop for books on book and bibliography. And in '78, Fleck began Oak Knoll Press, focusing entirely on printing and publishing books on books titles.

Collaborating with established publishers, he began with reprinting the great classics of the genre such as Bigmore and Wyman's *A Bibliography of Printing*, the definitive work on printing history, and Fredson Bower's masterpiece, *Principles of Bibliographical Description*, again the best-known book on the subject. In the early 90s, Oak Knoll had a breakthrough when Fleck, along with Nicolas Barker, the editor of 'The Book Collector' (the leading journal on bibliophily) persuaded Eton College, the literary estate of John Carter, to let them reprint *ABC for Collectors*, perhaps the finest book on books ever published. It is with this edition that Oak Knoll Press comes into its own: the reprint is beautifully and stylishly designed.

Carter's primer on collecting finally gets its bibliographic due in this elegant Oak Knoll makeover. (What a great pity that this legendary bookman is not alive to behold this deluxe edition.) It's often been said of *ABC for Collectors* that 'if you have one book about books in your library, this is the one'. To this I'd like to add, if you have one edition of this book about books in your library, the Oak Knoll is the one. It was clear that there had all along been a great void in the book trade that Oak Knoll was now filling, because Robert Fleck and his team found a deep and wide customer base for their books.

Soon Oak Knoll had the largest stock in every category of books on books, while scholars and writers from different countries were either submitting their manuscripts here or making book proposals. For several classic titles they have partnered – and continue to partner – with The British Library, the Library of Congress and the Tate Gallery. The range of titles, both in subject, design and format, will impress even the most extravagant bibliophile. Books in all shapes and sizes: octavo, folio, quarto. Some titles are just little keepsakes in octavo, others regular reading copies in folio, then there are handmade fine press books and suddenly oversized quarto books that are a visual knockout with full-colour illustrations and photographs.

One such marvel is *The Dark Page*. A stunningly produced book (photographed by Dan Gregory, text by Kevin Johnson) featuring 'full-page 9x12 three-dimensional images' of the true first editions that inspired the great cycle of American film noir classics and crime movies. To see images of these scarce first printing copies with their pulpy covers in such dimensions is to behold them in all their riotous and garishly-coloured glory. What one film critic described as 'a dark dream come true'. When I first saw *The Dark Page*, I could very easily see why someone will think up such an idea for a book – it's fabulous and overdue, and yet no one had done it until Kevin Johnson of Royal Books. But who could you possibly find to print and publish it?

The traditional publishers, however large, would dismiss it as too specialized, too expensive. That's where Oak Knoll steps in, and now bibliographers don't ever have to wonder if such splendid and extravagant books about books will find the right publisher. Johnson, Gregory and Fleck have brought out *Dark Page 2* and there's a 3 in the works. Oak Knoll now publishes more than forty books on books titles a year! This is staggering, both in volume and quality, since so many of them are fine press books, painstakingly designed and printed.

Oak Knoll is a member of the International League of Antiquarian Booksellers, and Fleck once served as its president. To mark their 30th anniversary, he wrote *Books About Books: A History and Bibliography of Oak Knoll Press*, which includes a fifty-page history of the press with a detailed bibliography of its most significant titles.

Fleck's commitment to private and fine press has deepened over the years with the Oak Knoll Fest, a one of a kind book festival held every year in the cobblestoned town of New Castle, where master printers from over the world gather to exhibit their newest work. 'It's a celebration of the art of fine press bookmaking,' says Fleck, 'where participants can browse exhibits from artisans specializing in engraving, binding, papermaking and letterpress. Our mission is to publish books that preserve the art and lore of the printed word.' As mission statements go, I said to him, reluctantly leaving the bookstore, this one will keep in an e-book world.

AT THE MUSEUM OF BOOKS

ONE SULTRY AUGUST Sunday morning (when most tourists wandering the city of Philadelphia were doing the usual sightseeing rounds) I set off to find the Rosenbach Museum and Library. It wasn't on any tourist itinerary, and when I asked for possible directions from the locals, nobody seemed to have heard of it. When I finally located it, I found a simple but elegant townhouse on a little street that is easy to miss. Only a small signboard gives it away. This little museum houses some very rare first editions and manuscripts from around the world, and is (remarkably enough) largely the collection of one legendary book dealer: A.S.W. Rosenbach.

Several hours later, I stepped out of the museum in a daze. I had never stepped into a museum quite like it.

To give you a quick highlight of what I beheld there: James Joyce's manuscript for *Ulysses*, personal letters of Lewis Carroll, a fine copy of a first edition of Cervantes' *Don Quixote*, original drawings and books by William Blake, portions of the manuscripts for Charles Dickens's *Pickwick Papers*, notes and outlines for Bram Stoker's *Dracula*, manuscripts of Joseph Conrad's *Lord Jim*, and rare and old editions of the novels of Jane Austen. There was plenty of Americana and antique furniture on display but that didn't interest me, so I lingered to look at the books instead.

Every hour on the hour, there is a guided tour and I signed myself up for one. The guide said he would save the best for last – the room on the ground floor that housed displays of original manuscripts of famous writers – and take us to the rooms that held rare first editions. I was allowed only to peer at them through the glass-fronted cases, not take them out and examine them. Still, it was an unparalleled treat to glimpse, close up, the spines of these rare Austen editions. 'Dr Rosenbach even once had in his possession the original manuscript of *Alice in Wonderland*,' the guide told us, 'but gave it to the British museum because he felt that was where it belonged.'

Rosenbach is often thought of as the father of modern book collecting and dealing. He was fond of saying, 'Next to love, book collecting is the greatest sport.' The Rosenbach museum, the guide informed us, even possessed at one time the *Bay Psalm Book* (the oldest printed book in America) and a copy of the *Gutenberg Bible*. And there is something else in the museum.

It has two very special rooms: the Marianne Moore room and the Maurice Sendak room. Moore was a great modernist American poet. She gifted to the museum not just her personal papers but everything that she had that made up her study. The museum has recreated, foot by foot, her study, which includes her typewriter, her books, and her furniture. I read her poems ('"Poetry": I, too, dislike it…') in college and it was a privilege now to be standing in her room, running my hands over her old typewriter.

The Maurice Sendak room holds several original drawings and sketches from his best known work and several first editions. Through the years there are several exhibitions and talks devoted to his work and life. Sendak and Rosenbach had become fast friends and the illustrator had even spent a few nights at the museum (when it was still the house of the Rosenbach brothers). On the ground floor is the museum's gift shop with replicas and posters of what the Rosenbach contains. Here I was thrilled to find five miniature Maurice Sendak books: these particular editions were tiny, only a little bigger than a matchbox, and they came in a miniature box set. I bought them in memory of Sendak's presence here.

Before we got to the manuscripts on view downstairs, the guide made a halt at one bookcase and pointed out, with uncontainable glee and pleasure, that what we were looking at was Herman Melville's own bookcase. He asked us to come closer and singled out one book inside: 'And that's Nathaniel Hawthorne's personal copy of *Moby Dick*'. On view, in a glass case, was a Shakespeare folio. As I was exiting I remarked in low tones to the guide that it was a pity one couldn't inspect the books. And the guide answered quite casually that I could. What! I exclaimed. 'Sure you can. The library collections are open to researchers. You just have to make an appointment with the librarian beforehand and she will personally show you the book or manuscript in question.'

I immediately made an appointment for the following day, and spent the rest of the day wondering which rare book or manuscript I should choose to view. When the librarian asked me what I wished to see, I told her what I wanted to look at more than anything else. And fifteen minutes later I was looking up close at, not without some disbelief, Bram Stoker's handwritten notes and plot outline for *Dracula*.

Strictly Books

Browsing in one of those large chain bookstores where every book is neatly in place, I sharply missed being in one of those small, cosy, intimate bookstores with overflowing, crammed bookshelves. But then, to be honest, there have been other times when I've wished I were in a superstore. That would be when I'm looking eagerly (or in a hurry) for a book in a local bookstore and being unable to find it (because of the clutter) or being told they don't have it (because of a smaller stock).

The superstore carries more titles, offers more browsing space, comfortable sofas and chairs to sit and read in, multiple checkout counters, a special corner for children, and author readings. But for all the conveniences of these large chain bookstores springing up in our cities, you are not reminded so much of ideas and literary beauty here as commerce.

A literary atmosphere and a sense of the personal has always been our most cherished notion of a bookstore. To walk in and be known, and to feel you are in a house of ideas. This is the bookstore experience we crave, and often miss from a superstore. In the end, though, both kinds of bookstores offer different browsing experiences. So why not wish for both kinds of bookstores to be around? That would be ideal if we could only take it for granted that the local, independent bookstore will be around.

I don't want to sound sentimental or nostalgic about independent bookstores shutting down, but in the struggle between independent versus chain bookstores, the local bookstore either loses or is always hit the hardest. If this were not so, the ardent browser would not take sides. As things stand, bibliophiles feel (or ought to feel) compelled to rally behind independent bookshops.

Will the local, independent bookstore in India eventually disappear? The independent vs. superstore struggle that once played out in America is fast becoming a reality here as well. (*Paperback Dreams* and *Indies Under Fire* are two documentaries about this David and Goliath struggle between independent and chain bookstores.) Already, I notice the local bookstores I used to patronize in various cities have either shut down or are in the process of shutting down. The emergence of the chain bookstore is only one factor in independents losing business.

Several of our legendary independent bookstores had central locations but steep rent increments that either forced them to relocate to the suburbs or compelled them to close down entirely. What we'll miss with their going is the picture of a bookshop that has been precious to us: intimate surroundings, a familiar old, musty smell, and running into idiosyncratic readers and eccentric booksellers. And, of course, browsing to our heart's content.

You can always tell a casual browser from a serious one, can't you? Once he's entered the bookstore, he'll head straight to the new arrivals shelf, scan the row quickly, and then hurry to a store assistant to ask for the book everyone is talking about. Worse, he doesn't even look around – he just asks the bookstore owner what's new and noteworthy. Any veteran browser can tell you that nothing spoils the pleasure of spending time in a bookshop than finding a book too quickly. The find has to come at the end of the search – even midway is acceptable. But to run smack into a book you definitely want to own… no, that just won't do.

The inveterate browser has her methods. Nothing

is more amateurish than to browse aimlessly all over the bookstore. The professional browser will head straight to her favourite shelf. Once there, she'll make herself comfortable (if it's one of those nice bookshops that provide chairs – or she'll just make do with a quiet corner), arrange a pile of books next to her, and then, and only then, will she begin browsing.

At the end of it, she may not even buy any of them: the point is to browse for the sake of browsing.

You have to look at each book carefully – not casually – internalize the contents, then stow it away in your mind for future reference. Browsing is more like a habit, a compulsion. What it takes is an ability to forget everything around you, even yourself, when you see a book you're interested in. To be seduced by jacket blurbs.

However, I do know friends who refuse to step into a bookshop if they aren't carrying enough money to buy a book. They're afraid of finding something they want and not having enough money to buy it. I, on the other hand, feel more compelled to be in a bookstore when I don't have money. I'm interested in the chase. My longing for a book increases when I can't buy it right away. Few things can match the intense anticipation of returning the next day, or a week later, to buy it. All the way to the bookstore you're wondering if it's gone or if it's still there. If the copy has been bought, then there's the excitement of the hunt. Where else can you find it, and how soon?

It's also a sensuous thing, this touching and fondling and smelling of books. Who can resist sniffing old books – especially comics – in used bookstores? It makes you nostalgic for childhood and gives you back the memory of your earliest encounter with books: the feel and smell of paper, the taste of words and sentences.

Many of my friends prefer bookshops as meeting

places. That way you don't have to wait if the other is late: you can browse. 'The tingle of anticipation that seizes you as you enter the store cannot be matched by any other feeling,' says my friend Malathy, another ardent browser. 'I can almost feel the books extending their arms to embrace me and begging me and daring me in turns to get to know them better. In an antiquarian bookshop, the possibilities for browsing are endless: out-of-print authors and centuries-old laboured scholarship bearing down upon you in solemn silence. But browsing always leaves me a little sad – there's so much you still don't know – is one lifetime enough for a real browser?'

My favourite independent bookstore, Lotus House Books in Mumbai – which I believe was the best *literary* bookstore in the country – shut down in 2005. It isn't clear why it closed down, since it had a large patronage of browsers, many of whom were serious readers, writers, intellectuals and even scriptwriters, directors and actors who bought their film books from here. The very first time I stepped into Lotus (in 2001) I knew I had found my favourite Indian bookstore.

I was in Mumbai on a book binge, doing the book-crawl the way some others pub-crawl. (Of course it is an entirely different matter that the book-crawl would usually end in a pub.) My friend and host, Rajib Sarkar (the editor of *Gentleman* then, and the only person I know who has mingled commerce, literary beauty and ideas in his life and work) told me the last bookshop on the crawl was special – a treat he had been saving for the last. Though I didn't tell him then, I was at once skeptical, since I had known disappointment again and again when other friends had introduced me to bookstores with the same promise.

What they usually had in mind was some fancy looking

bookstore, which, on closer inspection, would reveal had the same stock of books that every bookstore around the country carried – only the décor would be different. But Rajib knew what he was talking about. Lotus looked cosy and intimate, and had the reassuring air of a serious bookshop. Ten minutes of wide-eyed browsing told me the bookstore was unique, and after a good four hours spent in the store, I realized it was the first hardcore literary bookstore I had come across in my countrywide book-crawl.

What set Lotus apart, I figured out quickly, was that it did not solely depend – like most Indian bookstores do – on the same half a dozen book distributors operating in the country. Instead, the managers, Virat and Dom (two of the most impassioned readers I know) ordered their own titles based on international book reviews, book catalogues, and advance galley proofs of books still forthcoming. (Virat actually has the galley proofs of *The Secret History* somewhere; 'You can have it,' he told me once, but has never been able to lay his hands on it. So far.)

The one foreboding aspect about Lotus, which kept some away from the store, was that these books were expensive. Since their inventory was procured directly from foreign publishers and didn't come through the local distributor – who usually offers deep discounts – you had to pay the full list price. But this was the only way a niche bookshop could ensure it had a stock of quality titles not carried by most other bookstores. Well, Lotus is gone now. For a time it seemed as though it would rise, Phoenix-like, from its ashes.

The common reader as opposed to the experienced reader has come to prefer a bookstore that also carries other merchandise. The booklover has tried to stay loyal to the bookish bookstore. However, if the local bookstore wishes bibliophiles to continue patronizing it, it should figure out small ways (at low costs) to fashion itself as an unmistakably literary store, creating a unique identity not shared by the superstores. Apart from a literary identity, the independents could specialize, look at niche markets. A bookstore, for instance, devoted only to science fiction, another to mystery and detective fiction, yet another that stocks only hardcore literature (regional literature in translation, a larger poetry section) or books on film and the performing arts, self-help and spirituality.

What about a community bookstore – where books are only an excuse for a community of readers to talk literature, politics, ideas? Irrespective of how specialised the bookstore, they would do well to focus on more literary ephemera – bookish accessories such as literary bookmarks, out-of-print books, a used book section, offer special discounts for regular patrons, sell esoteric literary magazines, and even perhaps create a literary blog for their browsers to interact in.

One existing inspiration that our independents could learn from is the way American independents have tried to hold their own against superstores: by creating BookSense, a counter-cultural community of independent bookstores around the country. 'Book Sense' (now renamed 'Indiebound.org') recommends their own books – Book Sense Picks – as an alternative to other bestseller lists such as *The New York Times* list, which is a list apparently made up of books that chain stores and the dot coms have decided must sell best. Book Sense Picks on the other hand are books that have been bought by readers from the myriad independent bookstores across the country, and books that the staff and owners of these stores have personally read and loved.

If Indian independent booksellers formed a similar community, it would help not just with their survival, but also in bringing the joy and thrill back into running the kind of bookstore we've always celebrated and will always cherish: a bookshop full of just books. Thus did my bibliophiliac heart leap at reading Kolkata's Seagull Bookstore advertise itself as: 'Independent. Fiercely so. Constantly battling the Lords of Stationery and the Coffee machines. Strictly books.'

Each of you might know (or recall) a small, local bookstore in your respective towns and cities that meant (or still means) something to your reading life, where browsing and buying books was (and is) a very personal, pleasurable, bookish affair.

THE ULTIMATE BOOKSHOP

THE UNEXPECTED JOY of finding yourself in an online booksite like Between The Covers is that it offers a browsing experience worthy of that great bookstore in heaven. BTC is undoubtedly one of the best online rare bookstores on the Internet today. I spend endless hours browsing (seldom buying) and losing myself here because it is really the first truly virtual bookstore. Reading their knowledgeable, witty, detailed description of each book (its condition and variants) is almost akin to fondling a book in a bookstore or hearing a passionate, literate booklover describe a highly desirable book.

There's even a rotating 3D image of several 'high spots' (very collectible true modern firsts, signed or association copies, scarce and rare editions) that allows the browser a virtual examination of a book's dust jacket, spine, front, back and even fore-edge! This is the booksite for the serious book collector in India. Founded by Tom and Heidi Congalton in 1985, BTC is an independent, high-end online bookstore selling first, rare and signed editions in highly collectable condition. An important part of the bookstore are the cats, Admiral Muffin and 'her sometimes aide-de-camp', Pirate Pumpkin, who offer the best rare book bargains in the vicinity.

The first thing you notice when you open the BTC site is how busy, colourful and graphic-filled it is. The writing on the site, whether it is descriptions of books, ephemera or notes on their staff, is unfailingly witty, gently self-deprecating, and entertainingly knowledgeable. The one responsible for creating this vibrant, one of a kind booksite is BTC's general manager, Dan Gregory. Gregory, who strikes me as a very promising, inventive and talented young bookman, is also credited with inventing the amazing 3D rotating book image.

BTC strongly feels that hunting for books with just a search engine is boring and unimaginative. Looking inside a virtual bookstore such as Between The Covers you discover not only the books you want but also books that you did not know you were lusting for.

Apart from its large catalogue of modern first editions, rare and antiquarian books, the booksite has all kinds of other literary diversions – an illustrated glossary of rare book terms, articles on rare book collecting, a series of trading cards with pictures of famous first edition jackets titled Classic Card Series, and a couple of literary games you can play, such as guessing the names of books with famous opening lines.

Their catalogues (hard and soft copies) are entertainingly written and beautifully produced, with literary sketches by the very gifted and witty illustrator Tom Bloom. Almost every book listed on their (virtual) shelves comes with a spanking image of the book's dustwrapper, and a detailed description of each edition's condition and value.

When I asked Tom to say something about his experience of running such a high-end bookstore, he dismissed it with a rather modest observation. 'When I started out, I wasn't a high-end bookseller, but rather something of a low-end bookseller. However, my interest in the books just led me into better and more expensive books, and the natural evolution of my career, our business, and our finances led us into more rarefied material. There is always something new to learn about the books, and the longer I do this, the less I realize I know about rare books. When I started out in business I was a "know-it-all" but knew nothing; now I am a fairly successful bookseller, and realize how little I know of the total amount there is to know on the subject – but hopefully more than I knew when I started!'

I often think that BTC is the Indiana Jones of Antiquarian Bookshops: they are intrepid hunters of 'high spots' in modern first editions. They'll track down that elusive, truly scarce to rare book, and proudly display it on their rotating 3D gizmo. For instance, they are often able to offer for sale that holy grail of modern first editions in its true first edition, first issue, with its original dust jacket: *The Great Gatsby*. This is an item seldom seen even by antiquarian booksellers. The asking price? $110,000,00.

The legend on the BTC t-shirt says, 'Not Just Another Bunch of Books Geeks'. From this and the knowing, hip tone of the booksite, one gathers the impression that BTC would like to erase the old image of the serious faced, bookish, stodgy antiquarian bookseller. I celebrate a high-end online rare bookstore such as this one because it allows bibliophiles – rich and poor – around the world to browse inside the store to their heart's content. You may seldom buy anything here but BTC still affords you the rare privilege of roaming the bookstore, inspecting first editions, and dreaming about owning them. Thus the act of reading about a particular (virtual) book is for me like hearing a knowledgeable booklover talk about her books.

I used to lament that book browsing and buying on the World Wide Web was fast replacing the actual physical act of being in a bookstore, but now this seems a typical Luddite response on my part. I had thought then that it could only benefit the book seller/dealer and not the buyer/browser. I could not have been more wrong. I've spent the best part of the last few years browsing for books on the Net, and have come away astonished and excited at the riches in store for a book collector there.

It's like a giant bookstore where you can track down and find any book you are looking for – used, hard to find, backlists of an author's work, out of print, rare and first editions. You are accessing the stocks of thousands of book dealers across the world. Some of them have up to 20 million books listed on just one booksite alone. Two hundred and fifty new dealers and 600,000 new books are added every month on the Net. Thousands of fresh books appear daily – the equivalent of a massive 'New Arrivals' shelf.

I have always supported local, independent bookstores. I first check to see if my favourite bookstore is carrying the book I want, and only then turn to online book search engines. In India we are mostly familiar with 'Amazon' and 'eBay' but there are other book search engines (some corporate, some independent) for used, out of print, rare and first editions that are really quite fabulous.

The first booksite that I stumbled on is Alibris (pronounced 'uh-LEE-briss'), which offers 'over 60 million used, new, and out-of-print books.' Biblio brings together 'over 5000 professional, independent booksellers from around the world' and lists their stock on their search engine. They offer over 45 million used books to choose from. Abebooks lets you browse and buy 100 million books from 13,500 booksellers. They also host online community forums to connect readers; their aim is to 'build the world's largest online community of book lovers.' Bibliopoly, Bibliophile, Biblion and Tomfolio (an international co-op of independent dealers) are also excellent booksites.

Which brings me to Bookfinder, 'The Google of Rare

Books': one master meta-search engine that combines all the search sites where you can compare price, shipping, condition and variants. It lets you browse every major catalogue online, letting you know which of these booksellers are offering the best prices and selections. When you find a book you want, you can buy it directly from the original seller. There are no mark-up fees involved. (Addall is another good booksite – 40+ sites and 20,000 dealers – for the same thing: browsing and comparing prices.) Just as fascinating is another 'Google for rare books': viaLibre, the only meta-search engine on the web offering bibliographical information about antiquarian books. It's a great resource for bibliophiles looking for editions as far back as incunabula!

What particularly interests me about Bookfinder.com (which turned 10 in 2008) is that it was launched (in 1997) by Anirvan Chatterjee, then a 19-year-old UC Berkeley undergraduate. Chatterjee notes that 'both *Newsweek* and *Money* called it one of the two best book sites online.' Anirvan, founder and CEO of Bookfinder, is a lifelong bibliophile, a big supporter of independent bookstores and a tireless reader – working his way through a hundred books a year.

All the booksites I've described are indispensable for the book collector: here you can find the exact edition of a book you are looking for. These book dealers are knowledgeable and take care to describe a listed book exactly right – not just the content but the condition of the book – because condition is *all* in collecting. The advanced search options on these sites allow you to browse by binding (hardcover, soft cover) dust jacket, first edition, signed, limited edition, publisher, year, ISBN, keyword, new, used, out of print, and price range.

You don't have to be a wealthy book collector to buy

from these booksites – there are thousands of hard to find books at low used prices ($2 to $5) and even decent (if not collectible) first editions for $10-$25. For Rs 200 I found a paperback of *Booked to Die* signed by John Dunning! I had to pay an additional three hundred as international shipping charges but Rs 500 is a steal for a signed copy of this title. (A fine copy of a signed hard cover first edition, first printing of this title is usually estimated at $800.) A pleasant (and welcome) surprise was discovering these sites list several used and out-of-print books by Indian writers, in both their Indian and foreign editions.

For many years I've wanted to own UK and US editions of R.K. Narayan but could never find them in our bookstores. Then, recently, I came across several of these editions (some even signed!) on these booksites. I bought a nice used copy of *The Bachelor of Arts* (University of Chicago Press) for Rs 80, plus international shipping.

Once, midway through searching these booksites I paused on the computer, suddenly realizing that I had spent hours lost in browsing – exactly what happens when I'm physically in a bookstore. Am I saying skip bookshops and buy books online? No. Drawing from my experience this past year, I'm saying: why not experience browsing and buying from bookshops as well as booksites? For me the booksite is like a book scout who roams far and wide to find you not just the exact book but the exact *copy* of that book. Booksites give you the kind of browsing buzz you're looking for in a good bookshop. The thrill of the hunt is there, too. Isn't it just possible then that the Internet book site (especially those as enchanting as Between The Covers) has become the ultimate bookstore?

The Book in the Movie

The scene comes early in *The Big Sleep*. Bogart as private detective Philip Marlowe walks into a Los Angeles rare bookstore and asks for a 'Chevalier Audubon 1840, full set of course', and a 'Ben Hur, 1860, the third edition with the errata on page 113'. No such editions exist and Marlowe knows this – he just wants to know if the bookstore clerk knows enough to know this. She hesitates. The previous evening Marlowe had done his homework at the public library: consulted Elkin Mathew's *Fifty Famous First Editions* for background information and comes up with the idea of making up editions. Standing now before the hostile store clerk, he is certain that A.C. Geiger Rare Books is a front for pornography and blackmail. Marlowe – that is Bogart – continues to irritate the nervous woman behind the desk. 'You do sell books, hmm?' he asks sarcastically and the clerk pointing to some books replies, 'What do those look like, grapefruit?'

Unfazed, Marlowe walks out with a grin, and it's pouring outside, so he darts across into another bookstore, this time a legitimate antiquarian bookshop, and poses the same questions to a pretty book dealer (the bookishly charming or the charmingly bookish Dorothy Malone), who grins and says she doesn't have those editions because there aren't any. 'The girl across the street didn't know that,' says Marlowe. She teases him with: 'You're beginning to interest me – vaguely.' With that she turns the 'Open' sign at the door to 'Closed', lowers the blinds, shakes her hair down, and pulls out a couple of glasses of whisky. Marlowe says, 'I'd rather get wet here with you than outside in the rain.'

Howard Hawks' adaptation of Raymond Chandler's detective classic is a witty, sexy tribute to books in cinema. (The movie's literary pedigree is further bolstered by its scriptwriter: William Faulkner.) Cinema borrows much from books but gives back little. When movies feature books – as physical objects that is – and bookstores as location or setting, the scene or action is all too fleeting. When you see a bookshop in a movie, it's usually for a few seconds as some movie character darts in and out of one. If the character happens to be a woman, you can at least hope to see her leave with a book. No lingering is allowed; nobody browses either. You don't see the camera pan over bookshelves or stop to look at the books on it. And you never see a book in close-up. What we get instead is the camera languorously moving over curtains, sofas, bathroom fixtures – you get the picture.

The thin fate of books, bookstores and bookish people in cinema is made bearable by a handful of films that go beyond using books and bookstores as just classy backdrops. (When Hollywood uses bookshops this way, it is to give the movie a little unearned class – like in *Notting Hill*. Except for an unusual meeting place for Julia Roberts and Hugh Grant, the little bookshop on travel literature serves no other purpose in the film. I'm still partial to Nora Ephron's *You've Got Mail* because it at least addresses the issue of how huge chain bookstores are putting little, independent bookshops out of business.)

I couldn't for the life of me recall a good bookstore scene in any Indian movie that I had ever seen. (I would have thought that's the kind of setting Ray would have delighted in.) The Japanese, on the other hand, have injected bibliophilia even into animation. She's been described as the bibliophile's poster-child and the uber-bookworm – by day Yomiko is librarian at the Royal British Library Division of Special Operations, and by night The Paper: her superpowers enable her to fight biblio-villains, and in her hands, even the library card becomes a dangerous weapon. The cult Japanese anime series *Read or Die* (by Koji Masnuari, Hideyuki Kurata and Masashi Ishihama) is unique for the way it uses the world of books as primary background for a comic book world. (In one episode involving India, the extra features on the DVD actually has a bibliographical reference to *A Passage to India!*)

The most fetching close-ups of books and bookshelves are to be found in Neil LaBute's adaptation of A.S. Byatt's *Possession*, where Gwyneth Paltrow visits several breathtaking old libraries. And then there's Angelina Jolie in *The Bone Collector*, frantically looking for an out-of-print pulp mystery in a dusty used bookstore, while Michael Caine and Barbara Hershey browse in a lovely, old New York bookstore in *Hannah and Her Sisters* and discover e.e cummings. Later, when Woody Allen heard his favourite neighbourhood literary bookstore, Books & Co., was going to close, he paid tribute to it in *Everyone Says I Love You*.

In a rather glossy but unsatisfying infidelity drama, *Unfaithful*, Diane Lane has an affair with a young rare book dealer. The three visits she sneaks into his apartment where he stocks his inventory shows us books stacked not just along walls and passageways but in the middle of rooms, as though they were furniture. How, you wonder, does he ever find the books he wants? George Orwell's early satire, *Keep the Aspidistra Flying*, was the basis of the movie, *A Merry War*, about a struggling poet and his wife (Richard E. Grant, Helena Bonham-Carter) who work in a London second-hand bookshop to make ends meet.

The films of Peter Greenaway have always featured books and (nude) bodies as erotic objects – from *The Cook, the Thief, His Wife and Her Lover* to *Prospero's Books* to *The Pillow Book*. (In *The Cook, the Thief* the scholarly lover is killed by his rival who shoves pages of a book down his throat until he chokes.) Polanski's *The Ninth Gate* (based on that wonderful Spanish biblio-thriller, *The Club Dumas*, by Arturo Pérez-Reverte) suffused as it is in exquisite shots of books in burnished gold lighting, is not as careful about its bibliographic details: the rare editions of *Don Quixote* that Johnny Depp as the book-hunter carts away right under the noses of its philistine owners are really later 19th century editions, which are not really valuable even if they look old. *Black Books* from BBC was a comedy about a peevish bookseller 'who loves his books and hates his customers'. And Ismail Merchant's *The Mystic Masseur* is a top-notch comedy about bookishness gone wrong.

Fast Company, Fahrenheit 451, 84 Charing Cross Road, Crossing Delancey, The Name of the Rose, Bookwars, Paperback Dreams, Read You Like a Book and *The Stone Reader* are films entirely about books or bookshops. *Read You Like a Book* is a rather obscure independent movie set entirely inside a real bookstore, the legendary Black Oaks Bookstore in Berkeley. A mysterious man turns up at the bookstore and leaves a strange book called *The Illustrated Book of Failure* at the counter. The book, we soon realize, has a way of making an impact on the patrons and the employees of the bookshop. The story is slight, but what makes the movie special are all the long, lingering close-up glimpses of books, browsers and bookshelves.

Though *Crossing Delancey* also uses a bookstore, albeit a very beautiful one, as merely background to the romance between Amy Irving and Peter Reigert, it offers characters that really care for books, and a plot that is fairly literary in tone. There are several scenes featuring the bookshop and some lovely lines strewn with literary references. The film opens with a literary party in progress at the store, and its owner (played to perfection by George Martin) welcomes the guests this way: 'It's an aesthetic shock to see so many writers, readers and critics gathered in the same room.'

It's a little surprising and unusual for a mystery novel from the '30s to feature rare books, but entirely unexpected and unusual (but delightfully so) to see a movie from that time set in the world of rare books. Marco Page's *Fast Company* is probably an early example of the bibliomystery in English (the first ever bibliomystery is from 1874: *Scrope, or, The Lost Library* by Frederic Perkins, followed by *The Colfax Bookplate*, 1926, by Agness Miller) while the movie adaptation of *Fast Company* is most likely the first bibliomystery in cinema. Both the book and the film continue to remain obscure. The film is completely out of print, while paperback copies of the book are not always easy to find. The hero and heroine of *Fast Company* are a husband and wife team of rare book dealers who solve crimes involving rare books. Joel and Garda Sloan are always full of clever, witty banter, and the tone of the book and the film is urbane, sophisticated, knowing.

While researching the early years of antiquarian book trading in Britain, I came across murmurs and sniffles from various bookmen on some inaccuracies in Helene Hanff's classic bookstore account, *84 Charing Cross Road*, about what went on at Marks and Co. Apparently, for some time now, a whiff of controversy has attached itself to how much is true in Hanff's account. First published in 1971 as a slim, elegant volume of 86 letters (from 1949-1969), *84 Charing Cross Road* is the account of a New York bibliophile's love affair with an antiquarian bookshop in London.

The film version stars Anne Bancroft as Helene, the charming, witty American book collector and Anthony Hopkins as the knowledgeable, reserved English bookseller, Frank Doel. Here you can feast your eyes on as many books as you want to. It spends so much time inside an old London bookshop, you begin to smell the books. A few British veteran book dealers – contemporaries of Benjamin Marks, the store founder, sneered at Hanff's portrait of Marks & Co. as being untrue to the firm. This outlook, however, was confined to the inner circle of London's antiquarian booksellers. The controversy began when his son, Leo Marks, noted cryptically in his autobiography that the story was a 'gentle little myth', adding no more than that.

Naturally disturbed, I probed this as thoroughly as I could, consulting several memoirs and articles from that period, and no one seemed to be able to say in what way Hanff had taken artistic liberties. It now seems to me just a silly harangue over nothing and I only even bother to mention it here so you could dismiss anything you might hear and just go on delighting in the book and the movie in the way you always have. In the course of looking up the controversy, I did learn a few interesting things: that Freud had browsed at Marks & Co. Frank Doel was a respected bookman in antiquarian circles, and not at all the dull book dealer as imagined by some. It was Doel who fetched books for Freud to look at. The movie takes pains to be literate and is careful to show actual rare and first editions (not dummy copies or incorrect copies) such as the *Elizabethan Lyrists* from 1919 by Amy Cruise and the Chatto and Windus paper edition of *Virginbus Puerisque* from 1905.

The impressive looking antiquarian book (the lost treatise on laughter by Aristotle) in *The Name of the Rose*, for instance, is a made-up book, a beautifully constructed dummy. The filmmakers gave the dummy copy to Umberto Eco as a souvenir, and he has it now in his Milan apartment alongside the 30,000 books on his bookshelves. The movie is a bibliographer's delight, soaking our eyes in vellum and parchment and illuminated manuscripts. The film's most moving moment is when Sean Connery as the bibliophile-scholar monk William of Baskerville, risks his life to save those precious books from perishing in the library fire, provoking even the movie's blind villain, the venerable Jorge (who bears more than a passing resemblance to Borges), to whisper, 'What a magnificent librarian you would have been.'

The books that burn in *Fahrenheit 451* are mostly the orange and green Penguin paperbacks! Truffaut's unimaginative adaptation of Ray Bradbury's sci-fi classic about a future world that has banned books, is about secret libraries run by readers. When they are found out, the fire squad burns the books – 451 degrees Fahrenheit is the temperature at which paper burns. The hero of the film is a fireman who hides one of these books and secretly reads it at night by torchlight. The book turns out to be *David Copperfield* and thus does he discover reading. The story's ending is one of the most unforgettable tributes to books – and it doesn't even involve books! And yet nothing could mean more to readers and writers.

Our hero escapes to a hidden island where the only inhabitants are bibliophiles whose only job is to commit to memory an entire book. The book-loving fireman watches women, men and children walk around the island, reciting the books out aloud. The readers introduce themselves to the fireman: 'By the way, I'm *Treasure Island*.' 'I'm *The*

Martian Chronicles.' Twins walk up to him and say: 'I'm *Pride and Prejudice*, Volume 1, and I'm *Pride and Prejudice*, Volume 2.' 'Oh, and I'm Sartre's *The Jewish Question*,' says a pretty young lady. These ardent, dangerous book lovers, these compulsive, subversive readers have become living, breathing, walking, talking books!

As an aspiring writer, you are brought up on the notion that you have to write several books – offer a substantial body of work – or you are no writer at all. To write just one book and stop with that seems a failure of a kind. But reflecting on these one-book writers, I realize this needn't always be true. Why not put everything you know – about life, about the writing craft, about character – into that one book? Perhaps that is how you write a really good book, perhaps even a memorable one

An intriguing case of the reclusive one-book writer is now a suspenseful, uncompromising literary documentary called *Stone Reader*. This one-of-a-kind documentary is a movie about a passionate reader in search of other passionate readers.

A man named Mark Moskovitz stumbles on an old paperback copy of a book called *The Stones of Summer* by someone named Dow Mossman. The blurb on the book by a *New York Times* writer says the book is 'an undiscovered masterpiece, a seminal work of literature'.

Moskovitz, who has been devouring books since he was a child, becomes intrigued: he has never heard of the book or the writer before. Reading the book, he becomes excited. It is, as the review says, an unknown masterpiece. He becomes hungry for more books by Mossman but is astonished to learn that Mossman has not written anything else. He becomes even more puzzled when he discovers that *The Stones of Summer* is out of print.

Bookstores don't stock it, neither have they heard of

it. Now, doubly curious about Mossman, Moskovitz gets on the Net, searching for information on the author and discovers that there is none. No one, not even his former publishers know what happened to him. That is when Moskovitz, who directs political commercials for a living, hits upon the idea to turn his quest for Mossman into a film. A film that would document his search, step by step. On eBay he finds three hardcover copies of the book for sale and buys them all. He contacts several people who might have a clue to Mossman's whereabouts: the literary critic whose blurb provoked Moskovitz to read the book in the first place, the artist who designed the cover jacket of *Stones*, Mossman's contemporaries at a writers' workshop, his literary mentor whom the book is dedicated to and so on.

In trying to hunt down a one-book writer, *Stone Reader* becomes a film that also illuminates the reading life. Moskovitz talks endlessly of his deep love for books and writers. Other readers – friends of the filmmaker – and several famous literary figures such as Leslie Fiedler, Robert Gottlieb and Frank O'Connor talk about the writing life.

The film is also a meditation on the relationship between author and reader. It is a deeply satisfying and electric moment when Moskovitz finally finds Mossman. Moskovitz proves that a book becomes everything the author meant it to be when it meets its ideal reader. For Mossman, Moskovitz turns out to be more than the ideal reader – he seems to be in another dimension entirely. Copies of *Stones* had lain about in used bookstores and people's homes for several decades, and yet, it was not until Moskovitz read it and became possessed by it, did it begin to actually exist again.

Though most writers write for themselves, the film

reveals that it is the reader who completes the book. There has not been, so far, such an uncompromisingly literary documentary. It fulfils a fantasy for bibliophiles: to see a movie where the camera sensuously caresses books. The camera dwells lovingly on bookshelves, there are close-ups of book covers and their spines, the title page and the endpapers. And readers are seen caressing their favourite books. Because of Moskovitz's film, Barnes and Noble brought *The Stones of Summer* back into print. Interesting twist, isn't it? That a movie should resurrect a book?

Deep into his quest, Moskovitz becomes sidetracked by his new fascination for one-book writers. And decides it is his mission to bring back into print all these little known one-book writers. He makes a list, tracks down the books these authors wrote (several of them are on his shelf) and takes them to one of New York's leading agents. In the agent's office Moskovitz pours out from the bag on to the agent's desk his 10 great one-book writers of the century. He is there to plead for their life; that they be rescued from obscurity. It's a delightful, gratifying sight.

Shakespeare & Co.

On a cold, grey winter Sunday in Paris, a young man who was nearly broke ducked for shelter into the nearest bookstore he chanced on, and it turned out to be none other than the legendary Shakespeare & Co. Looking for something legitimate to do so he could hang on inside and out of the cold, he bought a 25 cent book and to his surprise was invited upstairs for tea with the staff. Walking up a few stairs looking for the tea party, he found himself in rooms crammed with not just books but beds, cots, mattresses, clothes, and toiletry. People lived here. Writers who were poor, unemployed and starving could come and find shelter at Shakespeare & Co. George Whitman, its owner, was a socialist who believed a bookstore was part of a community's strength and resource.

Jeremy Mercer's memoir, *Time Was Soft There*, is an account of living poor and as a bum at Paris' best known English bookstore. Shakespeare & Co. has been home to many Left Bank writers and intellectuals (Hemingway, Fitzgerald, Stein, Pound) though this was at a time when Sylvia Beach (1919-41) was the owner. Beach, if you remember, published *Ulysses* when no one else would. Whitman bought it over from her (in the 1950s) and decided to run it also as a free hostel for struggling writers. I had expected *Time Was Soft There* to be a lot about book talk but it's really more a funny, charming account of living broke and bohemian in Paris. And in the bargain, it is a moving, inspiring biography of the kind of bookseller, the kind of literary radical we can't hope to find anymore.

For three years Mercer and the other bums at the bookshop witnessed George being frugal with what he spent on himself so he could save every franc to keep the free hostel at the bookstore going. He drank the cheapest beer, bought grocery at discount markets, and didn't throw away even plastic bags because they could be used to wrap books for customers. He kept an entire floor in the bookstore for books that were for reading only, not for sale. He didn't even like selling the books, and would like to have given them away, but then what would all of them live on? Even with the landlord breathing down his neck to shut the bookstore, George only wanted to expand it!

The Shakespeare bums initiate Mercer into the ways of living the bum's life: pretending to be a student and eating a large but cheap meal at the 'students only' cafeterias around Paris. Then, the bookstore had no heating (it also did not have a telephone or a credit card machine) so you slept with blankets in the dead of winter – for all this hardship, says the writer, time was soft there. Criminals divide time into hard time and soft time; soft time was time 'that went easily, that was a pleasure to do. Time at Shakespeare and Company was as soft as anything I'd ever felt.'

There are many interesting characters that roomed at the bookstore. What got you in was a simple declaration to George that you were a serious writer or meant to pursue writing seriously. He would invite you to stay and point out which part of the bookstore you could sleep in. Whitman took it on faith that you were a writer and not a bum; only a month after were you required to show something you had written, or at the least write a few pages about yourself. Over the decades, George had collected hundreds of such writer's biographies.

All the denizens of the bookshop were no older than 35, except Simon the English poet who was in his 60s, and kept himself locked away in the antiquarian book room. George wanted him evicted: he wasn't allowing customers to come inside and browse. But no one could catch him: he would sneak out of the shop before anyone awoke and sneak in after everyone had gone to bed. No one knew where he went for the day or what he did. Finally, Simon convinces George that he has nowhere to go, that Shakespeare was his only home.

Whitman lived alone in a small apartment above the bookstore. He was estranged from his daughter, who he thought of often. When the book ends, George is 90, and is joyously reunited with his daughter who takes over the bookshop. Over a beer, with the sun setting, George tells the writer: 'I look across at Notre Dame and I sometimes think the bookstore is an annex of the church. A place for the people who don't quite fit in over there.'

The Lame Duck

I FOUND THE Lame Duck Bookstore when I wasn't looking for it. Searching for Raven, a popular used bookstore in Harvard Square, Cambridge, I found myself before the Lame Duck. The sign said, 'Rare, Out of Print and Antiquarian Books'. I had never been inside a proper antiquarian bookstore before – had not dared to because I was certain I could never afford a really rare book.

But now I couldn't resist a peek, and pushed open the door, ready to flee if the staff made me out as a cheap customer. I was greeted affably by a young man at the desk, who asked me to feel free to ask him where what was. I asked if they carried modern first editions and he replied that the store was full of nothing but modern first editions, especially in philosophy, poetry and fiction.

An hour more of poking around and talking to Tom Mattos, the gracious, literate and kindly bibliophile at the desk, I discovered I was in no ordinary rare bookstore but in one of the most significant antiquarian bookstores in the world. Lame Duck Books are 'internationally known specialists buying and selling important modern books and manuscripts'. They feature the 'most significant selection of 19th and 20th-century Spanish language literature in the world, as well as important holdings of 17th and 18th century English poetry'.

Its owner, John Wronoski (whom I caught a quick glimpse of, when he dashed in to and out of the store) is considered one of the most important book dealers in the world. Reading their catalogues that Tom handed me, I saw how detailed, knowledgeable and passionate Wronoski was in describing each item there.

Since Lame Duck Books, I have been inside many rare books stores but what is so singular and marvellous about the Lame Duck is how even very rare books, often signed and inscribed copies or association copies, are to be found strewn all over the floor in piles, waiting to be priced or sorted. The very first time I spoke to Tom was when I brought over a first edition of Bernard Malamud's *The Assistant* to ask him, in a hesitant fashion, if they perhaps also had a first edition of his *A New Life*?

'Hmmmm,' he said, 'Not at the moment but if Malamud is your man, we have something else that might interest you.' He stepped over a small pile of books on the floor, swept them up in his arms and off loaded them into mine. 'These all came from the library of a close friend of the Malamuds – many of these books have Malamud's handwriting in them.'

Just like that, books once owned and touched and used by Malamud were sitting in my hand.

Of course, each of these books was priced at over 100 dollars, so I had to put them back on the floor. An hour or so later, in another part of the bookstore, I came across a book – in a pile of unsorted books – Bernard Malamud's own copy of a book on literary style that he had heavily underlined and scribbled marginalia in. A very rare and precious book priced at $150. More than fair in dollars but converted to rupees, forbidding – at least for me.

However, the real excitement at the Lame Duck was yet to come. It was by sheer chance that I brought up the name of Salinger in some context and Tom, after a pause, said: 'The only really interesting thing we have by Salinger is a letter by him to his daughter.' I couldn't believe it. Anything written and signed by J.D. Salinger is truly rare, what the book trade calls 'a high spot' in literary ephemera. 'Would you like to see it?' he asked. It would be a privilege, I said, if it would not be putting him to too much trouble. 'My pleasure,' he said and disappeared into the office to get it out of the safe.

Tom knew well enough by now that I could never really afford their books, but he was still kind enough to entertain me. He let me hold the letter and read it for myself. It was placed in a clear acetate cover to protect it. It was priced $17,500. Let me quote from their catalogue to accurately describe what I was holding in my hands that day.

'One page typed letter, signed, 7x10 on yellow paper, undated, but circa 1960,' addressed to his daughter Peggy. Salinger encloses a couple letters for his daughter, which he ironically describes as exciting. The rest of the letter alludes to a decision his daughter must make on her own, and which he is confident she will manage well, as 'she is not gaga, and never ha(ve) been, and that in any crisis or near-crisis you're pretty detached and (hurray) self-protective'. Signed, Daddy in Salinger's distinctive block script. An affecting document which we'd love to return to its author as a gesture of solidarity, though we see no means of nor higher rationale for doing so. Near fine.'

I could never hope that I would ever again in any bookstore get a chance to hold a letter by J.D. Salinger. Only a handful of his letters exist for the public to see, and, suddenly on that afternoon, I was privy to one of them. I owe a deep debt of gratitude to Lame Duck Books, John Wronoski and Tom Mattos for making this possible. It was at that moment that I realized that I was standing inside a very special antiquarian bookstore, staffed by very special people.

Lame Duck is full of first editions of Proust, Kafka, Kierkegaard, Sartre, Rilke (I actually pulled out of the shelf a first ed in German of the *Sonnets of Orpheus*!)

Mann, Nietzsche, Eliot, and Kafka. Lame Duck has the only known manuscript of several of Jorge Louis Borges' most important work. I had seen several photographs, sketches and even a fascinating installation of Borges all over the store.

Tom then informed me that Borges was the Lame Duck's patron saint. And then it made sense why I was so happy and wonderstruck browsing inside the Lame Duck. Because it is Borges who said, 'I don't know why I believe that a book brings us the possibility of happiness, but I am truly grateful for that modest miracle.'

Afterword:
At the 50ᵗʰ New York Antiquarian Book Fair

Like everyone in the room I lusted after these books, but was too shy, even terrified, to touch them. They were beautiful, rare, uncommon. And very expensive. $500 for a book was cheap here. The average price of most of the books I was looking at was $15,000. Several were half a million. Like the Latin bible dating from 1230 was 850,000 euros at the Jörn Günther Rare Books booth, the manuscript of Joyce's *Ulysses* or the fourth Shakespeare folio that beckoned from the window at the Peter Harrington booth. In the next booth was another legendary antiquarian book seller from London: Bernard Quaritch, in the business since 1847. If you walked down a row of very high-end book dealers, you met the other legend in the antiquarian book trade: Maggs Bros.

They were all here, 200 rare book dealers I had only heard or read about, from London, Paris, Barcelona, Frankfurt, Tokyo, Milan, New York, San Francisco, Copenhagen, Amsterdam and Spain. They had brought with them the brightest and best copies of some of the rarest books in the world to show and sell at the 50th New York Antiquarian Book Fair. The New York Antiquarian book fair is perhaps the most important and prestigious rare book fair in the world. It takes place every year in April for four days at the Park Avenue Armory, a cavernous stone structure in the heart of Manhattan.

On a mild April day in 2010, I stood outside the Armory waiting for its doors to open. I was trying to rein in my excitement which was tinged with a little nervousness as well: I had never been to a rare book fair, and it was

Afterword: At the 50th New York Antiquarian Book Fair / 279

a little intimidating to find myself now suddenly at the Mecca of rare books, an accidental pilgrim standing on holy ground. In their engaging accounts of travels in the book world, Lawrence and Nancy Goldstone, visiting this fair in its thirty-sixth edition had made particular note of the attitude of the dealers here as being prissy and unfriendly, especially if they seized you up as a browser more than a buyer. Perhaps at the heart of my excitement was the possibility that I would meet here, at the end of the day, Nicholas Basbanes, who would be present to sign his new book.

Basbanes is arguably the most widely read and enjoyed bibliojournalist today, and his best-selling series on book culture has made the arcane, high-end and exciting world of bibliophily more visible, popular, magnificent. Waiting to be let in, I killed time gazing at the large, bookishly elegant yellow banner fluttering again the Armory wall, announcing the fair with an illustration of a rather serene and cool looking monk reading a book. Perfect. Once the doors opened, I wanted to dash inside but feigned a cool I didn't really possess; one that I would drop the moment I saw the books.

But even before I got to the books, I was seduced in the passageway by voluptuous and lavishly illustrated catalogues stacked on several tables that you could help yourself to. Expensive to print and design, these were collectibles in their own right and I grabbed an armload of them. From Paul Foster a lovely little catalogue on A.A. Milne and E.H. Shepard, focusing on signed first editions and original drawings of *Winnie the Pooh*. Inside were pages and pages of photographs showcasing scarce and expensive signed sets of *The House at Pooh Corner*. 29,000 pounds. Now all I had to do, using the pocket-sized fair directory, was to locate the Paul Foster booth and make physical contact with the actual editions. It was as simple and as forbidding as that.

When I finally got to the long row of booths upon booths all brightly lit, with books stylishly displayed on designer wooden and glass bookcases, I found myself predictably overwhelmed. I was in bibliographical shock. Anywhere I turned, the shelves were overflowing with out-of-print, difficult to find, limited, scarce, fine and rare editions. Our browsing experience in regular book fairs is handling shiny multiple copies of new titles; the individual copy matters not at all. If someone buys a copy before you, you just buy the next one on the pile. And if they are all sold out, the book seller asks you to 'Hang on a minute, there are more where that came from', and uncrates a new box.

The wonderfully peculiar nature of a rare book fair is that each copy of a book is unique; it can't be replaced. And very often there aren't more where *that* came from. Each copy of the same book is also different from the other – a different edition, a different state.

Each copy of the *same* edition is different: there's the copy with the endpapers slightly foxed, the copy with a little tear in the corner of the dust jacket, the copy with the restored binding, the copy that has a little rubbing to the board edges, there's the copy with a previous owner's bookplate, and the copy that describes itself as 'pristine'. Not just every varying edition, but every single copy in a rare book fair has character, individuality, uniqueness.

After an hour of wandering in a bibliographic daze, I realized the editions on the shelves were just the icing: Locked in glass display cases, each book dealer was showcasing letters from literary masters, illuminated manuscripts and antique maps. Surprisingly, the most incandescent books here were incunabula: the first printed books of the 15th century. You would have thought these books wouldn't have the finesse of the printed book as we know it today, but here each book was an artefact; a jewel. They were either folio-sized or miniature, with woodcut illustrations in gold, blue and red. *The Book of Hours* is particularly stunning for its illuminated illustrations. They are sold upwards of $30,000 with some going as high up as $350,000.

There was even a copy of the *Nuremberg Chronicle*, a landmark in early printing. And somewhere in the fair, and I can't remember in whose booth, I finally set my eyes on that Book Art masterpiece: William Morris's *The Kelmscott Chaucer*. The only two other famous rare book artefacts I did not see here was a full *Gutenberg Bible* and Poe's *Tamerlane*. The only existing copies are most likely with institutions but the reason why a book dealer did not possess one here was not because they couldn't afford to stock one, even though these are valued in the millions, but because they are simply rare – so truly rare – that even a single other copy cannot be turned up. (Except in a broken form, which is bibliospeak for parts or pages torn or broken from the original work, like a page from the *Gutenberg* that can sometimes turn up on the antiquarian market.)

I might have spent the rest of the fair just gawking if it wasn't for Angel, the witty, erudite and vivacious young woman at the Bauman's Rare Books booth who simply threw open the closed glass shelves, encouraging me to handle the books. She knew the provenance and bibliographical points of these editions intimately. She took out from the shelf a signed and inscribed copy of *The Fountainhead*, and handed it to me noting that Ayn Rand had inscribed it to Ely Jacques Khan, the architect for whom she had interned without pay to research the book. Price: $56,000.

Soon, I was handling copies of first printings of books that I had once known only in text book form. In my hand, for instance, was a first edition, first issue of Keats' *Endymion*, 1818, Octavo, uncut, top edge gilt. A copy that possibly the poet himself may have once touched. A few minutes later, I was holding a signed, inscribed first edition of Forster's *A Passage to India*, Edward Arnold, 1924, Octavo, original half brown cloth, gray paper spine label. Oscar Wilde's *Poems*, 1892, signed. (Signed!). I put it back and picked up a copy of *A Room of One's Own*, Hogarth Press, 1929, limited issue. One of 492 copies signed by Virginia Woolf in her characteristic purple ink. Original cinnamon cloth. I exchanged that for a copy of *The Wasteland*, signed by Eliot.

And just a little later the book in my hand was the true first edition of *Alice in Wonderland*, the earliest known edition, preceding the first published London edition, 1866, beautifully rebound with 42 illustrations by John Tenniel. And finally, a limited first edition of Rilke's *Sonnets of Orpheus*, signed and inscribed, 1923, gilt-ruled covers, raised bands, patterned endpapers, top edge gilt, uncut and unopened. I realized, with a shiver, that I had just touched the very same copies that these authors had once held in their hands.

I was only one among several browsers here lucky enough to make contact with these editions, and it seemed to me that this fair was a gateway through time for readers to suddenly, just for one Harry Potter moment, be in the presence of these beloved writers when holding the same copies they had once physically touched and used. These editions, these particular copies, were doorways – time machines – that teleported you in an instant to the past, and connected you to them and them to you. It was more magic than anything J.K. Rowling could conjure up.

I was grateful for Angel's unfussy ways of breaking the ice at the fair, and helping me overcome my timidity with handling these books. Angel Webster was a born bookwoman if I ever saw one, and the pleasure and joy she took in her job reached out and took hold of you. Though it must have been plain to Angel that I couldn't afford to buy anything she was showing me, it didn't stop her from entertaining me with rich bibliospeak.

When I exclaimed at her generosity, she dismissed it saying: 'I have come to view Antiquarian book fairs as a very well organized rummage for old and interesting books. After so many years of attending, and, at first, being terrified of the importance of the books, the quality and accents of the booksellers, I can now see it for what it truly is: Another happy hunting ground for book hunters. It's true that the books are usually so rare that the prices of the books must reflect the responsibility that goes with owning them; nonetheless, it is a huge, fantastic rummage that one should enjoy for the sheer sake of the books.

'To the point, there is nothing I like better on my own lunch hour at the rare book store, which houses incredibly rare and expensive books and letters, than going into some hole in the wall store or dusty, forgotten corner of a library sale so that I can do some rummaging. I'm like everyone else who loves books – a hunter at heart.'

I mentioned being warned to expect stuffy, inaccessible staff.

'Really? I always have some jazz music blasting when I'm working. And I can talk endlessly about a book. The stories of how they were written and created. How they have travelled, how they have persevered through adversity. In some cases, how they have been saved from fire and flood or rescued from the tide of indifference.

How they have escaped inside the helmets of soldiers, the trunks of immigrants, on the backs of bicycles, inside the heads of actors. The human impulse to record and write and collect fascinates me. Perhaps it is linked to our constant need to experience, even if it is vicarious experience. As for myself, this urge usually presents itself as a small need to read a story, then manifests itself, like a plant going from seed to bloom, as a desire to hold and keep. The word as object.'

Angel would be the best person, I realized, to tell me something about how truly scarce the *Gutenberg* and *Tamerlane* really were. Was it just possible that some dealer at the fair actually had one of these famed rare treasures? *Tamerlane* was Poe's first published work but it went unidentified for a century because he didn't put his name to it. (There was a mythical time when treasure hunters were turning up copies from flea markets, and now it's entirely possible there are no surviving copies left to discover.)

'Both are nearly unobtainable,' she said, 'as you guessed. And the prices would be… well… pretty "dear", as my English friends put it.'

Had she been lucky enough to see them?

'I recently took a trip to the Morgan Library and Museum to look at the *Gutenberg* they have, and to also see the *Catherine of Cleves*, a 15th century Book of Hours. The funny thing about the *Gutenberg* and the Book of Hours is that they are both books of devotion… and yet… how different! The Cleves Book of Hours is the most fantastically illuminated book I've seen outside of the *Book of Kells*; it's almost a devotional to art, rather than to the Holy Spirit. The *Gutenberg*, on the other hand, is quite humble in comparison. At least, to the uninitiated (my husband walked right past it). I pointed it out, among the other Bibles.

'How can you tell, he asked me.

'Easy, I said. Two columns of 42 lines. Evenly spaced. Excellent printing. It looks almost modern in the spacing. Look at how the other Bibles look kind of slapped together. The Gutenberg is perfect in its solemnity.

'And I've been lucky enough to have seen the *Book of Kells* at the British Museum – this was a long time ago, back in those trusting days when they were foolish enough to allow a 20 something punk girl alone with national treasures.

'As for *Tamerlane*… the last and only time I saw it was last year, at Christie's. I rushed over because I might not see another one for many years. I think it went for about $600,000. With less than 12 left in the world, it's as scarce as one of those mystical, ivory-billed woodpeckers. Although, I'd like to see one of those as well.'

I saluted her and headed to the booths dealing in modern first editions. But now thanks to Angel, I was browsing more unselfconsciously, focusing on the books, and tuning out the chatter and crowds around me.

I discovered that most of the dealers at the fair were actually friendly if not as chatty as Angel. They mostly left you alone to browse. I thought they were really generous and brave: if I dropped a book accidentally or creased a page it could devalue the book at once by hundreds of dollars. Especially with modern firsts where each of these dealers had the same titles but in varying condition. 'Condition isn't all, it's everything' as they say in the trade. Some rushed to ask you if they could help you find anything. A genuine offer to help you make up your mind – or perhaps to keep you from rummaging through the shelves? It was easy spotting the dealers specializing in modern editions: their shelves were colourful with the bright and rich dust jackets of modern firsts.

I lingered a while at Quill and Brush, introducing myself to its famous owners, Allen and Patricia Ahearn, publishers of the definitive book on modern collecting prices. There were so many dealers with so many bright copies of the high spots of modern firsts, that they nearly became commonplace! Only at the New York fair! And most of the copies here were not only in mint condition, they were also signed. First printings of *The Big Sleep*, *The Maltese Falcon*, *The Mysterious Affair at Styles*, *The Hobbit*, a whole run of Ian Fleming, Philip K. Dick, Pynchon, Wodehouse, all signed. Bright first issues of *Dharma Bums*, *Naked Lunch*, *Huck Finn*, *The Whale or Moby Dick*, *Dracula*. Advance reading copies of the first *Harry Potter* book. Hooray! I even saw a Faber first edition of *English, August*, inscribed and signed by Upamanyu Chatterjee. Five hundred dollars.

Anywhere else, these copies would be considered hard to find, but here it was raining high spots. At Biblioctopus you could browse through a complete set of Edgar Rice Burroughs' *Tarzan*, dust jackets intact and signed! It was a particular treat to browse at Royal Books, who have this marvellous and unusual focus in collecting film-related books, letters and manuscripts. For instance they had Patricia Hitchcock's own copy of the shooting script of *Strangers On A Train*, with Hitchcock's signature, a copy of that famous study of the director signed by Eric Rohmer and Claude Chabrol, a UK first edition of *2001: A Space Odyssey*, inscribed by Stanley Kubrick. From the shelves I turned up a copy of Satyajit Ray's *Stories*, Calcutta, Seagull Books, 1987 – signed by Ray. Ten thousand dollars.

Having had my fill for the moment of modern books, I gravitated towards my new interest: fine press and children's picture books. My hunch that the more artistic children's picture books really belonged with the artists' book seemed to be proved here, because nearly every book arts dealer also dealt in picture books. One of the fabulous things about a book fair of this scale and depth is the rare opportunity of seeing not one, not two, but half a dozen dealers specializing in book arts, many of them the best and most respected in this esoteric field of collecting. Priscilla Juvelis, a contemporary legend in the trade for artists' books, is the first booth I stopped at, looking for the bookwork of, among others, Richard Minsky.

Also present was The Kelmscott Bookshop with a focus on William Morris, Pre-Raphaelites and illustrated books. Kelmscott had some very enchanting artists' books for pocket-friendly prices. One little keepsake for an affordable fifty dollars was one artist's tribute in the form of a charming sketch book of the various Mr Darcys of film and television, from Laurence Olivier to Colin Firth. Unfortunately, I didn't have the pleasure of meeting Kelmscott's gracious owner, Fran Durako at the fair. (But I was lucky to meet her a month later at the opening of her second bookstore, The Bookshop in Old New Castle, a co-op made of four extraordinary rare booksellers, probably the first of its kind for the way it combines books arts, modern firsts, children's books and books about books).

After just one round of the booths, I had handled books that few people ever see, much less touch: Darwin's own copy of *Origin of Species*, a copy of the New Testament that Martin Luther had used, an illuminated *Book of Hours* from 1455, original Pooh drawings of EH Shepard, the very scare privately printed copy of Beatrix Potter's *Peter Rabbit* (80, 000 pounds!), the very scarce first printing of *Don Quixote*, the Olympia editions of *Lolita*, first editions of Kierkegaard's *Either/Or* and Kant's

Critique of Pure Reason, two letters by J.D. Salinger (one typed, one handwritten), signed sets of Kipling, Jane Austen, Brontë, Dickens, Flaubert, Sylvia Plath, and near complete sets of *The Strand Magazine* where the Holmes stories were serialized first at the turn of the century. They were sold on the pavements then for half a shilling and now a single copy of the magazine could go for as much as five hundred dollars.

And finally, I went looking for that holy grail of modern first editions: the true first edition of *The Great Gatsby*, in that scarcest of dust jackets. And found it, naturally, at Between the Covers Rare Books. The price? $175,000. BTC also possessed one of the highlights of the fair: an inscribed first issue of Hemingway's *The Sun Also Rises* in that very, very scarce dust jacket. I was also in search of my own personal holy grail among modern firsts: a signed first edition of *The Catcher in the Rye*. Ken Lopez Bookseller, that other legendary book dealer in modern firsts, sharing the booth with BTC, told me he had recently possessed one, but the copy wasn't at the fair because it had been pre-sold.

But he had, what was at least for a Salinger devotee like me, the next best thing: the first state printing of Salinger's *Raise High the Roofbeam Carpenters* in the hard to find edition lacking the dedication page. Only 20 or so copies of this state are known to exist in the market. I opened it, saw it lacked the dedication myself, and handed it back, feeling very privileged. Peter Harrington had a Shakespeare folio, something I had only seen pictured in catalogues before. And no one seemed to mind when I cautiously took it out of the glass bookcase and carefully, very carefully, turned the pages.

At day's end, I looked again at my acquisitions: four books. For what I had paid for them, I would have got a few boxes worth of new books at a regular fair. But I had no regrets. I would not trade them for a shelf full of new books. A handsome edition of *The English Patient* signed by Michael Ondaatje, a lovely autographed copy of Susan Sontag's *The Volcano Lover*, a beautiful limited edition of *The House at Pooh Corner*, and a first edition of Marco Page's *Fast Company*. It was time to quit, but not before my last rendezvous at the fair: meeting Nick Basbanes and getting my first edition of *Patience and Fortitude*, my favourite of his book about books, signed.

I dash out to the coat check room where I've stashed the book in my backpack and join a row of bibliophiles queuing up to get their copies of *About the Author* inscribed, his new book made available for the first time exclusively at the fair. And then I see him: a distinguished-looking man with a kind and friendly smile, exchanging banter with his readers, effortlessly inscribing book after book. From my correspondence with him I already know him to be generous, witty, and modest. I wonder for a moment if he would mind that I wasn't bringing his new book to the table to be signed (after all that's why he was here), and notice to my relief that at least one person in the queue before me has brought along *A Gentle Madness*. He would understand – after all he was, like Umberto Eco, the universal bibliophile.

Drawing closer to the book signing table I see sitting beside him, Rebecca Rego Barry, the editor of my favourite rare book magazine, *Fine Books and Collections*. I grab the moment to tell her how much pleasure the magazine gives me. When I hand *Patience and Fortitude* to Nicholas Basbanes, he raises his eyebrows to ask: 'Did you schlep this all the way from India?' I did indeed, I reply. He looks impressed and pleased. And with a flourish inscribes and signs it on the half title page. Later, when I look at what he's written, I am gratified and moved to see he refers to me as his colleague in India, and a fellow chronicler of the gentle madness.

Our meeting was serendipitous, not scheduled. An unexpected privilege. In fact, every moment at the 50th New York Antiquarian Book Fair was a rare privilege, a bibliographical high; enough to make even the most jaded bibliophile swoon.

BIBLIOGRAPHY

Adair, Glibert, *Love and Death on Long Island*, Grove Press, 1998

Adair, Gilbert, *And Then There Was One*, Faber & Faber, 2009

Allen, Woody, *The Insanity Defense*, Random House, 2007

Baker, Nicholson, *The Size of Thoughts and Other Lumber*, Vintage, 1997

Bartlett, Hoover Allison, *The Man Who Loved Books Too Much*, Riverhead Books, 2009

Basbanes, Nicholas, *Editions and Impressions: Twenty Years on the Book Beat*, Fine Books Press, 2008

Baudrillard, Jean, *The System of Objects*, Verso, 2006

Bayard, Pierre, *Who Killed Roger Ackroyd?* The New Press, 2000

Bayard, Pierre, *Sherlock Holmes Was Wrong*, (translated by Mandel, Charlotte), Bloomsbury, 2008;

Belanger, Terry, *Lunacy and the Arrangement of Books*, Oak Knoll Press, 2003

Benjamin, Walter, *Illuminations: Essays and Reflections*, Schocken, 1969

Blom Philipp, *To Have and to Hold: An Intimate History of Collectors and Collecting*, Overlook Press, 2003

Bradbury, Ray, *Fahrenheit 451*, Random House, 1953

Bright, Betty, *No Longer Innocent: Book Art in America 1960–1980*, Granary Books, 2005

Chekhov, Anton; Mamet, David, *Uncle Vanya*, Samuel French Inc Plays, Dodo Press, 2004

Connolly, Joseph, *Eighty Years of Book Cover Design*, Faber & Faber, 2009

Darnton, Robert, *The Case for Books: Past, Present and Future*, PublicAffairs, 2009

(Ed.): Dilworth, Leah, *Acts of Possession*, Rutgers University Press, 2003

Dinesen, Isak, *Babette's Feast, Anecdotes of Destiny and Ehrengard*, Vintage, 1993

Dirda, Michael, *Readings: Essays and Literary Entertainments*, W.W. Norton & Company, 2000

Dirda, Michael, *Bound to Please: An Extraordinary One Volume Education*, W.W. Norton, 2007

Dyer, Geoff, *Anglo-English Attitudes*, Abacus, 2001

Eco, Umberto, *The Mysterious Flame of Queen Loana*, Harcourt, Inc, 2005

(Eds.): Elsner, John; Cardinal, Roger, *The Cultures of Collecting*, Reaktion Books, 1994

Epstein, Joseph, *In a Cardboard Belt: Essays Personal, Literary and Savage*, Mariner Books, 2008

Fadiman, Anne, *Ex Libris: Confessions of a Common Reader*, Farrar, Straus and Giroux, 2000

Fadiman, Anne, *Rereadings: Seventeen Writers Revisit Books They Love*, Farrar, Straus and Giroux, 2005

Fforde, Jasper, *The Eyre Affair*, Penguin, 2003

Fleck, Robert, *Books About Books: A History and Bibliography of Oak Knoll Press*, Oak Knoll, 2008

Gekoski, Rick, *Nabokov's Butterfly and Other Stories of Great Authors and Rare Books*, Carroll & Graf Publishers, 2004

Goldstone, Lawrence and Nancy, *Used and Rare: Travels in the Book World*, St. Martin's Press, 1997

Grafton, Anthony, *Worlds Made By Words: Scholarship and Community in the Modern West*, Harvard University Press, 2009

(Eds):Gupta, Abhijit; Chakravorty, Swapan, *Print Areas: Book History in India; Movable Type: Book History in India II* Permanent Black, 2004, 2008

Hanff, Helene, *84 Charring Cross Road*, Moyer Bell (25th Anniversary edition) 1995

Heller, C. Anne, *Ayn Rand and the World She Made*, Nan. A. Talese/Doubleday, 2009

Hemingway, Ernest, *A Moveable Feast*, Scribner, 1964

Iyer, Pico, *Abandon*, Alfred A. Knopf, 2003

Jackson, H.J., *Marginalia: Readers Writing in Books*, Yale University Press, 2002

Jackson, Kevin, *Invisible Forms: A Guide to Literary Curiosities*, Thomas Dunne Books, 2000

Kalman, Maira, *Swami on Rye*, Viking, 1995

Kelly, Stuart, *The Book of Lost Books: An Incomplete History of All the Great Books You'll Never Read*, Random House, 2006

Kendrick, Stephen, *Holy Clues: The Gospel According to Sherlock Holmes*, Vintage reprint, 2000

Kidd, Chip, *Book One*, Rizzoli, 2005

Kumar, Amitava, *Bombay, London, New York*, Penguin, 2002

Levin, Ira, *A Kiss Before Dying*, Simon & Schuster, 1953

Maar, Michael, *The Two Lolitas*, Verso, 2005

Manguel, Alberto, *A History of Reading*, Penguin, 1997

Manguel, Alberto, *The Library at Night*, Yale University Press, 2008;

Manguel, Alberto, *A Reader on Reading*, Yale University Press, 2010

McDade, Travis, *The Book Thief*, Praeger, 2006

Mercer, Jeremy, *Time Was Soft There: A Paris Sojourn at Shakespeare & Co.*, Picador, 2006

Miller, Laura, *The Magician's Book: A Skeptic's Adventures in Narnia*, Back Bay Books, 2009

Mishra, Pankaj, *An End to Suffering*, Picador, 2004

Muensterberger, Werner, *Collecting: An Unruly Passion*, Princeton University Press, 1994

(Eds.): Ondaatje, Michael; Redhill, Michael; Spalding,

Esta & Spalding, Linda, *Lost Classics: Writers on Books Loved and Lost, Overlooked, Under-read, Unavailable, Stolen, Extinct, or Otherwise Out of Commission*, Anchor, 2001

Orsini, Francesca, *Print and Pleasure*, Permanent Black, 2009

Pascoe, Judith, *The Humming Bird Cabinet: A Rare and Curious History of Romantic Collectors*, Cornell University Press, 2006

Pearce, Susan M., *Interpreting Objects and Collections*, Routledge, 1994

Petroski, Henry, *The Book on the Bookshelf*, Vintage, 2000

Pierpont, Roth Claudia, *Passionate Minds: Women Rewriting the World*, Vintage, 2001

Rattigan, Terrence, *The Browning Version*, Nick Hearn Books, 2008

Rosenbaum, Ron, *The Secret Parts of Fortune*, Harper Perennial, 2001

Rosenbaum, Ron, *The Shakespeare Wars: Clashing Scholars, Public Fiascoes, Palace Coups*, Random House, 2008

Ryokan, *One Robe, One Bowl*, Weatherhill, 2006

Salinger, J.D., *Raise High the Roofbeam Carpenters*, Little, Brown, 1963

Salinger, J.D., *Seymour: An Introduction*, Little, Brown, 1963

Seligman, Craig, *Sontag and Kael: Opposites Attract Me*, Counterpoint, 2004

Smith, Zadie, *Changing My Mind*, Penguin Press, 2009

Sontag, Susan, *The Volcano Lover*, Picador, 2004

Stark, Ulrike, *An Empire of Books: The Naval Kishore Press and the Diffusion of the Printed Word in Colonial India*, Permanent Black, 2007

Steward, Susan, *On Longing: Narratives of the Miniature, the Gigantic, the Souvenir, the Collection*, Duke University Press, 1993

Sterberger, Paul, Drew, Ned, *By Its Cover*, Princeton

Architectural Press, 2005

(Eds.): Suarez, Michael; Woudhuysen H. R., *The Oxford Companion to the Book*, Oxford University Press, 2010

Suzuki, Koji, *Ring*, (Translated by Rohmer B. Robert, Walley, Glynne Walley), Vertical Inc., 2003

Tanselle, G. Thomas, 'A Rationale of Collecting', *Studies in Bibliography 51*, 1998

Vienne, Veronique, *Chip Kidd*, Yale University Press, 2003

Vila-Matas, Enrique, *Bartleby & Co.*, (translated by Jonathan Dunne), New Directions, 2007

Watterson, Bill, *The Calvin and Hobbes Tenth Anniversary Book*, Andrews McMeel Publishing, 1995

Wendorf, Richard, *The Literature of Collecting*, The Boston Athenaeum and Oak Knoll Press, 2008

Winterson, Jeanette, 'The Psychometry of Books', *Art Objects*, Vintage, 1997

Zaid, Gabriel, *So Many Books*, (translated by Natasha Wimmer) Paul Dry Books, 2003

Acknowledgments

Thanks to Shivmeet Deol, a true bibliophile and my gifted editor at Hachette, for her passionate and thoughtful engagement with this book. To Lovy, for a gift of time, energy, and funds generously and affectionately given. Nirmala Lakshman at *The Hindu* for her long support and encouragement. Netra Shyam for cover illustration and design. Rosamma Thomas for being there. The warmth and brilliant companionship of friends: Rajib, Kala, Prasanna, Kapu, Zac, Anjum, Chandra, Anu, Suresh, Nazarius, Rajaram, Vinaya, Harish, Malathy, Ruth, Sugandhi, Cheriyan, Sathish, Nilam, Jaya, Siddhartha, Asha, Naman, Srinivas, David, Leslie and that really silly but fabulous fellow, Galli. And the comfort and connection of family: Appa, Deepak, Ruth, Preeti, Tarun, Naveen, Mini, Priya, Asha, Ranjini, Michael, Malini, Nalini, Mama, Athai, Dody, Dinky, Kumar anna, Babu akka, and of course (including helicopter, i.e., inspector sir) Ajoy.

Several of these pieces first appeared in a slightly different form in *The Hindu*, *Deccan Herald* and *Businessworld Online*, and I'm grateful to them for giving me column space.